# STUDIES IN BRETHREN HISTORY

Schwarzenau in the Early Twentieth Century

# STUDIES

# in

# BRETHREN HISTORY

Floyd E. Mallott

Professor of Church History
BETHANY BIBLICAL SEMINARY
Chicago, Illinois

BRETHREN PUBLISHING HOUSE
ELGIN, ILLINOIS

2865

Printed in the United States of America

# INTRODUCTION

Two things largely determine the course of a movement, the forces within itself and the influences that come upon it from without. *Studies in Brethren History* deals with both of these factors. The author very clearly treats the sources of the Brethren movement and points out the basic ideas, convictions, and ideals that characterized the Brethren in their beginnings and gave them unity, strength, and drive. He also deals with the forces that have beaten upon the Brethren as inhabitants of a changing world and members of a dynamic society. In particular, he points out the effects upon the church of the industrial revolution with its resulting changes in American life. Such powerful, swirling currents in the stream of life were bound to have some effect upon the course of the Brethren movement. The treatment of this subject in this volume should give Brethren a new understanding of themselves and a new sense of direction as a result of the corrected compass reading it makes possible.

The author does a bit of evaluating at times but, for the most part, after plainly but tactfully raising questions, he allows the reader to draw his own thoughtful conclusions.

The appearance of this book is timely, for all the major general histories of our Church are out of print and there has been a widespread demand for an available authoritative work in this field.

Dr. Floyd E. Mallott, from whose voluminous classroom lecture notes and manuscripts these pages have been distilled, is recognized as the leading authority on Brethren history living today. A native of Ohio, he was born and reared in the Brethren tradition. His academic education was secured at Manchester College, Bethany Biblical Seminary, and the University of Chicago. Pastoral experience in the First Church of the Brethren, Chicago, Illinois, and in Battle Creek, Michigan, and a term of service on our Africa mission field have given him more than an ivory-tower acquaintance with the life and movements of the Church.

Since 1928, Dr. Mallott has been Professor of Old Testament and Church History at Bethany Biblical Seminary. Hundreds of students have enjoyed his classes and profited by his breadth of scholarship and keen insights. His knowledge of Brethren history is an integral part of his scholarly familiarity with the details of both general Church history and the wide sweep of world history. Since he is a historian with a philosophy of history, this book presents not just an orderly record of events, but an interpretation of history. Dr. Mallott's students and the Church as a whole should welcome this volume as the well matured fruitage of years of patient research and constant classroom testing.

The appendix provides some material appearing for the first time in published form and much never before available to the average reader of our generation.

C. *Ernest Davis*
Elgin, Illinois

# CONTENTS

## The Text

## CHARTS AND MAPS

## ILLUSTRATIONS

*To that large company of my students in Bethany Biblical Seminary and Training School and that multitude in summer camps and institutes during the past quarter century whom I have instructed and who have instructed me as we talked about*

THE CHURCH OF THE BRETHREN

*this volume*
*is affectionately dedicated.*

# Chapter 1

# WHO ARE THE BRETHREN?

We set ourselves to the task of telling once more the story of the Brethren. Such a story cannot be told in isolation. We need to examine with care the origins from which the denomination grew, its situation in the modern world, and its relationship to certain other Christian bodies. Then we may be able to discover what it is in its essentials.

How may we define the Brethren? They are a company of Christians, who, taking the New Testament as their authority, seek by democratic processes to achieve the good life. The Brethren are rated as a Church. From the beginning in 1708 they realized the folly of the Separatist renunciation of all organization. Yet the organization they developed has at times been more of a family fellowship than an ecclesiastical institution.

From the theological viewpoint the Brethren must be catalogued as mystics. A mystic seeks direct inward experience of God without intermediaries. A mystic is not necessarily ecstatic. Brethren have generally been quite rational and have disapproved emotional demonstrations. Their mysticism must be characterized as Biblical and Pietistic. They have always been people of the Book. In their use of the Bible they anticipated modern "progressive revelation" by their insight that the New Testament is on a loftier plane than the Old. Their persistent counsel has been, "Search the Scriptures." Their Pietistic spirit was evident in the fact that for them regeneration, brought about by searching the Scriptures, must bear fruit in moral conduct. One could not claim conversion without showing ethical character, no matter how orthodox his opinions. From one viewpoint the movement at Schwarzenau was a reaction against Pietism, but it was thoroughly saturated with the ethical earnestness of the Pietists.

We thus think of the Brethren as Biblical Pietistic mystics, but a simpler characterization is available. They are imitators of primitive Christianity. There is probably no clearer statement of this than that which comes from the Germantown church, the first congregation organized in America, in a record dated December 13, 1761:

> According to a council of love at Germantown in the community of Brethren (Gemeinschaft der Brueder) who have vowed to die and to live according to the doctrine of Jesus Christ and to follow in everything the manner and institution of the apostolic congregation of the first Christians, there has been elected by vote and lot as minister to the poor of this congregation of Germantown, Brother George Schreiber, besides the formerly appointed Brother Henry Schlingluff.[1]

The idea here expressed is amply documented and clarified from the earliest extant literature of the Schwarzenau brotherhood. The writings of Alexander Mack, Sr., were issued in 1715 by the brotherhood at Schwarzenau. His two pamphlets have not been adequately appreciated as sources of doctrinal and historical information. In his booklet, *A Conversation Between a Father and Son,* the inquiring son is made to say: "Give me still better instruction. . . so that with the testimony of the Holy Scriptures and of the primitive Christians I might be established in my faith."[2]

Alexander Mack, Jr., writing in 1774 a preface for a colonial issue of his father's writings, said:

> Under these circumstances some felt themselves drawn prayerfully to seek the footsteps of the primitive Christians and desired earnestly to receive in faith the ordained testimonies of Jesus Christ according to their true value . . . and when they found in authentic histories that the

---

[1] M. G. Brumbaugh, *A History of the German Baptist Brethren in Europe and America,* second edition, 1910, Brethren Publishing House, Elgin, Illinois. Page 175.

[2] *Rites and Ordinances.* Page 14 (the paging here and later is that of the Ashland, Ohio, edition, 1939).

primitive Christians in the first and second centuries, uniformly according to the command of Christ, were planted into the death of Jesus Christ by a three-fold immersion into the water of holy baptism, they examined diligently the New Testament and finding all perfectly harmonizing therewith, they were anxious to use the means appointed and practiced by Christ himself, and thus according to his own salutary counsel, go forward to the fulfillment of all righteousness.[3]

It is proper, then, to describe the Brethren as a company of Christians who seek to live according to the pattern of the primitive Christians. We almost have to coin a word to feature properly the Brethren. We might say that Brethrenism is imitative *primitive Christianism.*

We are here very close to the characterization which seems to this writer clearest of all. It is to be found in their emphasis upon the Sermon on the Mount as the law of the Christian life. This feature seems not to be abundantly documented in early Brethren history; it was one of the unspoken assumptions of the early Brethren. Our whole history is pervaded by the spirit which can come only from this idea. Groups of medieval Anabaptists from whom our early Brethren derived much expressed the idea often. Indeed, there is some documentation for it in Mack's writing. The pre-eminence of the Sermon on the Mount is plain in his *Brief and Plain Reply to Gruber's Ground Searching Questions Proposed to the New Baptists of Wittgenstein, to Be Answered Separately.*[4]

"Question 13. If baptism in water be absolutely necessary, why has Christ made no mention of it in his Sermon on the Mount, when speaking of the blessings: Matthew 5. . . ."

Mack's answer, in part, was:

. . . we confess, that Christ alone is the Savior and whoever wishes to be blessed, as he preaches, Matt. 5, must necessarily accept him in true faith, and submit to him in obedience as clay in the hands of the potter, and He it is who must make all things new, and save all, and to him all

---

[3] *Op cit.* Page 18.
[4] *Op cit.* Page 82.

the prophets have pointed. Now since Christ the Savior and good physician deems baptism also necessary for the believer. . . .

The Brethren are truly characterized as a company of people who seek to exemplify the type of life expounded in the Sermon on the Mount.

Time gives perspective. We are now far advanced in the third century of the life of our religious fraternity. Its history has been lived on several continents, under varying political jurisdictions, against diverse cultural backgrounds, during the most changeful and dynamic period of recorded time. But the thread of unity that binds Brethren of every time and place appears in this designation. In so far as we are Brethren, we seek to live by the Sermon on the Mount.[5]

---

[5] The writer of these lines was received into the church in 1911. The venerable Elder David Lytle, who gave the instruction and administered baptism, had then been in the ministry for over thirty years and was a stalwart and competent exponent of the "tradition of the elders." His instruction indicated that the writer was joining a church that had no creed but the New Testament. He called particular attention to the Sermon on the Mount. He designated it the constitution of the Kingdom of God. The nonswearing, nonresistance, nonconformity, and nonsecrecy in which the writer was carefully instructed were buttressed by liberal quotations from the Sermon on the Mount.

From the eighteenth century may be traced a Brethren predilection for Romans 12, which we recognize as a Pauline version of the Sermon on the Mount.

## Chapter 2

## ORIGINS OF BRETHREN IDEOLOGY

*It is, therefore, very good to look wholly and alone to the express words of the Lord Jesus, and to his own perfect example, and to follow that only. . . .*

*This then is the way to God for every soul, namely, to do and act agreeably to the will of God.*

*Hence, in conclusion, I will advise thee to look only unto Jesus, our Redeemer and Savior. Hebrews 12:2.*

*—Alexander Mack, "Rites and Ordinances"*

The Brethren idea of living according to the Sermon on the Mount, of imitating Jesus in love and reverence, is now widely acclaimed among common people as right and inevitable. Theologians and creedalists do not so recognize it. But that has not greatly bothered the Brethren. From the beginning Brethren had no basic test of a Christian except to ask whether he would try to live in exact imitation of and obedience to Jesus. Our grandparents were fond of calling themselves a *peculiar people*. They were more peculiar than they were aware.

Whence came the idea that the essence of Christianity consists in the imitation of Jesus? It was not original with Brethren. As far as we can tell it came into existence about the twelfth century, though there are indications that Tertullian (third century) sensed it in part. Three twelfth-century personalities stand out, two of them within the Roman Catholic Church and the other branded a heretic and schismatic by the Church. These were St. Bernard of Clairvaux (1091-1153), Saint Francis of Assisi (1182-1226), and Peter

Waldo (converted about 1176, and deceased by 1218). These were truly ancestors in spirit of the Church of the Brethren.

Bernard was a great thinker. He held that the essence of the Christian faith was imitating Jesus. For a thousand years Jesus had been worshiped in the Church as the second person of the Trinity, the eucharistic Christ of the altar. But it remained for Bernard to discover Jesus as the Man of Nazareth, our Companion, Brother, Teacher, and Example. This discovery initiated a new phase of Christian history. Of course Bernard never doubted the divinity of Jesus. But he found a fresh interest in Jesus as man and our exemplar. It was Bernard's idea that Charles Sheldon picked up in the twentieth-century book, *In His Steps*.

To Bernard the most striking traits of Jesus were humility and love. Contemplation of these traits led him to oppose persecution of the Jews and forcing them to become Christians. It raised his voice in behalf of kindness and gentleness in dealing with children. It caused him to advocate earnestly feet-washing as a sacrament mirroring the character of Jesus. But Bernard was a regular "organization" man as far as the Church was concerned. He headed the monastic school at Clairvaux and one of his early pupils became pope. This pope leaned heavily upon Bernard for advice. Bernard did not question formal theology. In the earth-shaking controversy between the Schoolmen, who were teaching salvation by faith in the tradition of the Church, and Abelard, who thought Christian faith must be rational, Bernard abhorred the rationalism of Abelard. In doing so he unwittingly weakened the traditional view. He proposed that men needed neither faith nor reason, but assurance.

Thirty years after Bernard's death Francis of Assisi was born. He was neither a thinker nor an organizer but a man of great earnestness and emotional force who concentrated his whole energy in living like Jesus. He sought to love God and his fellow men completely. He was a passionate devotee of Jesus and was able to present Jesus so vividly and persuasively to people of every degree and class that he and his early associates changed the outlook of a large part of their generation.

It was an accident of the times that his society of "brothers" became a monastic order. He never so planned it. In the feudalistic society of his day the owning of property made necessary the rendering of military service either in person or by a substitute. Francis saw that military service was a violation of the law of love such as Jesus lived. Hence he renounced property in order to avoid military service.

Both Bernard and Francis were mystics of a sort—Christ-mystics, one may say. Their mysticism was a union with God in Christ, a union not of metaphysical substance but of affection and will. One learns to love the things Jesus loved and to do the things he would do. Mysticism of this sort calls for positive social living.

Peter Waldo is the man we must associate with these two great medieval saints of the Church. Perhaps we can call him a saint, too, although the Church did not so regard him. In point of time, Waldo came between Bernard and Francis. Bernard was a famous churchman when Waldo was a young merchant. Francis was born six years after Waldo's conversion. They lived in the same general region of Europe.

Waldo's ideas resemble those of both Bernard and Francis. He, like them, drew friends about him. He emphasized imitating Jesus' words and deeds. Like them he preached that men should live according to the Sermon on the Mount. But while the pope gave status to the "brothers" of St. Francis as a monastic order within the framework of the Church, the ecclesiastical authorities flatly forbade the Waldensians to teach or preach. Waldo and his followers could say only, "We must obey God rather than men." They became rebels and schismatics from the Roman Church.

When challenged for their authority, they pointed to the New Testament.

Waldo is thus the closest ancestor of the Brethren. Here is where the idea of a Church founded upon the New Testament was born into Christian history. This was more than seven centuries ago. Note that the adoption of the New Testament here was a practical, devout attitude not determined by scholastic theory or doctrine of inspiration. The New Testament was valued because it testified of Jesus, gave his words, and set forth primitive Christianity.

It was in just such a mood that the founders of the band at Schwarzenau turned to the New Testament. They were motivated by no theory of the New Testament. They took it as the book that presented a picture of Jesus and of primitive Christianity.

Wherever this Bernardine-Franciscan-Waldensian emphasis has appeared in these past seven centuries, there has come forth a certain type of Christian life. It has been, first of all, an ethical and humanitarian emphasis. Jesus, the man, has been in the foreground, and the standard of ethics has been his character and his words. Second, the method of this Church life has been democratic. That is a corollary of the first emphasis. Third, it has been a nonconformist Church. The degree of nonconformity has varied from generation to generation. The tension between Church and society has been present always and has been keen at times. It was for this nonconformity that Brumbaugh called us "a church of protest." The nonconformity is a result of the spirit of Jesus within. The usages, ambitions, and viewpoints of the environing society are felt to be at variance with the spirit of Jesus.

Ethical highness, humanitarianism, democracy, and nonconformity seem to be qualities of that Church life which feels itself based on the New Testament.

# Chapter 3

## THE BACKGROUND OF SCHWARZENAU

In the previous chapter we found origins of cherished ideas of the Brethren far back in the history of the Christian Church—in Saint Bernard, Saint Francis, and Peter Waldo. In this chapter we undertake to get the more immediate historical setting for the movement originating in Schwarzenau.

First, as a matter of perspective, let us try to see the main Church trends from medieval times to the present.

In the medieval world all mankind was regarded as necessarily belonging to a single Church, the rightful head of which was the bishop of Rome, the pope, by divine appointment successor to Saint Peter, Prince of the Apostles. This was a unified world, a single vast political order or State called the Holy Roman Empire. It was an aristocratic world with each man filling the place for which Providence had destined him by birth or by attainment. Commoners obeyed the lords; the lesser lords, the greater; and all, the emperor. The feudal lord was legislator, judge, and executive.

A new element had been growing quietly from the twelfth century. Political unity was threatened. Feudal States were becoming powerful and achieving virtual nationhood. Then in 1517 Martin Luther launched a course which divided Western Europe religiously. The Church was reconstituted in many places on *reformed* or *evangelical* lines. But the Protestant Reformation turned out to be quite as much a political as a religious movement. One hundred years after Luther nailed his theses to the door of the Wittenberg church came the Thirty Years' War. That destructive war was fought over the issue: Shall Europe be forced back into the medieval theocratic Church-State, or fall apart into independent geographical Nation-States politically and a number of national or regional Churches religiously?

Aristocratic world unity was lost through the Thirty Years' War. The Treaty of Westphalia (1648) recognized that certain civilized areas did not owe allegiance to the Holy Roman Empire. With the coming of nationalism the dream of a single world Church also was shattered. Although the first reformed Churches were organized on State or regional lines, denominationalism here came into being. These were the "protestant" Churches, protesting against the authority of the Roman Catholic Church.

The following diagram classifies the Christians of the Reformation period.

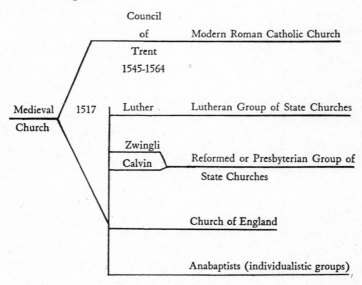

The Thirty Years' War lined up Protestant against Catholic. It brought petty rivalries and confusion. Organized religion got the blame and came to be counted a curse by many thoughtful people. Here was fruitful soil for the seeds of the Renaissance to bring forth rationalism. Thoughtful people on every hand turned away from religion. Protestant pastors preached in a perfunctory way to small, listless, and bored congregations. The majority expected nothing from the Church and got it. The Church came to be little more than a political utility. In Roman Catholic lands the situation was much the same. The period from Westphalia (1648) to the French Revolution (1789) was one of the dreariest in Christian history.

| Christianity as individualistic, subjective, ethical mysticism | I. Quakerism. | Emphasizes the inner light, the guidance of the spirit. Individual conscience supreme. |
| | II. Pietism. | Emphasizes goodness, resulting from regeneration through the Word, the Bible. |
| | III. Methodism. | Emphasizes holiness and the love of God exhibited in the crucified Savior. |
| Effort to escape from subjectivity to objectivity by a chiliastic scheme of history drawn from the Bible | IV. Chiliasm. | English—Plymouth Brethren, J. N. Darby, etc. American—Adventist, William Miller, etc. |
| Effort to escape from subjectivity to objectivity by returning to emphasis upon the institutional Church | V. Anglo-Catholicism. | Regards the Church as an unbroken historical continuity and development under apostolic succession. Tractarianism or Oxford movement. J. H. Newman, great leader. |

Since Westphalia the Roman Catholic Church has been in fact a denomination. The *reformed* Churches have continued, some following the *Lutheran* theology, others the *Genevan* or *Calvinistic,* and still others the *Anglican.* In addition to these older creeds, *five movements* may be distinguished in the non-Roman world. Through divisions, imitations, and various combinations of emphasis, geography, language, and administrative procedure, scores and even hundreds of denominations have come into being, but all can be grouped under these movements.

It is necessary to draw upon both these charts to get the antecedents of the Brethren. The final line on the first chart contributes the Anabaptist, individualistic element, and number two on the second brings the Pietistic element. We now trace out, in reverse order, these two lines of influence upon the Brethren of Schwarzenau.

The Pietistic movement is said to have originated with Philip Jacob Spener (1635-1705) and was advanced under his colleague and successor, August Hermann Francke (1663-1727). These men reacted against the academic and scholastic creedalism into which the Reformation forces had developed. Confronted by the appalling conditions following the Thirty Years' War and the widespread loss of faith in the Church, they found new life in the emphasis upon Christianity as an inner experience of godliness. Spener, from his youth, read the Catholic devotional writers and was attracted by the Franciscan-Bernardine emphasis on living like Jesus. Pietism thus came to be a projection of the earlier Christ-mysticism against a Lutheran Church background. It had become more Biblical, but was a projection of the imitation-of-Jesus type of teaching. Its emphasis was on the Church-in-the-spirit, as over against the formal or institutional Church.

In 1675 Spener published a small volume, *Pious Desires*, in which he set forth his hopes for a Church purification. He pleaded for recognition that Christianity is chiefly a matter, not of knowledge, but of life, an exemplification of the principle of love. His chief reliance for bringing about the changes desired was prayerful reading of the Bible. He hoped that ministers would come to preach simply, seeking only moral instruction and spiritual edification. This sounded revolutionary in his day.

From the title of Spener's book, his enemies dubbed his disciples Pietists. *Piety,* in the vocabulary of that day, was an honored synonym for *goodness*. The jeering epithet then meant *goody-goods*. But the title won respect; Pietism has colored the thinking and determined the lives of millions of Christians, especially those of German origin.

Spener and Francke never dreamed of leaving the Church or of encouraging anyone else to do so. They maintained that to be a good Christian was necessarily to be a good man or woman. The orthodox or creedalist party attacked them bitterly. Certain of their own followers went to an extreme that dismayed the leaders. They assumed that one can be good even though he is not a member of the Church. These came to be called Separatists. The term *Separatist* thus has a meaning in Germany different from that in England. These Separatists separated themselves not only from the State Church but from organized religion. They repudiated clergy, sacrament, organization, church buildings, bells—everything that suggested organized religion. They branded the Church as Babylon.

The Separatists were pure individualists. But they did not intend to repudiate the Bible. Though denouncing the Church, they continued to count themselves Christians—in fact, the only truly regenerated ones—and proceeded to preach, witness, and argue, and to berate State Churches. Their earnestness and their continued absorption in the Bible distinguish them clearly from the ones we know in the twentieth century who repudiate organized religion and straightway fall away into humanism, agnosticism, or materialism. The seventeenth-century Separatists remained under the shadow of the Church, a thorn in the flesh of all ecclesiastical authorities. The modern ones count the Church inconsequential and proceed largely apart from it.

In the time of the seventeenth-century Separatists the Church was decidedly a political force. So they found themselves inevitably clashing with the law. Few were slaughtered; the day of martyrs seemed to be past. But many who would

not conform to State Church regulations were fined, imprisoned, and abused in numerous ways. Such individualism as
theirs was counted wild-eyed craziness or willful heresy which,
if unchecked, would destroy the social order and civilized
living.

Schwarzenau and a few other places in the Germanies
became congregating places for those who were chronically in
conflict with the religious laws. Schwarzenau was in Wittgenstein, a county of Westphalia. The county had considerable
autonomy under Count Henry, its ruler. Modern research has
thrown unfavorable light on Henry's character and suggested
selfish financial motives for his sheltering of the Pietists. But
the original accounts speak of him as a "mild count" and
regard him with gratitude and respect. They speak also of the
women of his family as "pious countesses."

In this quiet, mountainous, forested, and semi-isolated
region of Wittgenstein all manner of religious dissenters and
rebels found shelter. Count Henry as a local leader was able
to protect them and the remoteness of the area made it easy to
overlook them. Alexander Mack came to Schwarzenau in 1700
as a Separatist refugee. All of the eight members of the founding company of 1708 were Separatists.

After the death of Count Henry there was a spasm of
enforcement of the religious laws which in 1720 drove the
Brethren of Schwarzenau to Holland.

Now we turn to the other line of historical influence on
the early Brethren, that of the Anabaptists and Gottfried
Arnold.

The Waldensians started something when they originated
the idea of a Church founded upon the New Testament. Their
preachers had familiarized a great many people of Europe with
this idea even before the Reformation. There began to appear,
particularly in the Germanies, groups of independent, individualistic Christians. These groups had in common the idea that
religion was to be a matter of adult conviction. This meant

that baptism administered to infants was not regarded as valid; there must be adult baptism. Hence they were called, at first in reproach, the Anabaptists, i. e., the "re-baptizers."

Among the Anabaptists, there were some whom writers call the soundly Biblical Anabaptists. The principal leader of these was Menno Simons (1492-1559). This man, a contemporary of Luther, had been a Roman Catholic priest. Moved by the martyrdom of some gentle "gospel Christians" to renounce the Church, he joined the seceders. The largest brotherhood descended directly from these sixteenth-century Anabaptists bears his name today—the Mennonites.

The Anabaptists generally agreed that the Church should be composed of the regenerate only. Infant baptism was counted the source of numberless errors. The true Church emphasized self-denial and brotherhood. It was entirely separate from the State. They generally carried this separation from the State to the extent of refusing military service, even in self-defense. These communities laid great stress on the imitation of Christ. They renounced earthly comfort and glory. Personal adornment, worldly amusements, wealth, and all forms of luxury were regarded as inconsistent with the Christian life. Standards of admission and discipline were severe. Excommunication of the false or the backsliders was practiced.

It looked for a while as though the Anabaptists were going to sweep Europe. But Europe was not yet ready for them. Then too, after a brief Pentecostal period, they developed their position negatively in opposition to the hierarchical and State Churches. By 1648 they had settled into a number of small quasi-monastic communities who were largely barred from participation in the political, social, and professional life of the times. They were in eclipse.

But in the latter part of the seventeenth century was born a remarkable man, Gottfried Arnold (1665-1714). Arnold was born in the State Church but read mystical writers and became a thorough Pietist and a personal friend of Philip Jacob Spener.

His first book, *The First Love for Christ,* was published in 1696. The most important among his fifty works were *The Portraiture of Primitive Christians* and *Impartial History of The Church and Heretics.* For a time he was professor of Church history at Giessen University, then a Separatist, and finally a settled pastor in the State Church.

He was an independent student. Some have called him the father of the modern historical method. Until his day, the principal use of Church history had been to buttress dogmatic and partisan claims. He exposed this procedure. He showed that the so-called heretics were often sincere people who differed from the institutional Church and sometimes had gleams of the truth which the Church had forgotten or neglected. His studies developed a clear picture of the early Christians that later research has largely confirmed and but to a limited degree supplemented.

The group formed at Schwarzenau were truly Anabaptist; they were called New Baptists in reproach. The principal reason they did not join any of the older Anabaptist congregations was the new light on primitive Christian life that Arnold had made available. It was Arnold's studies and writings which had recovered the knowledge that in the first and second centuries Christian baptism was trine immersion. It was not only a believer's baptism, but also a threefold immersion. Also the group at Schwarzenau began with a clear understanding, aided by Arnold, that the agape or love feast accompanied the communion of the bread and the wine.

A quotation from Alexander Mack's *Conversation Between a Father and Son,* page 23, demonstrates the use the early Brethren made of Arnold's writings:

Son: Do we not find in histories that the primitive Christians did baptize their children?

Father: We find in Godfrey Arnold's Portraiture of Primitive Christians that infant baptism began to be practiced in the end of the second century after the birth of Christ.

# Chapter 4

# THE ORGANIZATION AT SCHWARZENAU

The origin of the Brethren as a Church was the work of a group of eight earnest souls—five men and three women. Alexander Mack was indeed a leading spirit among them, but precaution was taken to minimize the personal factor. There was to be no founder of the Brethren. This fact contributed to the character of Brethren history.

There is one authoritative and friendly account of the organization at Schwarzenau. It was written by Alexander Mack, Jr., on January 30, 1774, out of information "from some papers, which were left by two brethren; namely, Alexander Mack and Peter Becker" and some given "to me orally by my parents, as well as by some other brethren, who have also fallen asleep in the Lord and who were themselves eye-witnesses." The account is in the preface to the first American issue of the writings of Alexander Mack, Sr.

The younger Mack recounts briefly some of the facts presented in our last chapter. There was great decay of true Christianity in almost every place. But some heard the call to repentance and began to look about for the true righteousness. Here and there private meetings were established in which newly awakened souls sought edification. These were held apart from the established Churches. The Church leaders embittered the rulers against these earnest souls and persecution resulted in various places such as Switzerland, Wurttemberg, the Palatinate, and Hesse. The persecuted and exiled found refuge in Wittgenstein, where a "mild count" ruled. Here at Schwarzenau, near Berleberg, liberty of conscience was granted. Though that country was poor and rough, it became widely known as a refuge.

Those who fled there from persecution differed in opinions, manners, and customs, but they were all Pietists and called one another brother. But there was no established order whereby they could apply the teachings of Matthew 18 to maintain brotherly relationships. There was disagreement over the degree of spiritual liberty that was desirable among them, and many thought it better to return to the denominations from which they had come.

From this point we quote from the preface written by the younger Mack.

Under these circumstances some felt themselves drawn powerfully to seek the footsteps of the primitive Christians, and desired earnestly to receive in faith the ordained testimonies of Jesus Christ according to their true value. At the same time, they were internally and strongly impressed, with the necessity of the obedience of faith to a soul that desires to be saved. And this impression also led them at the same time to the mystery of water-baptism, which appeared unto them as a door into the church which was what they earnestly sought. Baptism, however, was spoken of among the Pietists in very different ways, and the manner in which it was sometimes spoken of, caused pain to the hearts of those that loved the truth.

Finally, in the year 1708, eight persons consented together, to enter into a covenant of a good conscience with God, to take up the commandments of Jesus Christ as an easy yoke, and thus to follow the Lord Jesus, their good and faithful Shepherd, in joy and sorrow, as his true sheep, even unto a blessed end. These eight persons were as follows: namely, five brethren and three sisters. The five brethren were George Grebi from Hesse Cassel, the first; Lucas Vetter, likewise from Hessia, the second; the third was Alexander Mack from the Palatinate of Schriesheim between Manheim and Heidelberg; the fourth was Andrew Bony of Basle in Switzerland; the fifth John Kipping from Bariet in Wurttemberg. The three sisters were, Johanna Noethiger or Bony, the first; Anna Margaretha Mack, the second; and Johanna Kipping, the third.

These eight persons convenanted and united together as brethren and sisters into the covenant of the cross of Jesus Christ to form a church of Christian believers. And when they had found in authentic histories, that the primitive Christians in the first and second centuries, uniformly, according to the command of Christ, were planted into the death of Jesus Christ by a threefold immersion into the water-bath of holy baptism, they examined diligently the New Testament, and finding all perfectly harmonizing therewith, they were anxiously desirous to use the means appointed and practiced by Christ himself, and thus according to his . . . counsel, go forward to the fulfillment of all righteousness.

Now the question arose, who should administer the work externally unto them? One of their number, who was a leader, and speaker of the word in their meetings, had visited in sincere love, different congregations of Baptists (Tauf gesinnten) in Germany, most of which admitted, that holy baptism when performed by an immersion in water and out of love to Christ, was indeed right; but they would also besides this, maintain that the pouring of a handful of water might also do very well, provided all else would be right.

The conscience however of them (the Brethren) could not be satisfied with this. They therefore demanded of him, who led in preaching the word, to immerse them according to the example of the primitive and best Christians, upon their faith. But he considering himself as unbaptized required first to be baptized of some one of them, before he should baptize another. So they concluded to unite in fasting and prayer in order to obtain of Christ, himself the founder of all his ordinances, a direction and opening in this matter. For he who was requested to baptize the other, wanted to be baptized by the church of Christ, and the rest had the same desire.

In this their difficulty, they were encouraged by the words of Christ, who had said so faithfully, "Where two or three are gathered in my name, there am I in the midst of them." With such confidences in the precious and sure promise of God, they, under fasting and prayer cast lots, which of the four brethren should baptize that brother, who so anxiously desired to be baptized by the church of Christ. They mutually pledged their word, that no one should ever divulge, who among them had baptized first (according to the lot,) in order to cut off all occasion of calling them after any man, because they had found that such foolishness had already been reproved by Paul in his writings to the Corinthians.

Being thus prepared, the Eight went out together one morning, in solitude, to a stream called Eder, and the brother, who desired to be baptized by the church of Christ, . . . when he was baptized, . . . baptized him, by whom he had been baptized, and the remaining three brothers and three sisters. Thus these Eight were all baptized at an early hour of the morning.

And after all had come up out of the water, and had changed their garments, they were also at the same time made to rejoice with great inward joyfulness, and by grace they were deeply impressed with these significant words, "Be ye fruitful and multiply!" This occurred in the year above mentioned, 1708. But of the month of the year, or the day of the month or week, they have left no record.

After this said eight persons were more and more powerfully strengthened in their obedience to the faith they had adopted, and were enabled to testify publicly in their meetings, to the truth; and the Lord granted them his special grace so that still more became obedient to the faith, and thus, within seven years time, namely, to the year 1715, there was not only in Schwarzenau a large church, but here and there in the Palatinate there were lovers of the truth, and especially was this the case in Marienborn where a church was gathered; for the church in Palatinate was persecuted and its members then came to Marienborn. And when the church here became large, it was also persecuted. Then those that were persecuted, collected in Creyfeld, where they found liberty, under the King of Prussia.

Moreover, the Lord called during those seven years, several laborers, and sent them into his harvest, among whom were John Henry Kalkleser, of Frankenthal; Christian Libe and Abraham Duboy from Ebstein; John Nasz and several others from Norten; Peter Becker from Dillsheim. And to these were added also John Henry Trout and his brothers, Heinrich Holsaple and Stephen Koch. The most of these came during those seven years to Creyfeld; John H. Kalkleser, however, and Abraham Duboy came to Schwarzenau; so did also George B. Gansz from Umstatt; and Michael Eckerlin from Strasburg.

But as they found favor with God and men on the one hand, so (on the other hand) there were also enemies of the truth, and there arose here and there persecutions for the Word's sake. There were those who suffered joyfully the spoiling of their goods, and others encountered bonds and imprisonment, some for a few weeks only, but others had to spend several years in prisons. Christian Libe was some years fastened to a galley, and had to work the galling oar among malefactors; yet, by God's special providence, they were all delivered again with a good conscience.

There is another account, to a degree unsympathetic but perhaps generally dependable in the facts it presents. It is in the *Ephrata Chronicle*. After mentioning the Separatist movement among the Pietists and the return of some of the Separatists to the pale of the Church, the narrative points out three gathering points for the rest: Marienborn, Schwarzenau, and Schlechtenboden. From that point we quote several paragraphs:

Among the Pietists gathered together in that region, two congregations were soon formed whose principles were radically different and contrary; namely, the Community of True Inspiration and the Baptists of Schwarzenau. . . . The Schwarzenau Baptists arose in the year 1708; and the persons who at that time broke the ice, amid much opposition, were Alexander Mack, their teacher, a wealthy miller of Schriesheim an der Bergstrasse, (who devoted all his earthly possessions to the common good, and thereby became so poor that at last he had not bread enough to last from one day to the next), his housekeeper, a widow Noethiger, Andreas Bone, John George Hoening, Luke Vetter, Kippinger, and a gunsmith, whose name is not known.

From these eight persons were descended all the various kinds of Baptists among the High-Germans in North America, who now are scattered from New Jersey to Georgia; but whether they were the first who restored immersion, as a candle to its candlestick, in Germany, that is a question demanding closer investigation. It is asserted that the godly Hochmann agreed with them on the subject of baptism, but as they carried the thing out while he was under arrest, he could not afterwards insist upon it any more; probably too, their sectarianism was a hindrance to him. Certain it is that God was with them at that time. Neither was there any difference between them and the congregation afterwards found at Ephrata, except with reference to the Sabbath. . . . They had their goods in common, and practiced continence, though, it is said, they did not persevere in this zeal longer than seven years, after which they turned to women again and to the ownership of property involved therein. And this is very likely, from the fact that, afterwards, when the great awakening in Conestoga took place, during which similar circumstances arose once more, they always declared that if it were possible to live in such wise, their fathers at Schwarzenau, who for a time had the same zeal, would have succeeded in it. . . .

This congregation of Baptists at Schwarzenau increased very much. A branch of it settled in the Marienborn district, but was thrice persecuted there, and finally found a refuge in Creyfeld in the year 1715. Here a division took place. Some say it was with reference to the question whether one might marry out of the congregation. Others maintain that the occasion of it was the marriage, contrary to the teaching of Paul

(I Cor. 7:), of a single minister of theirs by the name of Hager. If this be so, there must still have been a considerable measure of awakening among them at that time, and their error consisted only in making a law out of the teaching of Paul, which it was not meant to be. In the year 1719 a party of them arrived in Pennsylvania with Peter Becker, who afterwards became their teacher.

This Ephrata account sharpens Mack's story. It throws into relief the strong bias of the Separatist-Pietists against organization. It points out that not only Schwarzenau but also Marienborn was the location of one of the first organizations. It introduces the "Community of True Inspiration" (which, by the way, is still the official name of the Amana Community in Iowa).

The ancestors of both Inspirationist and Dunker shared the narrow confines of a few European villages two and a half centuries ago, and their struggles helped to give form to our faith. However much was held in common by the two groups—individualism, aversion to a State Church, indifference to creeds, belief in firsthand mystical experience with the Spirit—the Inspirationist view that revelation was continuous impelled Mack and his associates to emphasize the canonical New Testament as the basis of authority. They wanted no spiritual anarchy. One of Mack's books was his *Brief and Plain Reply to Eberhard Ludwig Gruber's Ground-Searching Questions.* Gruber and Johann Rock were the co-founders of the True Inspiration community. The Inspirationists came to the climax of formal organization about 1714.

The name *Hochmann* appears in the quotation from the *Ephrata Chronicle.* This was Ernst Christoph Hochmann (1670-1721). He was an outstanding example of the extreme Separatists. As a law student he had been expelled from the University of Halle for his erratic views of nonchurch Christianity. He is known to have been a friend of Alexander Mack. M. G. Brumbaugh may be right in conjecturing that he joined the Schwarzenau Brethren before his death. It can hardly be proved that Mack derived much from Hochmann. They, rather, were both sharers in the extremist views of the times.

The fact that the Schwarzenau brotherhood began by experimenting with community of goods and celibacy shows at the same time their earnestness and their intellectual bewilderment. Alexander Mack's greatness lies in the fact that he was one of the few leaders who were stable enough to pick a sane path through the mazes of morbid emotionalism and unbalanced fanaticism. The Schwarzenau brotherhood clung fast to the essential truth of their mystic experience. They avoided extremes and discarded that which led off upon tangents. Their spiritual health was found in following the simple precepts of the New Testament.

The decision to organize came about in order to make it possible to live by the New Testament in all things. The eighteenth chapter of Matthew, the fifteenth chapter of Acts, and the Scriptural injunctions about baptism could not be followed without an organization. From such scriptures came forth a sort of basic-government framework for the brotherhood at Schwarzenau.

To maintain a proper balance between spirit and form is a perennial problem for religionists. If one leans too far in emphasis on spirit his religion soon becomes a sentiment or a mood; this is the danger of the mystic. If he emphasizes form too much he becomes a formalist, then a legalist. It would not be truthful to say that the household of Schwarzenau has always maintained the desirable balance. But the New Testament that it exalts is the best basis for resolving the problem. Here are reconciled content and the technique of expression. Here may be resolved the relationship of individual and community. The answer of the Schwarzenau Brethren grew out of extremity.

In one of his really eloquent passages, the eminent historian, M. G. Brumbaugh, says:

. . . they were by no means satisfied with the formalism and ritualism with which their spirits were oppressed. On the other hand they could not fully and unreservedly adopt the faith of the Pietists whose utter hatred for all church organization had led them to abandon the ordinances of the house of God. Rejecting on the one hand the creed of man, and on the other hand the abandonment of ordinances, they turned to the Bible for guidance. . . . Adopting the Bible as their rule and guide they organized a church with no creed, and with all the ordinances as taught by Jesus and his followers, as recorded in the New Testament. Their position is unique. . . . They are Pietists without the ultra church-in-the-spirit doctrines of Spener and his followers.[1]

---

[1] M. G. Brumbaugh, *A History of the German Baptist Brethren*. Pages 33 and 34

## Chapter 5

# THE EUROPEAN PERIOD OF THE BRETHREN

The story of the Brethren in Europe extends from 1708 to 1729. The five or six hundred refugees gathered into Schwarzenau and Berleberg were fertile soil in which the new Brotherhood could propagate its views. We know of four congregations or centers. Perhaps it would be more accurate to call them brotherhoods or communities rather than congregations. Besides these gathered brotherhoods there were individual believers in various places.

The Schwarzenau congregation became the largest on the European continent. It became a compact, well-organized fellowship under the oversight of Alexander Mack. Mack is reported to have spent his entire wealth for the welfare of his brethren. This may have been in the period of community of goods. From Schwarzenau went forth preachers who toured the Rhine Valley, even into Switzerland. In the year 1720, after Count Henry died, the Schwarzenau group met persecution and found it necessary to migrate in a body. They went to Westervain in West Friesland, Holland, where they could enjoy toleration. There they lived quietly until 1729, when they migrated to America.

The administrator of Count Henry at Schwarzenau in 1720 left a revealing report:

For a long time many pious people have lived around here, of whom no one heard anything bad, but perceived that they conducted themselves in a wholly quiet and pious manner, and by no one had a complaint been made of them. There were about forty families of them, about two hundred persons, that lately have betaken themselves entirely out of the land, of whom it was said that they were Anabaptists. The rest of those who yet lived about Schwarzenau are Catholics, Lutherans, and Reformed in religion. However, whether any of the above named persons, who are forbidden the Kingdom, stay about here, is unknown to me.

Marienborn, located in the Palatinate, became the site of a congregation. Reference was made in the quotation in the previous chapter to a large church there. John Naas served as minister at Marienborn, and Peter Becker joined the Brethren at that place.

There was also a congregation at Epstein for a time. Christian Libe was in charge there, assisted by Abraham Duboy.

Persecution caused the majority of the Marienborn group to take refuge in Creyfeld in the county of Cleves under the tolerant King of Prussia. It is probable that the Epstein Brethren joined them. Creyfeld thus became the fourth congregation that we can identify. At Creyfeld the Brethren moved into a new world of influence. Creyfeld was a considerable city, a center of textiles and various other industries. The Brethren thus found themselves transplanted from a farming and vineyard area into an industrial setting. The Creyfeld group maintained themselves here from 1715 to 1719.

Long before 1715, Creyfeld had been a Mennonite center. There are several indications of fraternization between the congregation at Creyfeld and the Mennonites. The unfortunate Hacker case occurred there. A young minister of the name of Hacker married the daughter of a Mennonite merchant. John Naas was the elder-in-charge at Creyfeld and Christian Libe was his assistant. Libe and four single brethren excommunicated Hacker. This was done under the spell of the ascetic views of the extreme Pietists, but it is said to have turned away from the Brethren more than one hundred persons.

Libe was an extremist. He had to spend two years in the galleys for preaching in Switzerland. The fervent temperament which drove him up and down the Rhine to preach, which kept him steadfast under persecution, which sent him back to preach at Bade, from whence he had been exiled as an Anabaptist, also made him an intolerant rigorist in his Church administration.

It was at Creyfeld that six members of the Reformed Church joined the Brethren and were immersed in the River Wupper. This was too much even for tolerant Creyfeld. The synod of the Berg Province and the general Reformed synod heard of this with regret. On February 26, 1717, the six were taken to Duesseldorf and imprisoned for four years. The names of the six were Wilhelm Grahe, Jacob Grahe, Luther Stetius, Johann Lobach, Wilhelm Kneffers, and Johann Henkels. They were compelled to work at hard labor and became ill in prison. Stephen Koch, Jacob Wilhelm Naas (son of Elder John Naas), and Gosen Gojen visited them. Gosen Gojen was a Mennonite preacher who became convinced that trine immersion was the correct apostolic baptism.

It was at Creyfeld that contacts were made which led to the first migration to America. Creyfeld Mennonites had bought land in William Penn's colony as early as 1681. In 1683, thirteen men with their families proceeded from Creyfeld to the New World and settled in what came to be called Germantown, six miles north of the square of the city of Philadelphia. Thus contact was made between Creyfeld and the religious freedom and economic opportunities of Pennsylvania. In 1719, Peter Becker with forty families, many of them Brethren, sailed for Pennsylvania.

There is a report in the annals of the Reformed Church of Creyfeld (Acts, Synod General, 1719, pages 21 and 44) that records the ecclesiastical farewell:

The preachers of the Meuro classe have received the confession of faith of the so-called Dompelaers staying at Creyfeld, and they have sent their remonstration to his gracious majesty the King of Prussia. However, this brotherhood of the Meuro Synod report with pleasure that

these Dompelaers, who have been so injurious to our church, have betaken themselves away . . . and are said to have sailed to Pennsylvania.

However, the brotherhood at Creyfeld did continue for
several years after this. But it did not prosper. John Naas and
Christian Libe quarreled openly. Naas called Libe a pillmonger
and went to Switzerland in discouragement and alienation.
The congregation weakened and some individuals followed to
America.

In 1729 the brotherhood at Westervain migrated in a
body to Pennsylvania. The lists of non-English immigrant
arrivals at the Port of Philadelphia from 1727 to 1808, printed
by the Pennsylvania German Society under the title, *Pennsylvania German Pioneers* (edited by William John Hinke),
is authority for the arrival of Mack's company in the chartered
ship *Allen,* with James Craigie as master. They left Rotterdam
and proceeded to Cowes, England, whence they sailed on July
7, 1729. They landed at Philadelphia on September 11 and
made the required affirmations on September 15, 1729.

A list of the *Allen's* passengers is given in the appendix
to this book. The maximum number of households to be
counted is fifty-seven. This would allow for Matthew Bradford
and Nicholas Bayly to have been casuals taken aboard at
Cowes. It would be an unfounded assumption to count them
as members. The proportion of young children among them
was certainly small. Only five—all boys—are listed as under
fifteen. This fact no doubt reflects the rigorist-Pietist emphasis upon celibacy.

There is no further record of Brethren on the continent of
Europe. A few other individual Brethren are known to have
come to America later. John Naas arrived in 1733 and was
met by Alexander Mack and reconciled to the Brethren.

Brumbaugh has compiled two hundred twenty-five names
of persons who were probably members of the Church in
Europe. This is the most complete data we have on the
European strength of the Brethren.

## Chapter 6

## PREVIEW TO BRETHREN HISTORY IN AMERICA

The Brethren came to the New World. The importance of that move can hardly be overestimated. They came from an old, aristocratic, stratified society, where they were with few exceptions in the poor laborer and peasant class. Their poverty had been rendered greater by the fines and persecution inflicted upon them. The colony to which they came was then one of the most democratic, liberal, and open-minded places on the globe. But in the new country they unexpectedly encountered the deadlier, though more subtle, dangers of wealth.

In the present chapter we shall try to get a view of the environment into which the Brethren came, then set the point of view of our study of Brethren history, and finally note the nature of the Industrial Revolution, which has conditioned the environment in which Brethren directions have been determined.

First, we look at the Penn colony. William Penn had founded it with rosy expectations. He called it the "holy experiment." In 1681 he got possession of forty thousand square miles of territory in the American wilderness in settlement for a debt to his father. He saw nothing inconsistent between the desire to increase the family fortune and the carrying out of his Utopian scheme. He believed his colony would be profitable. He wanted to prove that religious liberty was practical, that pure Christianity could be maintained without a State Church, that government could be carried on without war and oaths, and that the power of the spirit was sufficient without a hireling ministry, dogmas, cruelty, or persecution.

He not only welcomed the persecuted Quakers from England and the Mennonites and other Separatists and the Pietists from Holland and the Rhineland as ideal citizens for his new society, but he also sent agents into those regions to sell land and induce migration.

But Penn believed too easily in the goodness and honesty of people. Many imposed upon him. He himself spent much time in England. His deputies and even his own children failed to catch the full spirit of his idealism. The popular atmosphere of Pennsylvania became one of wealth-getting. He was dismayed at the slowness of the realization of his dream. He failed to see that to lay the foundations of a holy society even partially upon self-interest and material advantage is to build on sand. His position was very easily interpreted as a tacit acceptance of the values of this world as the *real* values.

The simple Quakers, most of them from the humbler walks of life, suddenly found wealth dumped into their laps. They straightway built stately homes and got costly furnishings. They conformed increasingly to the fashions of the world and lost their spiritual fervor. Christopher Sauer in 1724 wrote thus of the change: "According to appearances plainness is vanishing pretty much . . . . The dear old folks, most of whom are dead by this time, have spoken to their children a good deal about plainness. It is still noticeable in the clothes except that the material is very costly, or is even velvet."[1]

It was into this kind of world that the religious radicals from the Rhineland came. The ennervating effects of wealth were to soften gradually their Biblical radicalism. But not without resistance. The "plain people" became a bloc of extreme Christian conviction. The designation, *a plain people,* did not apply to costume only. It meant nonconformist people as over against those who conformed to common, worldly society. The more distinctive Quaker and Anabaptist sectarians

---

[1] *Pennsylvania Magazine,* Volume XLV. Pages 252 and 253.

felt themselves akin and stood over against the whole world of conventional Church Christianity.

Philadelphia came to be known for its luxury. Its fine and ornate buildings were objects of comment; its elaborate menus became celebrated; foreign travelers observed its people to be rich in apparel and elegant in manners. Card-playing and dancing came to be countenanced by many even in Quaker circles. So also fox-hunting, horse-racing, health-drinking, and office-holding. But theatrical performances did not become legal in Philadelphia until 1789.

Germantown was not a new community when the first Brethren arrived there in 1719. In the previous chapter we noted its establishment by Mennonite settlers from Creyfeld. These original settlers were mostly of the linen-weaver and mechanic classes. Since it was not easy for German city dwellers to start farming in the wilderness they proceeded to practice their respective trades in the new land. They settled somewhat as an Old World village.

Writing in 1684, Pastorius said that the village then had forty-two persons in twelve families and that each family had an estate of three acres. Later, the town seems to have been resurveyed into fifty-five lots of fifty acres each.

The German settlers who were farmers were dazzled by the prospect of owning land in the New World. The usual holding was from two hundred to one thousand acres. Penn sold land at one hundred pounds sterling for five thousand acres, subject to quit rent of one shilling for each hundred acres per year.

The first dwellings were caves or huts. The log cabin of Swedish and Finnish origin came later. Before 1700 the improvised houses of Germantown had begun to give way to impressive stone and brick dwellings such as are still counted typical of southeastern Pennsylvania. The German settlers made some modification of the architecture of the region but their main contribution was the great barns. As soon as the thrifty and industrious immigrant could attain to it, he equipped his homestead with a large barn and a commodious house, which probably represents the highest average of housing comfort the working people of the world have ever attained.

The colony of Pennsylvania grew rapidly. From two hundred in 1681 to seven thousand two hundred in 1685, to twice that many in 1700, it increased to fourth rank in population among the colonies by 1740. The size of the early German migrations is not known, but there were several groups. In 1714 to 1719 German immigration really got under way. Since the land around Germantown was already largely sold, most of the later arrivals went into the wilderness. In 1719, one of the members of the Provincial Council wrote: "We are daily expecting ships from London which bring over Palatinates, in number six or seven thousand. We had a parcel that came about five years ago who purchased land about sixty miles west of Philadelphia, and proved quiet and industrious." The numbers expected seem fantastic—unless they are to be understood as a summary of the entire number of immigrants from the Palatinate.

We assume that the ship bearing Becker and his brethren was one of those expected in 1719. If so, this is our only strictly contemporary reference to their landing. The "parcel" that had come five years before have been identified as a company of Mennonites who settled in what is now Lancaster County. The Lancaster Mennonite settlement had been begun as early as 1710. This area became really the second homeland of the Brethren in America.

Peter Becker's party seems to have scattered after landing. A nucleus of several families settled at Germantown. Others went to the "back country," where land was more easily obtained.

The party of 1729 seems to have distributed themselves in

similar fashion. There were congregations in the back country by 1729. Migration meant added strength to them.

We have pointed out the great change of environment which came to the first generation of Brethren in their transfer from the continent of Europe to the New World. In a very real sense the history of the Brethren in colonial Pennsylvania was a prelude and a prophecy of their entire history. Except for those living in eighteenth-century Europe and in the mission fields today, the Brethren have lived their entire life in America, one of the most favored economic areas on the globe. They have lived under a mild and tolerant government which has hitherto given a very large measure of freedom to the individual citizen. This tolerance has made life easy. It has also meant that the temptations to which the Brethren have been exposed have been for the most part very subtle ones.

Let it be said clearly at the outset that there has been a continuing and unbroken thread in Brethren history from 1708 to the present. This continuous element is easily identified in the ideal to live as a community after the mind of Jesus Christ—the resolution to live according to the Sermon on the Mount. It is not to be asserted that each generation has used identical language in proclaiming this core of truth. Nor is it to be held that every period has thought alike. The changing environment has brought changed ways of thinking and doing. In a historical survey we must seek to discover the changes and try to interpret them.

It has been customary to outline Brethren history as a *colonial period* from the beginning in 1708 to the confiscation of Christopher Sauer's printing press in the Revolutionary days of 1778; a *western-migration or wilderness period* from 1778 to 1851, when Henry Kurtz launched the *Gospel Visitor;* and a *period of revived activity and progress* from 1851 to 1918 (the end of World War I) or some more recent date. Brethren generally have been apologetic for the middle period, un-

necessarily so in view of the major work then done in planting
the church geographically. And they have been too ready to
accept the designation *progress* for the last period. It remains
to be seen whether or not the changes in this period add up
to progress.

There is a very simple outline, the noting of which clarifies
the events of Brethren history. It is based on a twofold time
division: from 1708 to 1851 and from 1851 to the present.

The year 1851 is a pivotal date. The beginning in English
of the Church press, the establishing of an organ of discussion
and exchange of thought, was significant. But there was a
deeper reason for this date as a turning point. The year 1851
marks the approximate time that the Industrial Revolution
struck America. In spite of the fact that the Brethren had
changed continents, the world in which they met for the Yearly
Meeting of 1851 was much nearer the world of 1708 than that
of 1950. From 1708 to 1851 the Brotherhood begun at
Schwarzenau lived in the midst of an agricultural society—
a thoroughly rural economy. The year 1851 brought a new era.

We shall attempt to lift the story of the Brethren out
of isolation and apply to it the principles furnished to us by
the present sociological-development school of historical writing. We frankly adopt the standpoint of *the Church in conflict
with its environment.* By *conflict* we mean *tension.* In every
generation the Church of Jesus Christ in all its phases must
come to some attitude toward its environment. The environing
society is the milieu in which any religious society must live
and work.

The Industrial Revolution is the outstanding feature of
Occidental history since the Renaissance and Reformation. It
is dated from the invention of the steam engine in England
in 1769. The use of the new steam power for manufacturing
was the beginning of that technological transformation which
has profoundly affected the inherited habits, manners, and
viewpoints of man. His manner of life has been modified in

a hundred ways. The consequent strain upon the intellectual and spiritual resources of Occidental men has been so great that it is a serious question whether man can endure the civilization that he himself has built. There is a straight line of development from the steam engine to the atomic bomb.

The United States gradually took on industrialization in the first half of the nineteenth century but the change came very rapidly after 1850. Brethren history has been enmeshed with the American development. Our life is lived in one of the great industrial nations of the globe. The real understanding of what has happened to Brethren Church life since 1851 is to be read as adaptation or adjustment to the growing urban-industrial society. It is adaptation rather than some rosily conceived progress or triumph.

The appraisal of the benefits of adjustment to the rising American order requires more wisdom than is now available. Perhaps such an appraisal must await the clarification of the destiny of our urban capitalistic industrial order.

# Chapter 7

# FIRST ORGANIZATIONS IN AMERICA

We shall never quite solve the puzzle that after migrating to Pennsylvania as a party, Peter Becker's group held no common religious services until the autumn of 1722. To be sure, there had been arguments at Creyfeld. But we are certainly correct in saying that the arguments had been adjourned and those who started together felt themselves sufficiently harmonious to travel together.

The *Ephrata Chronicle* is our source here. The *Chronicle* with its absurd veneration and exaltation of Conrad Beissel must be read with discrimination. But its main errors are in interpretation and in imputing motives, rather than in factual data.

Telling of Beissel's coming to Germantown in 1720, the *Chronicle* gives us a very penetrating analysis of the Pietists and the Brethren in the free and materialistic atmosphere of Pennsylvania. We quote:

For many, who had maintained a very proper walk in Germany had here hung up their holy calling on a nail, and, what was worst, would give no one credit for zeal or diligence. Among these were several who in the Palatinate had let themselves be driven from house and home, but here left great wealth behind them after their death. All this caused him [Beissel] much concern; for he everywhere saw the pious sitting at the helm and exercising magisterial offices. As he saw clearly that his trade[1] would not be of much use to him in this country, he determined to learn the weaver's trade, and so put himself under the instruction, for a year, of Peter Becker, a member of the Baptists. These good people showed him much love, and confessed all their condition to him, namely,

---

[1] Beissel had been a skilled baker.

how upon the ocean they had lost their love for one another, and now had even become scattered over the country. That the great freedom of this land was one cause of their being thus sold under the spirit of this world, through which all godly influences had been lost, and each one depended upon himself. "See, dear Friend," they further said, "thus it has happened to us; we have become strangers one to the other, and nearly all love and faithfulness have been lost among us."[2]

The *Chronicle* goes on to claim for Beissel the credit of stirring "the Baptists" to hold a meeting. But since the first meetings were held more than a year after Beissel had left Germantown, this may be doubted. In the autumn of 1722 Peter Becker with two other Brethren made a visit to all the scattered Brethren. House-meetings were held in Germantown alternately at Becker's and Gomorry's until the winter set in. In the summer the meetings were resumed at Becker's home.

In August 1723 a rumor spread that the eloquent Christian Libe was coming to America. Some of the people from the interior came to meet him. The rumor was false. But Becker and the Germantown Brethren kindly entertained them and a meeting was held at Becker's house. This led to a second meeting soon afterward. Four weeks later a group from Germantown visited the "newly awakened" on the Schuylkill. Six of the attendants desired baptism.

This issued in the first American organization. Peter Becker was chosen to baptize the candidates. The story of those events has perhaps never been better told than by Martin G. Brumbaugh. Since Brumbaugh's book is out of print, we quote:

Doubly memorable Christmas Day, 1723! Christ's anniversary and the date of the birth of His church in America! There is an activity at Peter Becker's house in Germantown. The spindles are still; and the voice of praise is raised. Six persons, Martin Urner, his wife Catherine, Henry Landis, his wife, Frederick Lang, and John Mayle, all from what is now the Coventry district, were in the midst of seventeen members, and they were preparing to hold the first immersion in the church in America. There was no ordained minister this side of the Atlantic. The

---

[2] The *Ephrata Chronicle*. Pages 15 and 16.

members hold a council. Peter Becker is chosen to act as elder. The preliminary examination is held, prayer is offered, and then these twenty-three souls walk out into the winter afternoon, in single file, headed by Peter Becker. They journey to the Wissahickon Creek. The group kneels. Overhead the solemn sentinels of the forest fastness—the pines and hemlock—are stilled. The ice-bound stream utters strangely solemn music. Curious eyes from the Kelpianites rest reverently upon the group. Peter Becker's voice breaks the stillness. The prayer is ended. The six candidates for membership in God's family are led one by one into the water and are baptized by trine immersion. The procession returns to Germantown. They assembled in the house of John Gomorry. It is evening now. The old-time tallow-dips are lighted. They gather around a long table, a hymn is sung, and in the silent evening hour, with no witness but God, and curious children, these people begin the observation of the ordinances of God's house on Christmas evening, 1723. The sisters on one side, the brethren on the other, arise and wash one another's feet. Then they eat the Lord's Supper, pass the kiss of charity with the right hand of fellowship, partake of the holy communion, sing a hymn, and go out. It is night! But under God's guidance their acts have been repeated in a thousand twilights, in all parts of this country in all the years that have come and gone; and, please God, we will repeat them again and again until He shall say, "It is enough. Come up higher."

Let us look yet more closely at this company. Who are they? Six are already named. They are babes in Christ. But the other seventeen are warriors of two continents. They had a remarkable career. At the head sat Peter Becker, pioneer preacher in America. He could have told of blessed meetings in Creyfelt and of sermons by Elders Mack, Libe, and Naas. He is not a gifted preacher, but he leads the sacred music that fills the dimly-lighted room with echoes of heaven's choir. His prayers are eloquent and overmastering. He loved God and talked with Him in the full faith of an expectant child of the King.

To his right sat John Jacob Price, who had prayed and preached in the Rhine Valley with Elder Naas. He was not large in body, but fervent in spirit. There was Stephen Koch, John Hildebrand, Henry Traut and Henry Holsapple, of whom the reader has already heard. They were rich in experiences with God's people in Germany. There was John Gomorry, in whose house they sat, near him were Jeremiah and Balser Traut, Daniel Ritter, John Kempfer, Jacob Koch, and George Balser Gans, all sterling men of God.

To the left of Peter Becker sat Maria Hildebrand, whose daughter was destined to wed a son of founder Mack. By her side sat Magdalene

Traut, Anna Gomorry and Johanna Gans. Seated in their midst were the six new members—twenty-three in all. Who can lift the veil and record this hour's holy service? What thoughts, what emotions, what religious experiences, what covenanted pledges, what rejoicings, moved lips and heart and head! To God only is known the ecstasy of that communion. "Ye know not now; but ye shall know hereafter." Blessed beginning of the church in America; may her latter days be like her first!

The congregation was now organized. The spirit of the Master was upon them. The next autumn the congregation decided to undertake a general visitation to all their brethren in the whole country. October 23, 1724, they started.[3]

The enthusiasm of this pioneer Brethren historian is justified. The Brethren are held in fellowship by the New Testament symbols or ordinances. It is impossible to conceive of a Church of the Brethren apart from the agape and communion table. Others may talk eloquently and poetically about the "altar." Our characteristic expression is the fellowship about the table—even as the gospels picture.

In the year 1724 a very active missionary spirit burned in the newly organized church. The *Chronicle* tells us that they wrote an epistle to the congregation in Holland. The old chronicler writes:

The next spring, of 1724, however when they resumed their meetings, there was given to them such a blessing that the whole region was moved thereby. Particularly among their youth was this movement felt, who now, to the great edification of their elders, began to walk in the fear of the Lord and to love the Brethren. And as the fame of this awakening spread abroad, there was such an increase of attendance at their meetings that there was no room to contain the majority. The following summer again many among them were moved, and love feasts were held, through which many of them were impelled to join them, and so their communion experienced a speedy increase.[4]

On October 23, 1724, the Germantown church sent its entire male membership (fourteen) to visit the scattered members in the interior. Evidently this was in anticipation of the impending winter, which would practically stop travel.

---

[3] M. G. Brumbaugh, *A History of the German Baptist Brethren.* Pages 155-160.
[4] The *Ephrata Chronicle.* Page 23.

The evangelizing party traveled, seven on horseback and seven on foot. The fact that seven could travel on horseback suggests the relative affluence of the community at this early date.

Their first visit was to Brother John Jacob Price on the Indian Creek. Thence they traveled to Falckner's Swamp and held services at the house of a Brother Albertus, where a meeting was held with breaking of bread; so also at Oley, and then at the Schuylkill (Coventry). On November 7 an organization was formed by electing Martin Urner as preacher. This is the second Brethren church to be established in America. Here on November 8, they also held a love feast, no doubt at the house of Martin Urner. At this place two persons were baptized. These two were Peter Heffly and Owen Longacre. Andrew Sell had formerly been baptized at Germantown. There were thus nine members at Coventry.

This was the end of their contemplated missionary tour.

At Coventry, however, news was received that in the Conestoga country were a number of awakened souls. The Brethren decided to continue their journey to the Conestoga. The party divided for the night. Those who were afoot spent the night at John Graff's and the riders at Jacob Weber's. On the 10th they united at Rudolph Nagele's, at that time a Mennonite. From Nagele's they went to visit Conrad Beissel and Michael Wohlfahrt, who at that time were living a solitary or hermit life. On the night of the 10th they lodged with Stephen Galliond. The next day they pushed on to Henry Hohn's. On the 12th a meeting was held at this man's house. Beissel was present. The revival spirit was powerfully manifested. The theme of the Brethren was baptism, the hope of fallen man.

At the close of the meeting five precious souls asked for baptism— Henry Hohn and wife, John Mayer and wife, and Joseph Shafer. They were baptized in the apostolic manner by Peter Becker in Pequa creek. This ceremony was so impressive that a sixth, Veronica, wife of Isaac Frederick, was also baptized. And now a strange event must be recorded! Conrad Beissel saw all this. He knew it was his duty to be baptized. But he had such an exalted opinion of his own religious experiences in his hermit life that he could not submit to baptism at the hands of Peter Becker, whom he regarded as inferior to himself in religious thought. In this perplexity he suddenly remembered that Jesus had submitted to John "to fulfill all righteousness." Consequently, after Sister Frederick came up out of the water, "Beissel came down from his spiritual pride, humbled himself before his friend Peter Becker, and was by him baptized on the same day in apostolic-wise, under the water" [quotation from the *Chronicle*].

That evening a love feast was held at Brother Hohn's house. This was November 12, 1724. The following Sunday a meeting was held at Sigmund Landert's house, and Landert and his wife were baptized. The stream was so muddy on this occasion that some of the members protested against its fitness, holding that baptism should be administered as Alexander Mack taught, "in a running stream of clear water." As these people were strangers to the Brethren, Peter Becker addressed the people as follows: "These two persons have applied to us for baptism; but as they are unknown to us in their walk and conversation, we make this announcement of the fact to all men here present, especially to their neighbors. If you can bear favorable witness concerning their lives, it is well, and we can baptize them with the greater assurance; but if you have any complaints to bring against them, we will not do it." This is the first recorded instance of a practice honored by the Brethren to this day. It evidently dates to the beginning in Germany. This is the beginning of the church in Lancaster County. Since the distance was so great, the Germantown members advised these to select a preacher and form a separate congregation. Conrad Beissel was chosen. Then the kiss of peace was given and the Brethren returned to Germantown.[5]

Thus the year 1724 closed with three Brethren congregations established in the New World: Germantown, Coventry, and Conestoga.

---

[5] M. G. Brumbaugh, *A History of the German Baptist Brethren.* Pages 160-165.

## Chapter 8

## THE BEISSEL MOVEMENT AND EPHRATA

We give attention to as much of the story of the Ephrata Society as seems to have bearing on Brethren history. It provides valuable documentation on Schwarzenau and early Brethren life in America.

Johann Conrad Beissel was born in 1690 at Eberbach on the Neckar, in the Palatinate. He was the post-humous son of a drunken baker. His first eight years he was cared for by a godly mother. At her death the orphan was left to an uncertain existence under the care of older brothers and sisters.

Apprenticed to a jovial, violin-playing, dancing baker, he became an expert baker and a musician. At twenty-five he experienced a typical Pietistic conversion. He became firmly convinced that he was a divinely chosen instrument, and seemed able to impress this conviction effectively upon others. He depended upon emotional experience to yield intellectual guidance. The results of such a course are sometimes unusual to the point of being bizarre. Such was the case with Beissel.

Beissel moved repeatedly and came to Heidelberg, where he worked for a godly baker. He was arrested for attendance at the Collegia Pietistica but refused ransom by his employer and received a sentence of banishment. He then sought refuge at Schwarzenau. There he was employed by a baker who was an Inspirationist. At Schwarzenau he met Johann F. Rock, one of the founders of the Community of the True Inspiration. Beissel leaned toward the Inspirationists but lacked the emotional discipline and the knowledge to remain long with them. He came in touch with the Brethren but never really accepted the Brethren's position on the New Testament as the sufficient rule of life.

Beissel circulated through Schwarzenau, Marienborn, and Creyfeld. Then he came to America with two friends, Stiefel and Stuntz, attracted by reports of the hermitage on the Wissahickon. This was the community called The Woman in the Wilderness, led by Johann Kelpius, and is frequently referred to as a Rosicrucian movement. When he arrived at Germantown he found that this establishment had disbanded. And so he apprenticed himself to Peter Becker to learn the weaver's trade.

In the autumn of 1721 he and his friend Stuntz went into the remote Conestoga country to live as hermits. Isaac Van Bebber and George Stiefel joined them. The four lived in meditation and prayer. One by one his companions left him, but in 1724 Michael Wohlfahrt, an extreme Pietist, joined him.

All this time Beissel was unhappy with what he regarded as the spiritual barrenness that he found in the New World and sighed for the fervid emotional religion he had known in Europe. Often he ate nothing for three days and said that he attained to a blessedness in his communion with God which neither the world nor time could ever outweigh. Then he became concerned about baptism as a transplanting into the death of Christ. But he knew no congregation or man that he counted worthy to baptize him. Once he baptized himself in Mill Creek but it brought him no satisfaction, with no witnesses to make it valid. The account of his submission to baptism by Peter Becker was given in the previous chapter. The *Ephrata Chronicle* concludes the account of this baptism occasion with the observation that Providence brought it about that those who had been baptized with him elected him as their teacher. "Without himself seeking it, he was thrust into the vineyard."

The years 1724 to 1728 were troubled years for the frontier

congregation under the leadership of the unstable, erratic Beissel. He had imbibed Sabbatarianism prior to his baptism, no doubt under the influence of the Seventh Day Baptists in the vicinity of Philadelphia. Beissel proclaimed the authority of the law of Moses and the superiority of celibacy. In 1728 he published a defense of the Sabbath. In December 1728 Jan Meyle, one of his followers, rebaptized him in the Conestoga Creek, and then Beissel rebaptized all who adhered to his views. This was "giving back to the Brethren" their baptism.

From 1728 to 1732 the secessionist congregation exhibited a peculiar evolution. Beissel recognized "three classes of members in his spiritual household; the Household members, or those who were married; the solitary brethren, who lived a single, chaste life; and the Spiritual Virgins, who from time to time fled to him and placed themselves under his guidance and vowed to live a pure, virgin life." The celibate estate was regarded as superior. As from the days of Hochmann, the ideal marriage was that of meek and quiet souls to Jesus. The life of the congregation was stormy. In fact, Beissel carried a tempest with him.

We are amazed at the near-idolatry that the simple-hearted followers manifested for this magnetic person.

He conducted all meetings . . . with astonishing strength of spirit, and used so little reflection over it, that even in the beginning he was not suffered to use a Bible; so that the testimony might not be weakened by written knowledge. He began his discourse with closed eyes, before a large crowd of hearers; and when he opened his eyes again, the most of them were gone, not being able to endure the Spirit's keenness.[1]

In 1732 Beissel called together the elders of his congregation, placed a New Testament in their hands and bade them rule by it. Then he disappeared. Some time later they found him eight miles away on the banks of the Cocalico Creek, whither he had gone to share hermit life with Emanuel Eckerlin. Meanwhile quarrels disrupted his congregation.

---

[1] The *Ephrata Chronicle*.

Some moved to join Beissel. And that was the beginning of Ephrata.

In 1735 there was a great religious revival which resulted in large accessions to the Ephrata community. Beissel seemed to have strange power, as when he established his hermitage at Cloister it was then a desolate region, yet men and women came from distant parts and voluntarily assumed hardships, bearing burdens, drawing plows, sleeping on rude benches with a block of wood for a pillow some of which used by the solitary for sleeping purposes are still to be seen in the Sister House at Ephrata.[2]

Beissel was tireless in proselyting, and he traveled extensively and frequently with his monastic companions. The years 1738 and 1739 saw a general exodus from the Germantown Brethren in which six families joined the Beissel Household and seven persons joined the Solitaries. The total is said to have been seventeen adults. Alexander Mack had been dead since 1735. With his steadying influence gone, the conditions in colonial Pennsylvania were changing rapidly. A deep nostalgia had risen in the souls of many.

The *Chronicle* credits this accession to direct divine influence.

It must be known that this Baptist removal to Ephrata was wholly unexpected to the Superintendent [Beissel] and to the congregation. Indeed they had resolved not long before, because those of the Baptists who had gone out to them had turned out so badly, that they would not receive any more of this people: but who can withstand the counsels of God? and who can set bounds to his Spirit? It was indeed a great marvel to the Superintendent that those who according to their spiritual age, could have been his fathers, now became as children unto him, and put themselves under his leading.

Among the well-known converts to Ephrata were Conrad Weiser and Peter Miller. The latter, a Reformed minister of great learning, took ten families with him to Ephrata. Upon Beissel's death on July 6, 1768, Miller succeeded him in the office of superintendent.

---

[2] S. G. Zerfass, *Ephrata Cloister Souvenir*, 1921.

Ephrata put out several branches and the movement persisted for many years, but in alliance with the Seventh Day Baptists rather than the Brethren. They, however, retained marks of Brethren influence. Their achievements in music and printing are well known.

Ephrata, with its strange combination of mysticism, Sabbatarianism, and monasticism, was an outgrowth of Separatist Pietism. From the quicksand of such unstable emotionalism the levelheadedness of men like Alexander Mack and Peter Becker guarded us. Had the Brethren not held firmly to the New Testament as their guide they would have been open to the same excesses of religious expression as were the Beisselites.

The state of Pennsylvania has now taken over the Ephrata Cloister and is restoring it as a historical site.

## Chapter 9

## GERMANTOWN—MOTHER CHURCH

Germantown has long carried the title "mother church" among the Brethren. Claim to the title rests on such bases as priority in date, the cultural importance of Germantown for German Americans, the personalities residing there, and the fact that the first Brethren meetinghouse was built there. The growing center of the church was elsewhere—in the Conestoga country (Lancaster County). The Brethren multiplied, not in an urban, but in a rural setting.

Germantown was without a rival as the German capital of America from its founding until after the War of 1812. The Germans from Maine to Georgia got their books, almanacs, Bibles, and newspapers in their mother tongue from Germantown. News and views from this locality gained disproportionate value. The trade of the prosperous German settlements of southeastern Pennsylvania flowed through it to the port of Philadelphia. Often its traders were the brokers for this "back country." Such items as ink, paper, and type from there were furnished to all Germans of the early American period and to some English-speaking people. Its knitting and weaving industries thrived. Thus an undue proportion of its residents became magnates of wealth.

Germantown reflected the glory of the flourishing port of Philadelphia until that city swallowed up its satellite. The great industrial growth of Philadelphia then threw Germantown into the shade about 1815. The flood of German immigrants into America after 1820 did not affect the situation, for these were of a temper different from that of pietistically inclined immigrants of the eighteenth century; they went westward to the Mississippi Valley and established their centers at Cincinnati, St. Louis, Chicago, and Milwaukee. Germantown became a small community of slowly assimilating Germanic people circumscribed by a larger population of English origin. This situation was not favorable to the growth of a large Brethren church.

The leadership of the eighteenth-century congregation at Germantown was outstanding. It included such personalities as Peter Becker, Alexander Mack, Sr., Alexander Mack, Jr., and the two Christopher Sauers. In 1788 the congregation elected to the ministry a man named Peter Keyser, Jr., whose ministry was destined to span the period of the eclipse of Germantown by Philadelphia. He was a minister in Germantown and Philadelphia for sixty-one years and the elder for forty-seven. No man is more truly a link between colonial and early American times than Peter Keyser, Jr.

Philadelphia was the first urban congregation of the Church of the Brethren. The church in Philadelphia stemmed from Germantown. Services were held in a Philadelphia schoolhouse in 1813, and house meetings may have been held for many years before that. There is no evidence of any formal organization prior to March 1, 1817. One of the truly fortunate circumstances of our annals is that we have an excellent record of this first church in an industrial city. Roland L. Howe has written *The History of a Church (Dunker)*, giving the record of the Philadelphia congregation through one hundred thirty years—almost the life span of American industrialism.

As noted at the beginning of the chapter, the first Brethren meetinghouse was built in Germantown. G. N. Falkenstein, in his book, *History of the German Baptist Brethren Church,* traces the steps that led up to this project. From 1722 to 1732 the meetings were held in the homes of the members, probably most of the time at the Becker, Gomorry, Gantz, Traut, or

Kalckgasser homes. The coming of the Mack party in 1729 increased the size of the group, though there was a notable movement then to the "back country" where more land was available.

Morgan Edwards,[1] looking back from 1770, observes that "the reason of their (i.e., the Tunker baptists) having no more places of worship is, that they chose rather to meet from house to house in imitation of the primitive Christians." This gives clear indication of the noninstitutional bias of our spiritual ancestors. It reminds us of the "House Amish," who even yet refuse to build church houses lest the direct face-to-face character of the church fellowship be lost. The building of the meetinghouse at Germantown was a mark of urban influence. In the western country of Ohio and Indiana some of the churches kept the primitive custom of house meetings until the 1830's or 1840's.

Here are the steps in the Germantown procedure. In 1732 Christopher Sauer erected a large house sixty by sixty feet in size. Of it Falkenstein says:

> The second story of this house was constructed with partitions hinged to the joist so that when necessity required, they could be swung open and a large audience room secured. Here the Brethren worshiped until 1860, when the second Christopher Sauer was an elder of the church. His increasing family and growing business demanded all the room in the house.

Then Peter Shilbert's property, a half acre lying about a half mile outside the main village, was given to the trustees of "the Religious Society or Community of the people called Dutch (German) Baptists and belonging to the Meeting of that people in or near Germantown." The four trustees were Alexander Mack, Christopher Sauer, Peter Leibert, and George Schreiber. The deed was dated August 11, 1760, and the four made a declaration of trust the next day. On this land stood what was known as the Pettikoffer house. Johannes Pettikoffer

---

[1] *Materials Towards a History of the American Baptists.*

and his wife, Ann Elizabeth, had sold it for sixty-five pounds when they left Germantown to join the Ephrata community in 1739.

The Pettikoffer house did not meet the full requirements of the Germantown Brethren for a house of worship, but they used it with some remodeling for ten years. The declaration of trust reads:

> One room in the said Messuage[2] to be made use of for a meeting place of the said people at or near Germantown . . . the which room may be improved or enlarged for the better convenience of the said meeting . . . and one room and kitchen of the said Messuage to be made use of for a dwelling place for some widow woman of the said society or community to live in rent free.

The last provision in this declaration of trust may be said to be the beginning of old people's homes among the Brethren. After the building of the stone meetinghouse in 1770 the erstwhile Pettikoffer house was set aside as a home for widows and remained in such use until 1861. Without questioning at all the benevolent motives of the congregation, the present writer would observe that this Pettikoffer house provided a convenient step in 1760 to the genuine meetinghouse of 1770. He would also express the hope that the spirit of fraternity that the Germantown Brethren exhibited in collectively meeting the complex problems of Christlike living would ever animate this fellowship as industrial conditions become more and more difficult.

The stone meetinghouse, built in 1770, was located in the rear of the Pettikoffer house. It was thirty feet square with an attic for storage and for miscellaneous uses and a full basement where cooking for love feasts was done. An outside staircase reached the attic. The membership at that time was fifty-seven.

In 1793 a cemetery was begun on the church grounds. In anticipation of a need for more ground, that same year an adjacent lot containing a log hut and a good stone house

---

[2] A rare term meaning a dwelling with adjacent buildings and adjoining lands.

was purchased for four hundred thirty pounds. Half the money was paid by voluntary subscriptions the year of purchase and the remainder on April 1, 1805.

**The Germantown Church**
The smaller left wing is the original church, built in 1770. The larger wing was added in 1897. Mack and other leaders of the colonial church are buried in the cemetery back of the church.

Later developments of the Germantown church house are related in M. G. Brumbaugh's history, page 169. He says:

. . . About 1880 a Sister Lehman and a few others had the meeting-house remodeled. The old attic was removed, the exterior plastered, and new appointments provided throughout. On May 16, 1897, a fine addition to the old meeting-house was dedicated. This addition was the gift of Jacob Z. Davis, a direct descendant of Alexander Mack. The dedicatory exercises on this occasion were conducted by the . . . pastor, George N. Falkenstein. The dedicatory sermon was preached by the writer of these lines from Psa. 122: 1-9.

Brumbaugh gives interesting facts about the financing of the Germantown congregation. It was the practice from early times to have a box in the meetinghouse into which the Brethren could drop money as they felt moved. There is extant a record of giving from 1747 to 1806. The church was generous to the poor. The deacons were custodians of the funds and distributed them to the poor.

Apparently a general donation occurred on the occasion of a love feast. The following contributions are recorded for the one held on March 26, 1749:

| Brother Gundy | 7s.6d. | Brother Schweitzer | 3s. |
|---|---|---|---|
| Sister White | 10s. | Brother Mack | 1s.6d. |
| Brother Snyder | 1s.6d. | Brother Weber | 2s.7½d. |
| Brother Schlingluff | 2s.3d. | Brother Richard | 2s. |
| Brother Gans | 5s. | | |

1 pound 15s.4½d.

For the feast there was expended:

For rice (3 pound) ......................................................... 9s.
For flour, spice, and butter ........................................ 1s.6d.
For bread and rolls ..................................................... 4s.10d.
For meat ...................................................................... 15s.

1 pound 10s.4d.

There was a meal given from this at noon and one in the evening.

In 1762 the contents of the box for 1761 and subscriptions paid for the repairs of the meetinghouse (the Pettikoffer house) the sum of forty-five pounds, thirteen shillings, four pence.

From time to time officials were elected. These seem to have been elders, ministers, and deacons; and the office of deaconess seems to have been recognized.

At a church meeting held in Germantown, April 2, 1826, all the members present;[3] our Brother Timothy Bangor was duly acknowledged and approved as a minister of the gospel in the church of German Baptist. And on the following sabbath evening, the church in Philadel-

---

[3] What a commentary on present-day councils!

phia, in convention ratified and approved in like manner Timothy Bangor as a minister and helper in the Gospel of Christ.

Signed on behalf of the church,
Peter Keyser, Secy.[4]

This minute makes clear that the Philadelphia church was an offshoot of Germantown. On October 12, 1826, the first love feast was held in Philadelphia. From then on Philadelphia had the spring love feast and Germantown the autumn one. The years 1834 and 1843 were exceptions, both feasts being held at Germantown those years. Philadelphia seems to have had both feasts in 1858 and 1866. The feast seems to have been neglected at Germantown after 1867. This indicates that the "mother church" was in eclipse and had come to be regarded as an annex to Philadelphia.

One of the staunch pillars, who lived far into the nineteenth century, was John Fox. We are indebted to him for the historical note he has inserted into the Philadelphia church records:

Names of Elders of the German Baptist Church in Germantown and Philadelphia from the year 1793 down to this date, Feb. 22, 1865:

| | | |
|---|---|---|
| Alexander Mack | John Sellars | Thomas Major |
| Philip Weaver | Peter Bruster | Sara Righter |
| Peter Leibert | John Van Lashett | John Fox |
| Thomas Langstroth | Timothy Bangor | Amos Crowell |
| Charles Hubbs | James Lynd | Henry Geiger |
| Justus Fox | John Heisler | David Harley |
| John Weaver | John W. Price | Christian Custer |
| Peter Keyser | John Righter | |

I have heard all these Brethren preach,

Your Brother in the Lord,
John Fox, Elder.

After Peter Keyser's death in 1849, and especially after 1867, the congregation seems to have been in a state of chronic weakness until the coming of George N. Falkenstein in 1893. From close investigation Elder Falkenstein wrote:

---

[4] *History of the Church of the Brethren in Eastern Pennsylvania.*

For many years the preaching was supplied, in part, by the Philadelphia ministers, John W. Price from Fitzwatertown, and others from adjoining churches. For a period of almost twenty years there was no resident minister. At times deacons conducted the preaching services. Finally there were no resident deacons, and when the present writer became pastor, in 1893, there was neither minister nor deacon in the congregation. For many years there are few, or no records at all.

There is evidence that from 1872 to 1877 J. T. Myers did the preaching and was virtually in ministerial charge at Germantown. He was a student during those years. Evidence is scant, but it seems that a Sunday school was begun in 1872. J. T. Myers was even then a partner in editing and publishing a church paper.

Howard Miller's *Record of the Faithful,* published in 1882, gives Germantown as having eighteen members and being without ministry. And this date was but two years after the remodeling of the church house in 1880! In Philadelphia there were two ministers and one hundred twenty-four members.

Just prior to G. N. Falkenstein's coming, an extraordinary personage came into Germantown's history. From January 1892 until about June 1, 1893, Wilbur B. Stover was in pastoral charge. He was a student in Temple College (later called Temple University) and the vision which led him to India filled his eyes and voice with glory. He lived in Philadelphia, but with him began a new day at Germantown.

Through the General Mission Board a resident minister was made possible for Germantown. George N. Falkenstein came and served very happily from June 9, 1893, until his resignation to go to Elizabethtown College, on December 1, 1900; he continued to fill the appointments until the following February.

T. T. Myers served for a year, followed by Walter Long for two years, 1902-1904. M. C. Swigart was called on November 13, 1905, and moved to Germantown on April 4, 1906. He remained as pastor and elder until his death on January 11, 1939.

A period of crisis followed, one feature of which was the rapidly shifting population of the urban area. B. F. Waltz became the pastor. The adjoining elders and then the general boards of the Church were enlisted in the preservation of Germantown.

The Annual Conference of 1947 approved a project of making Germantown a historical shrine and museum of Brethren history. This project has not called forth much local enthusiasm or general support. Little progress has been made on it.

In the meantime filling stations, stores, and lodging houses have crowded in upon the disintegrating neighborhood. Suddenly an immigration of Negroes started. And now the membership is widely scattered. Germantown at the mid-century is in a precarious situation. Its lot is a parable of the situation that faces members of American churches of all denominations in our great industrial centers. Shall the churches be sold and new centers be formed in the suburbs to which the members have moved? Or can the church continue its witness in the changed industrial community? Germantown might be made a historical museum, but God forbid that this should be the fate of the Church in the industrialized community in general!

## Chapter 10

## COLONIAL CONGREGATIONS:
## IN ENGLISH-URBAN AND GERMAN AREAS

We have already noted that the language and land factors directed the growth of the church toward the frontier region where the Germans were finding land available. There were some Brethren, however, in the English-urban area, and these took a course somewhat different from that of their brethren in the more remote German settlements.

Around Philadelphia itself, including Germantown, Coventry, and their offshoots, there came to be a small body of members who were in semi-isolation from the main body of the Brotherhood. It was the activity of the early elders in preaching and in the rising Annual Meeting that preserved the unity between these Brethren and the rest.

A tendency toward cleavage was apparent as early as 1791, in a record written by Alexander Mack, Jr., and quoted in Brumbaugh's history, page 504. On June 11, 1791, many Brethren from far and near came together at Germantown, including elders of several congregations. For some unexplainable reason Brumbaugh called this a "committee." It was clearly the Annual Meeting of 1791. In 1813 there is a minute about Annual Meetings. Article 3 says:

It has also been again requested of, and counseled by the old brethren that the great (annual) meeting should be continued in the order as it has been heretofore declared and laid down by the old brethren . . . those that will come should endeavor to arrive on Thursday evening so near to the place of meeting as to be able to be at the place Friday morning at 9 o'clock.

In 1791 that would have been June 11. One more Annual Meeting record uncovered!

The Mack record says:

A question was brought up by the brethren of the Germantown congregation to the assembled brethren coming from other places. The good purpose in this question consisted principally in this—How we could here in Germantown resist by a joint effort the very injurious evil which by the conformation to the world is worked upon the minds of the young, as we are living so near to the capital of the country.[1]

After careful deliberation the visiting brethren gave us, in the fear of the Lord, an advice to which they signed their names. We Germantown brethren also have signed in the name of the entire congregation, to bear witness that we have received their advice in submissive love and are willing to submit to the same loving advice, in the fear of the Lord, as the written testimony reports in detail, which is preserved in Germantown.

On that same evening, we broke the bread in the congregation at the Lord's supper which was specially appointed for the purpose, and have thus bound ourselves all together in love and faithfulness.

It is but natural that the problem of conformity to the world would be felt most acutely in the urban environment. One's heart is touched by the sincerity of heart and mind manifest in this early Annual Meeting. Of a variety of further items that might be cited, let one prior to 1892 suffice.

The Yearly Meeting of 1875 sent as a committee to the Philadelphia church: H. D. Davy, James Quinter, Moses Miller, C. Bucher, and J. R. Hanawalt. Nine items were presented by an aggrieved group, the first of which, significantly, was the bringing in of a paid pastor "called from a distance." The points were examined individually; the summarizing exhortation of the committee's report is eloquent:

Considered, that from the foregoing grievance, and from the departure we see, we would most earnestly and affectionately urge the brethren and sisters of the Philadelphia church to adhere to the doctrine of non-conformity to the world in dress, in spirit, and in every way that

---

[1] The capital in 1791 was Philadelphia.

doctrine can be applied, as this constitutes such a prominent doctrine of the gospel, and one of the peculiarities of our Brotherhood.[2]

In the *Gospel Messenger* of January 26, 1892, is found a letter from Isaac Frantz entitled "Impressions by the Way." The first church mentioned in the letter was in the German area, but the others were in the English-urban section. Here are some statements:

By request of the Executive Committee of the Book and Tract Work, I visited some of the churches in Eastern Pennsylvania.

Our first work was in the Chiques church, which has a membership of over 500 members. Here the true merits of Tract Work, as adopted by the church, were not so well known, but, I am thankful to say, due respect was paid to my weak efforts, and here, as in my entire trip, when the merits of the Work were known, encouragement and financial aid were given, and I am convinced that the same will be the result all over the Brotherhood, if we all do our duty. One of the salutary influences here is the fact that the elders are loyal to the church and said, "Our heart is in the work." This is as it should be, for the lambs will be strong according as they are fed by the shepherds.

I was also impressed by their comfortable, neat, and clean houses of worship. As a people, we take great pains to have our meeting-houses attractive, neat and comfortable, which is a Christian duty. . . .

At the Green Tree and Coventry churches our mind was much impressed with the words, "The memory of the just is blest," by the repeated references to the departed, who gave their lives to the cause— Quinter, Umstead, and Price. . . .

In these churches some of the ancient landmarks of our church, especially that of non-conformity, are not so fully adopted, but the spirit manifested and the love enjoyed were such as shall never be forgotten.

I speak of this with much interest, because I feel that one of the greatest wants of our church is more true sociability, for can we not say, with the Apostle Paul, "Though we make every sacrifice and have not love, it profiteth nothing?"

This cluster of urban or near-urban churches came to be regarded as English and were set somewhat over against the other Eastern Pennsylvania churches, which were spoken of as German. In 1896 a petition was presented to the Eastern

---

[2] *Minutes of the Annual Councils of the Brethren,* printed by the Christian Publishers Association, Dayton, Ohio, 1876.

Pennsylvania district meeting asking for a division of the Eastern District between the English-speaking and the German-speaking churches. The petition was unanimously adopted. Thus arose the District of Southeastern Pennsylvania, subsequently called Southeastern Pennsylvania, New Jersey, and Eastern New York.

Now we turn to the German churches. We observed in an earlier chapter that Conestoga was the real "mother church" as far as growth was concerned. It was the third church to be organized.

Speaking at the Bicentennial Annual Conference in 1908, J. G. Royer summed up Conestoga's growth thus:

> Conestoga was one of the first organized colonial churches. In 1730 it had about thirty-five communicants. In 1748 it had 200, in 1770, having by that time received over 400 into fellowship it had only 86 communicants. From the very beginning, Conestoga church was now weakened by emigration, then recruited and strengthened by the faithful, earnest application of the home-community missionary method.

> What can we say for Conestoga today? for we still have her with us. Her territory has been divided and subdivided until there are now within her original boundary twenty congregations with a total membership of nearly 5,000 souls.[3]

The Conestoga brotherhood numbered about twenty when Michael Frantz took charge, and it had increased to about two hundred at his death. The church had the good fortune to have a worthy successor to Michael Frantz in the person of Michael Pfautz. He presided over the congregation from a few weeks after his ordination on September 25, 1748, until his death on May 14, 1769. The congregation grew surprisingly. In the first year of his eldership, fifty-seven persons were added to the church. From 1749 to 1755, one hundred more were baptized. The story goes that there were then seven years of barrenness, followed by another fruitful period. We are not sure whether Jacob Sontag or Christian

---

[3] *Two Centuries of the Church of the Brethren: Bicentennial Addresses.* Page 78.

Longenecker succeeded Michael Pfautz immediately, but soon after 1770 it was Elder Longenecker.

One of the very valuable evidences of research in Brumbaugh's history is his listing of the names of four hundred sixty-three persons who joined the Conestoga church from the days of Michael Frantz to the year 1799. In 1770 there were only fifty-three families and eighty-six persons on the communion roll. But that is eloquent testimony to the influence of Conestoga. The members had migrated south and west, and they carried their faith with them.

The study of the names on colonial church rolls is most instructive. These old church records contain the names of ancestors of a goodly part of the present membership of the Church. This is not surprising. Faith and family have always been intimately related. The inspired volume that we call the Old Testament, recording the history of a cluster of families, is an illustration of this linkage of faith and family. History moves forward on the twin bases of biological inheritance and religious ideology. The history of the Church is no exception.

A statement by J. G. Royer, found on page 78 of *Two Centuries of the Church of the Brethren: Bicentennial Addresses,* well illustrates the secret of the successful expansion of the Church of the Brethren: "In 1846 the Annual Meeting was held in the reduced territory then known as the Conestoga church. But the Conestoga of 1846 is today seven congregations with a membership of over 1600. Growth — growth by the home-community missionary method."

## Chapter 11

## COLONIAL CONGREGATIONS:
## WESTWARD IN PENNSYLVANIA

The fourth colonial congregation to be organized was Oley, in Berks County. It took its name, apparently, from the township in which it was located. The organization was effected on the occasion of the first communion service, presided over by Peter Becker. In 1742 a general exodus of members to more attractive farm land occurred. Many went to the valley of the Conacocheague. Presently there was another general exodus, caused by favorable reports from the first group. This congregation chronically lacked ministers, although Martin Gaby and John Jodder were elected to the ministry here. In 1770 Morgan Edwards listed only twenty members and the two ministers. We do not know how many persons entered into the fellowship of the Brethren in this congregation and then moved on westward, helping to establish new congregations.

In this territory the second meetinghouse of the Brethren was built. It stands near the village of Pricetown and is the oldest unaltered meetinghouse of the Brethren and one of the oldest unaltered houses of worship in the United States. It came into being largely through the enthusiasm of Martin Gaby (or Gaube), who began to desire earnestly a special meetinghouse already about 1766. In 1775 he built himself a large house on his farm, which included what is now Pricetown. A large oak tree stood near the site where he planned to build the meetinghouse. In the nice weather of summer the

*Photo by E. G. Hoff*

**Pricetown Meetinghouse, Maiden Creek Congregation**

Built in 1777, this is the oldest church house in the Brotherhood that remains unaltered and one of the oldest churches in the United States. Its stark simplicity reflects the ideas of the early Brethren, who were so impressed with the rational element of worship and the fact that the church was a fellowship that they feared to follow the more institutional and formal pattern of popular Christianity.

meetings were held in the shade of the oak. In bad weather they were held in Gaby's house. Then the meetinghouse was built in 1777. .

The fifth church may be said to have been Great Swamp in Bucks County. There was an "awakening" among a few persons here in 1733. They sent to Germantown for someone to instruct them. John Naas had recently settled in New Jersey and he was their first visiting minister. He baptized six and established a meeting. In 1735 Peter Becker and Martin Urner visited them and baptized five. A love feast was held with the group of eleven and an organization was then effected. Abraham Duboy settled here in 1738 and was their first elder until his death on March 21, 1748. Then John Frick became their minister but was not ordained as an elder until 1770. In 1770 Edwards listed twenty-eight members.

It is chronicled that this congregation had great trouble with the Moravians at Great Swamp. In 1742 Count Zinzendorf persuaded some of the Brethren to go to Bethlehem, but most of them soon returned. In the later years of the eighteenth century the records lapsed, and tradition is confused. The Brethren still exist in Bucks County, but their relationship to the original congregation is not clear.

The sixth church of the colonial period was the Amwell church in New Jersey, begun in 1733. The well-beloved John Naas was the founder. Naas landed in Philadelphia in September 1733 and soon went with four families to New Jersey. These families became the nucleus of the church. Naas was elder until his death on May 12, 1741. John Beckleshammer was the only other elder the church had until after 1790. Naas had many talents and was sound and spiritual. The leadership that followed was apparently not equal to that of Naas.

In 1790 Morgan Edwards visited the New Jersey Brethren. He found that they had no one then who could speak English. The statistics he gathered, dated February 2, 1790, are as follows:

| | |
|---|---|
| Churches of the Tunker Baptists in New Jersey | 1 |
| Members | 46 |
| Families | 28 |
| Souls (allowing five to a family) | 140 |
| Ministers, ordained | 0 |
| Ministers, licentiate | 2 |

The two ministers were William Housel and Abraham Lausche.

A great change came in the matter of language. Amwell came to be the first congregation using English. In 1811 Israel Paulson, Sr., gave ground for a meetinghouse. He was elected to the ministry at an unknown date, but probably before 1811, and was the elder for many years. Being unable to speak German, he had to preach in the only language he knew— English. He died on February 14, 1856. The linguistic difference accentuated the geographical isolation. There were divisions in the church itself that hinged on the personalities of its ministers. And so the church in New Jersey never grew much. Migration may have been an added factor. Today there is a small congregation at Amwell.

The seventh colonial church is White Oak. It acquired its name from the fact that the white oak grew in northwestern Lancaster County. The Lancaster County of colonial times had three "brotherhoods" within its borders. The creation of Dauphin County reduced its area and took away from it the Big Swatara congregation. The White Oak cluster of members settled near Lititz as early as 1729. Among the pioneers were George Reyer (Royer) and John Langanacre. In 1736 there were enough baptized members to hold the first love feast. Michael Pfautz presided. He served as their minister. He continued to live in the Conestoga territory and was elder there, but remained elder of White Oak until his death in 1769.

This poses the question whether Conestoga and White Oak were one or two congregations. The Brethren were not concerned with "congregations"—only with fraternalism. In 1772 there was a triple division in which the expanding and spreading brotherhood was to be recognized as three: Conestoga, White Oak, and Swatara. This seems chiefly to have been a division of labor among the ministers. In 1772 it was written that "the Lancaster and Schaefferstown road" was to be the dividing line.

The first resident minister of White Oak was Peter Hummer. He moved into the territory and bought a farm in 1753. The date of his election to the ministry is not definitely known, but may well have been immediately after 1753. He was the father of Catherine Hummer.

Catherine Hummer illustrates how close the colonial church still was to the atmosphere of Ephrata. White Oak was not far from Ephrata, and Beissel was then at the height of his power. Catherine Hummer's visions threw the whole Brotherhood into confusion. It was the business of the Yearly Meeting of 1763, held at Conestoga, to compose the differences and allay the clamor which had arisen over her visions. The visions were spread over several years. Peter, the minister-father, accepted them without question. But the summer after the Yearly Meeting of May 27-28, 1763, it developed that there was a moral defect in the seeress. When she was in her trances, no one save one young man, Sebastian Keller, could enter the room lest the trance be disturbed. Catherine subsequently married this young man and they lived long and honorably and reared six children. After Catherine's marriage, her visions ceased. The seeress who had talked with the spirits of the saints was disciplined. The blow was so heavy upon her father that he is reported never to have preached again.

The lack of baptisms at Conestoga for seven years (1775-1763) may well have been due to the trouble over Catherine Hummer's visions. The peculiar reticence and the involved rhetoric of the old narrative seem to point to this as the source of Michael Pfautz's great "tribulation." A tremendous problem of personalities, emotions, and faith was involved.

Other ministers at White Oak were Peter Eichelberger, who was baptized in 1752, and Jacob Stoll, who was baptized in 1748. Both of these subsequently removed to Conestoga and became elders. Johannes Tug was baptized in 1749 and elected a minister in 1770. George Miller was baptized in 1752 and elected a minister at an unrecorded date. Christian Longenecker was baptized in 1754 and elected to the ministry in 1764. He was ordained as an elder, and succeeded Michael Pfautz in 1769.

In 1770 Morgan Edwards listed sixty-five members in the

White Oak congregation. The White Oak family names are found in every area of the Church of the Brethren. The congregation was at the "growing point" of the church. Its ministers were worthy. But in the late 1790's a serious rift arose between the aged ministers, Christian Longenecker and Johannes Tug. The Yearly Meetings of 1799, 1803, and 1804 were occupied with the trouble at White Oak. Elder Longenecker died in 1808, aged seventy-six, and his death happily seems to have terminated the discord in the ministry.

There was no meetinghouse in White Oak until 1859, when two were built—Kreider's near Manheim, and Longenecker's near Lititz. Today White Oak stands with five meetinghouses, and in the *Yearbook* of 1950 it reports five hundred thirty-one members. It is perhaps as fine a specimen of Dunker church life of the rural order as could be cited. It deserves a volume of its own annals.

We break with chronology here in the order of churches, for the sake of logical sequence. See the table at the end of the chapter.

The next church we list is Big Swatara. As already noted, it was located in what became Dauphin County. It grew out of the White Oak-Conestoga fraternities. The baptism of George Miller in White Oak in 1752 was noted above. Other members from White Oak settled near Miller and his wife. In 1756 Michael Pfautz began to preach for them regularly. By 1770 George Miller and Adam Hammacher were ministers but not yet elders. There were then thirty-nine members. In 1780 George Miller was ordained to the eldership by Christopher Sauer and Martin Urner. At the same time Johannes Tug of White Oak was ordained. In the rearrangement of 1772, Big Swatara had achieved a larger degree of independence. Its records are few but a sturdy church represents it today. The histories of these congregations become genealogical studies for the Church of the Brethren.

The next church to note is Northkill, named after a small

river in the townships of Tulpehocken and Bern in Berks County. Its beginnings go back to 1748. Michael Frantz was the first elder. George Kleine, baptized by John Naas at Amwell, New Jersey, in 1739 and elected to the ministry there, moved to Northkill in 1750. Martin Frantz and Martin Urner ordained him to the eldership in 1757. He became elder of the congregation, which was carrying on in 1770 with eleven members. Northkill was on the frontier and suffered from constant removals and all sorts of religious excitements that seemed to strike the neighborhood. The old church is well known in memory, but the territory of Northkill and Oley is included in what in the nineteenth century came to be called the Maiden Creek congregation.

Another congregation was Little Swatara. We are told by Morgan Edwards that the members of this congregation lived in Tulpehocken Township in Berks County and overflowed into Besher Township, Lancaster County. About 1745, immigrants into this neighborhood were George Besher, Michael Frantz (not the before-named elder), Peter Heckman, John Frantz, and others. George Kleine came over from Amwell and preached, baptizing those named. The church was formed in 1757. Kleine was their elder in 1770 and Peter Heckman was their minister. There were forty-five members at that time. On August 12, 1780, the Michael Frantz mentioned above was ordained as an elder by Elders Sauer and Urner. Records are lacking, but a present-day congregation is descended from this colonial mother.

Brethren migrated, along with other Germans, to the newer agricultural lands to the south and west. One of the early movements, a very daring one, was across the Susquehanna River. This brought the Brethren into York County. There came to be four colonial churches in York County.

The oldest York County church was Little Conewago, located twenty miles from York and one hundred seven miles southwest of Philadelphia. The beginning here was in 1738, when, under the leadership of Daniel Leatherman, "one Eldrick, Dierdorff, Bigler, Gripe, Stutsman, and others united into a church." After Daniel Leatherman migrated, for a time Nicholas Martin was their minister. In 1770 there were fifty-two members. Today in the District of Southern Pennsylvania there is one of those deeply rooted churches, one of the finest products of the Christian faith, that is directly descended from Little Conewago. In some unrecorded manner the original name was changed to Upper Codorus.

*The History of the Church of the Brethren in the Southern District of Pennsylvania* has such a good sketch of this congregation that we quote it as an example of Christian life and fraternity among our early Brethren:[1]

Meetings were held in rotation over the district at private places— in barns or dwelling houses which were often built with an idea to throw two or more rooms together by large folding doors to accommodate a place for the meeting. A goodly number of brethren would come the evening before and a social time would be spent in Scriptural discussions and song and worship before retiring. Next morning breakfast was furnished by the host, assisted by guests, with the greatest delight to all present. The crowd began to swell to such a size that our attendance of today would be surprised. The hospitality of the host was specially fine. Dinner was furnished, free to all, at meeting. Their horses were cared for during the night and all well fed at meal time. A number of hostlers were always engaged prior to meeting to help to care for horses. The greatest respect was shown to everyone present, members, as well as neighbors. Sometimes these rotations would come around every sixteen weeks; later ten to eight weeks; finally the church houses were built. The old brethren were afraid when churches were built "something might be lost."

These rotations of meeting places were scattered over a distance of 50 miles between Westminster, Carroll County, Maryland, and York, York County, Pennsylvania. Christian Royer, John Myers, and Samuel Miller in Manchester district, Maryland; Henry Hohfs, Adam Buchers, Abraham Geimans, Samuel Myers, Jacob Millers, John Millers and Jacob Bussers, in Manheim township, Pennsylvania; Aaron Baughers, Philip Millers, in Codorus township, Pennsylvania; Jacob Stauffers, and

---

[1] Pages 191-193.

*Photo by E. G. Hoff*

**Folding Doors in the Home of Elder Aaron S. Baugher**

The Baugher home in York County was used as a meeting place. These doors could be thrown open to provide a large room.

Danners, in Heidelberg township, Pennsylvania; Andrew Millers, George Mummerts, and John Millers, in Jackson township, Pennsylvania; and other places. . . .

In 1865 about 40 families, members of this congregation, moved to Illinois, lured there by greater inducements for financial gain, by the broad fertile acres. This was quite a draw on our congregations as among them were a number of ministers and deacons. A number settled around Astoria where we find them connected with church history there. Among these were Hamms, Danners, Stremmels, Mummerts, Lerews, Millers, Fitzes, Geimans, Eberts, etc.

The Little Conewago Congregation or Upper Codorus Congregation, as now called, lies in part of two counties, York County, Pennsylvania, and Carroll County, Maryland, embracing a stretch of country about 50 miles square. The following churches were built in this area: Beaver Creek, Pleasant Hill, Black Rock, Chestnut Grove, Stoverstown, Melrose and Wildasin's school house.

The second church in York County was Conewago, some-

*Photo by E. G. Hoff*

## A Corner of the Tulpehocken Meetinghouse

The basement of this meetinghouse was used for school purposes, the main floor for church services.

*Photo by E. G. Hoff*

## Interior of the Tulpehocken Meetinghouse

times called Big Conewago. The first minister here was George Adam Martin. He united with the church in 1735, was ordained in 1739, and became an elder in 1741. He first lived in the Coventry church, then in Conestoga. Big Conewago was already a large church, because of immigration, by 1741. The rash and unruly Martin had to be expelled in 1760; he could not content himself with some of the practices of the Brotherhood.

Some Seventh Day sympathizers removed to York County, and settled near the Big Conewago. In 1758 Beissel organized these into the Bermudian Seventh Day Baptist Brethren church. After his expulsion in 1760, Martin went to Ephrata and was received as Beissel's disciple. Some of the Brethren at Big Conewago felt he should not have been expelled. Beissel sent him back with a letter commanding the Bermudian church to receive him as an elder. His preaching was popular. The situation was fraught with danger. At this point John Mack, son of Alexander Mack, Jr., and a Brother Staub visited all the members and explained the dangers of the Beissel movement. This blocked any mass movement to follow Martin, although all continued to attend his preaching.

In spite of this friction, the Bermudian Seventh Day Baptist Brethren and the Conewago Brethren worshiped together in the houses and barns of the area for many years. About 1820 the Seventh Day organization ceased, having been gradually absorbed by the Brethren.

Presiding elders of Big Conewago, in turn, were Daniel Leatherman, Nicholas Martin, George Brown, Isaac Latshaw, and William Trimmer. The last named was elder until the congregation was divided in 1849. The congregation then became the Upper Conewago and Lower Conewago congregations. This old church is distinguished by having had seven Yearly Meetings within its boundaries.

The third church in York County, Codorus, was organized in 1758. The people who settled here were among the sturdiest

*Photo by E. G. Hoff*

**Beds in the Attic of the Black Rock Church**

About fifty people could be accommodated over night in this attic on love-feast occasions. The Black Rock church is now the Upper Codorus church.

*Photo by E. G. Hoff*

**Old Brick Stove in the Black Rock Church**

The meals for the love feast and other occasions were prepared on this brick stove in the basement of the church.

and best of German immigrants. Among the earliest members
of Codorus were Rudy Yunt, Peter Brillhart, John Brillhart,
and Henry Neff. The first elder was Jacob Danner, son of
Henry Danner, who was a prominent man in the history of
York County and one of the five commissioners to view and
lay off the county in 1749. After Jacob Danner moved to
Frederick County, Maryland, Henry Neff was called to the
ministry and was in charge of the church until after 1775.
In 1770 the membership was listed as thirty-five.

The Codorus Brethren did not build a meetinghouse
until 1872. There are still an unusual number of sturdy old
Pennsylvania homes in the community, the partitions of which
are removable or show marks of having been removable for
holding church services—a testimony of the fraternity of the
days that our ancestors knew. Today three meetinghouses
accommodate the membership of three hundred seventy-five.

The fourth York County church is Bermudian. We have
already spoken of it in connection with Big Conewago, and
it is doubtful whether Bermudian should be listed as a separate
church. Beissel organized the group in 1758 and in 1762 sent
George Adam Martin to supervise it. When Martin found that
he could not carry all his former Brethren with him into the
Seventh Day church, he grew tired and went farther west to
what we know as Bedford County. After Martin's removal,
Henry Lohman was chosen minister. He was not an elder in
1770, although Morgan Edwards listed the membership at that
time as fifty-eight. We have already noted that a half century
later Bermudian merged with the Conewago congregation.

The Stony Creek church in Bedford County was a
western outpost of the Brethren in the colonial period. It was
on the fringes of European settlement. Indeed, settlement
beyond the Alleghenies was then of doubtful legality. But
there were venturesome settlers. Here George Adam Martin
came and preached in 1762. He soon had a small Seventh Day
church. Before many years the congregation began to observe

**Handmade Bench, Heidelberg Meetinghouse**

This is one of the two old handmade benches stored in the attic of the Heidelberg meetinghouse.

**Soup Dishes Stored in the Attic of the Heidelberg Meetinghouse**

The long hand-made table on which the soup dishes stand was also long used at the love feasts of this Eastern Pennsylvania congregation.

**Pewter Communion Cups, Heidelberg Meetinghouse**

**A Farm Near Brodbecks, Pennsylvania**

Love feasts of the Upper Codorus congregation were held in this barn on the Miller farm.

the first day and was recognized as Brethren. Morgan Edwards recorded it in 1770, when the seventh day was still kept, as having seventeen baptized members.

In summarizing his researches, that invaluable and industrious historian, Morgan Edwards, says:

Thus we see that there are in this province fifteen churches of Tunker Baptists, to which appertain eight ordained ministers, elders, or bishops, and thirteen exhorters, or probationers. . . . We see also that their families are about four hundred nineteen, which contain about two thousand and ninety-five souls allowing five to the family, whereof seven hundred sixty-three persons are baptized and in communion.

His fifteen churches included Ephrata, which is credited with one hundred thirty-five members.

We append a table of colonial churches in the area covered in this and previous chapters plus Antietam of the next chapter, as of 1770. When we consider the conditions and the stability which time has exhibited, the growth was really amazingly good.

| Congregation | State | County | Date Organized | First Minister | Membership in 1770 |
|---|---|---|---|---|---|
| Germantown | Pa. | Philadelphia | 1723 | Peter Becker | 57 |
| Coventry | Pa. | Chester | 1724 | Martin Urner | 40 |
| Conestoga | Pa. | Lancaster | 1724 | Conrad Beissel | 86 |
| Oley | Pa. | Berks | 1732 | Peter Becker | 20 |
| Great Swamp | Pa. | Berks | 1733 | Abraham Duboy | 28 |
| Amwell | N. J. | Hunterdon | 1733 | John Naas | 46 |
| White Oak | Pa. | Lancaster | 1736 | Michael Frantz | 65 |
| Little Conewago | Pa. | York | 1738 | Daniel Leatherman | 52 |
| Conewago | Pa. | York | 1741 | Geo. Adam Martin | 77 |
| Northkill | Pa. | Berks | 1748 | Geo. Kleine (Kline) | 11 |
| Antietam | Pa. | Franklin | 1752 | William Stover | |
| Great Swatara | Pa. | Dauphin | 1756 | George Miller | 39 |
| Little Swatara | Pa. | Berks | 1757 | Peter Heckman | 45 |
| Codorus | Pa. | York | 1758 | Henry Neff | 35 |
| Bermudian | Pa. | York | 1758 | Peter Miller | 58 |
| Stony Creek | Pa. | Bedford | 1762 | Geo. Adam Martin | 17 |

# Chapter 12

## COLONIAL CONGREGATIONS:
## SOUTH AND WEST

If ever a person outside our fraternity deserved our vote of gratitude, it is Morgan Edwards for his careful survey of "Tunker baptists." It is a sad misfortune that his manuscript on "Tunker baptists" in Maryland (and presumably south of Maryland) was never published and was destroyed by fire as it lay in the files of the Baptist Publication Society in Philadelphia.

Nevertheless, Edwards' record is not above criticism. He knew the Pennsylvania Brethren much better than he knew those living south of Pennsylvania. Why he overlooked the Antietam church in Franklin County, Pennsylvania, is difficult to see—unless he counted it with Maryland. He seems also to have overlooked the Ten Mile church in Washington County, far west of his outpost of Stony Creek. Accordingly we give attention to these two churches in this chapter apart from the Morgan Edwards' data.

The original Antietam brotherhood was one of the sturdiest and most fruitful colonial churches. Concerning this church we quote rather fully from *The History of the Church of the Brethren in the Southern District of Pennsylvania*.[1]

Antietam Congregation, according to the best information obtainable, existed as a mission of the churches of Eastern Pennsylvania and of York County some years before its organization in 1752. It was then known as the Conococheague District. In 1752, John Price moved to Antietam District from near Philadelphia. About this same time Bishop

---
[1] Pages 7-9.

Abraham Stouffer of Conewago or Germantown, who had been ordained by Peter Becker, moved into this community and effected a church organization. It is said that Geo. Adam Martin assisted in this work for awhile. In a few years because of ill health Abraham Stouffer returned to Conewago and William Stover was chosen to the ministry and ordained Bishop of the Congregation.

In 1754, William Stover and his family came here from Germantown, having a short time before come from Switzerland. He took up land about two miles west of the Prices. They soon became connected with the Church of the Brethren.

.    .    .    .    .

For the first fifty years the brethren suffered many privations on account of the French war in 1755, the Revolution 20 years later, and subsequent Indian wars together with many inconveniences incident to a newly settled country, as our part of the state was at that time. The dread of the Indian's tomahawk and scalping knife, was everywhere felt. In the morning before going to the fields to work, the farmer and his sons often bid good-bye to the balance of the family, fearing they might not return, or if permitted to do so, would find their loved ones murdered by the Indians. (From Brethren Almanac 1879.)

Under the guiding hand of their first resident Elder, Wm. Stover, the congregation worshipped in houses. Brother Jacob Miller was elected to the ministry, and in 1765 moved to Virginia. . . .

As was customary with other congregations, the Elder was elected for life. The seniority in the ministry was very much in evidence, even to the seating behind the table. The next oldest in the ministry always sat next to the Elder and was considered in authority according to his place in the pulpit. The deacons likewise recognized seniority. The oldest in office was seated directly across the table in front of the Elder with the next oldest beside him, and so on to the youngest. This order continued for nearly 100 years.

The Church was democratic in form but when the Elder, after consultation with the other ministers and deacons, made any declaration, it was usually accepted by the Congregation. The members of the Antietam Congregation, being of German descent, all spoke German in the early days. The sermons were all delivered in German until about 1830 after which time both German and English were used. After 1875, all English was used in the pulpit. In making the yearly visit by the deacons confirming the members in the Faith, the language most agreeable to the members was used. In 1900 very few members could even converse in German.

In 1881 about 100 members withdrew and formed what is known as the Old Order German Baptist Church. A record of events was preserved from this date. All definite records prior to the summer of 1880 have been lost to the Church. At that time Brother D. P. Saylor, of Monocacy Congregation was chosen Presiding Elder and retained this position until 1882 when Brother J. F. Oller was ordained.

. . . . .

There were four Annual Meetings held in the Antietam Congregation as follows: 1810—In the Antietam Meeting House; 1829—On a farm owned by Brother George Royer about one mile west of Antietam or Prices Church; 1847—On the farm of Brother Isaac Deardorff, two miles west of Antietam or Prices; and 1866—On the farm of Brother Jacob Price, one-half mile east of Prices Church. These pioneers were willing to open their homes in a hospitable manner in accord with the teachings of the New Testament. They not only "entertained strangers" but opened their homes to the community where all who would could meet and worship God and study His Word together. During the first 47 years of the existence of Antietam Congregation, all of the public worship and funeral services were held in the homes of the people.

Many of the homes were built to meet the needs. Often the partitions of adjoining rooms were made so that they could be moved. Benches were used for seats. These could easily be stored away when not in use. At very large meetings the services were held in the barn to accommodate more people who sat on the benches without backs, on the hay, or any other available space. Services were held in the open when occasion demanded.

Morgan Edwards makes a general statement that is provocative. After enumerating the churches as one in New Jersey, fifteen in Pennsylvania, seven in Maryland, and ten in the more southern states, he observes:

Their church government was purely republican as I observed in my first volume; but in Maryland (and I suppose in other states) they have a superintendent whose name is Daniel Leatherman; to him is referred the decision of variances among the ministers and the people, and as the Dunkers call all their ordained ministers bishops, it follows that Leatherman holds the rank of archbishop.

Daniel Leatherman is said to have been bishop of seven congregations in Maryland. These were probably not distinct congregations but rather neighborhoods in which services were held. Five more or less distinct centers can be named if Antietam is included. These would be Pipe Creek, Beaver Dam and Israel Creek, Middletown Valley, Baltimore, and Antietam. The four centers other than Antietam were east of the Blue Ridge Mountains. There may have been transient centers of which we do not know; we certainly cannot name ten south of Maryland.

In the eighteenth century Maryland meant the middle and eastern part of the present state. The idea that Daniel Leatherman was bishop of all the Maryland churches agrees with the tradition that originally all Maryland was included in the Pipe Creek congregation. Edwards' idea that Leatherman was an archbishop rests either on his own quaint conceit, on a misunderstood tribute to Leatherman's personal influence, or on his preponderant influence in the Yearly Meeting.

There were practically no Germans in Maryland prior to 1720. They were in Virginia first. Indeed, there was a small German immigration into Fredericksburg, Virginia, as early as 1614. In 1717, a party of twenty families—eighty souls—settled toward the Blue Ridge and became prosperous farmers. These Virginia Germans established communications with their kinsmen in Philadelphia. They opened the trail through Lancaster, York, Hanover, and the Monocacy River, across the Potomac.

Down this trail traveled the German pioneers from York and Franklin counties in their restless search for new lands and scenes. The frontier to the south was better protected than that to the west. Jost Hyte of Pennsylvania became interested in moving to the Valley of Virginia. In 1732 he led a party of sixteen families and settled near Winchester. That same year Lord Baltimore offered land on liberal terms in the unoccupied area in Maryland. From that year Maryland received a host of German-speaking immigrants.

Pipe Creek was our mother church in Maryland. Some members are thought to have settled near Linwood as early as

1745. Two of the earliest names are Ulrich Crumpacker, who had come directly from Germany in 1732, and Andrew Wolfe, who came from Coventry and probably had been baptized there. Wolfe's wife was Mary, daughter of Elder Martin Urner. The Pipe Creek church was in existence in 1745, and probably much earlier. The second Martin Urner is mentioned as its first elder. After ten years he was succeeded by Daniel Leatherman. Leatherman had moved to Maryland in 1756. From 1756 to 1793 meetings were held in homes. About 1793 a log school-house was built near the site of the present Pipe Creek church house; meetings were held in it from 1793 to 1806. In 1806 the first meetinghouse was built on the present grounds.

Beaver Dam is the second recorded Maryland church. Jacob Danner settled on Israel Creek in 1762. There is no record of separation of the group around Beaver Dam and Israel Creek from the Leatherman group that was called Pipe Creek. Its separation must have been a process of localization due to distance and numbers. Danner was the first elder. He was succeeded by Daniel Seiler. Seiler had come from Conestoga, where he had been baptized by Michael Pfautz in 1752. He was a minister when he came to Maryland. He was succeeded in the eldership by his son Daniel.

A log meetinghouse was in existence in 1790, and this was replaced by a large stone church in 1828. The succeeding order of eldership after the Seilers was John Garber, Jacob Sayler, Isaac Pfoutz, and then the famous Daniel P. Sayler. Daniel P. Sayler was a minister from 1840, but was not made an elder until the division of the original Beaver Dam church in 1855. In 1855 the congregation had nearly four hundred members and was one of the largest churches in the Brotherhood. At the division in that year, the part named Monocacy elected Daniel P. Sayler as elder. Isaac Pfoutz continued as elder of the main part of the congregation and at the division of 1881 Elder Isaac Pfoutz led a considerable part of the congregation into the Old Order fraternity.

The third Maryland congregation can be distinguished as Middletown Valley. As early as 1760 a group of twenty members lived in this pleasant and fertile valley. Daniel Leatherman was their elder. One of the first family names here was Grossnickle. Gradually there developed three farm homes where meetings and love feasts were held—Peter Grossnickle's, Michael Harshman's, and Jonathan Moser's. No meetinghouse was built until 1839. A second meetinghouse, more centrally located, was constructed in 1847 and led to the abandonment of the first in 1863.

The story of the early impermanent beginnings in Baltimore is reserved for the appendix.

The church began in Virginia in pre-Revolutionary times. Only two separate organizations can be distinguished in the eighteenth century.

About 1765, Elder Jacob Miller moved from Franklin County, Pennsylvania, to Franklin County, Virginia. This was far down in southern Virginia. A few years later he won a remarkable convert, William Smith. Smith was from Floyd County, southwest of Franklin. He could speak only English. Jacob Miller and William Smith preached together in German and English and did a great deal of effective evangelizing. Miller was one of the remarkable men of colonial America. He reared nine sons and three daughters, most of whom became effective church workers. Two sons, David and Aaron, became noted ministers. Jacob Miller, about 1800, took several members of his family and pioneered for the Brethren in southern Ohio. He even helped to open up Indiana. But his work in Virginia remained to grow and prosper.

John Garber, from York County, Pennsylvania, moved into the Shenandoah Valley about 1775. He was already an elder, and his settlement in the northern part of the Valley was as significant as Jacob Miller's in the south. The troubled times of the Revolution were at hand. Pennsylvania law required an oath to the new government. To avoid participation in swearing or in the war, the peace-loving among the Germans were glad to go to Virginia, where land was cheap and government was still lax. We have record of thirty-seven families who by 1787 had moved from Maryland and Pennsylvania and settled in Shenandoah and Rockingham counties, the greater number in Rockingham. By 1780 there was also a small group in Botetourt County near New Amsterdam, which was later named Daleville.

It is recorded of Elder John Garber that during part of his life he was a shoe cobbler, which also meant a shoemaker. Like his colleague to the south, he also raised a numerous family—seven sons and three daughters. Six of these sons became preachers, the other a deacon, and two daughters married preachers. Four of his sons remained in the Shenandoah Valley, one went to Tennessee, and two moved to Ohio.

John Garber died in 1787. His death may have been the occasion of the first definite church organization in the Valley. In 1788 a line running through Harrisonburg, Rockingham County, was decided upon as the boundary separating the Lower Rockingham or Shenandoah Brethren from the Upper Rockingham or Augusta Brethren. North of the dividing line we find such family names as Flory, Myers, Miller, Bowman, Neff, Glick, and Wine. South of the line the ministers' list contains such names as John Bowman, Abraham Neff, Daniel Barnhart, John Eller, Austin Hylton, Samuel Crumpacker, David Rife, Henry Snider, and Christian Bowman.

For a quarter of a century after 1788 there was no further church organization. The Brethren held forth in these two great multiple-centered clusters. Then gradually an increase in membership tended to localize the monthly or bimonthly meetings. The increase in both ministers and members no doubt added meetings until these became fortnightly. Thus congregations stemmed and branched. The first meetinghouse recorded in Virginia was built in 1824 at Middle River in the Middle River congregation, Augusta County.

Three more churches remain to be considered in this chapter. One is a church whose candlestick has been removed. The Yearly Meeting of 1785 sent a letter to "the loving brethren, Valentine Power and Martin Power," on the subjects of war and oaths. The greeting included "the beloved members, brethren and sisters on the South Branch." Again in 1790 the Yearly Meeting dealt with the same Valentine Power. The South Branch is the South Branch Valley of the Potomac. In 1772 Valentine Power had purchased land there and he and Martin were the ministers of an arm of the fraternity which flourished in an area that would now fall within West Virginia. But the memory of this congregation is all that remains.

Beaver Run in Hampshire County, Virginia, was begun as early as 1785. (In 1866 this site was included in Mineral County, West Virginia.) Nicholas Leatherman, a minister and a son of the famous Daniel, moved near this locality with his wife and baby son, Abraham, in 1784. In 1785 from Frederick County, Maryland, came three brothers, Elder Samuel Arnold, Elder Daniel Arnold, and Deacon Zechariah Arnold, with their two sisters, Betsy and Mollie, also members of the church. Records are scanty but we know that the organization here formed was the first one west of the Shenandoah Valley; it has been in continuous existence since that time. The homes of the three Arnolds were the meeting places until a log meetinghouse was erected in 1834. From John Kline's diary it seems that the love feasts continued to be held at Daniel Arnold's even after the meetinghouse was built.

Finally we must note the Ten Mile church of Washington County, Pennsylvania. Washington County is in southwest Pennsylvania. From Blough's *History of the Church of the Brethren in Western Pennsylvania,* page 44, we quote the following paragraph:

Elder John Wise, who grew to manhood and spent much of his life in this county, is authority for what I will here record. At the Des Moines (Iowa) Annual Meeting in 1908, the last one he ever attended,

I had a lengthy interview with him concerning the early history of Western Pennsylvania. He was then past 86 years of age, but his mind was clear and he made his statements without hesitation. He told me that the Ten Mile congregation was organized about 1759 or 1760. He also said that a man by the name of Helft was the first elder. The old brick meeting house, he said, was built in 1832. . . . this puts the Ten Mile congregation at the head as the oldest congregation in Western Pennsylvania, and the brick meetinghouse as the first one erected west of the Alleghany Mountains.

The dates here seem incredibly early. Yet the only point that can be urged against them is the Indian perils of the French and Indian War, which ended in 1763. The famous Braddock Road led directly into this region. One must allow for the hardihood of the pioneers and their ever-restless craving for new and better land. It was not very far from the Brethren outposts of Somerset County and of Virginia. Such a settlement is necessary to explain the Far Western Brethren, whom we meet in the nineteenth century out of touch with the Eastern churches.

If one were to urge that 1760 was too early for Washington County's entrance, he would have to admit at least that the tradition certainly points to a very early settlement of the Brethren there. It certainly must have been pre-Revolutionary. To be sure, this indicates a squatters' settlement. But to the vanguard of Western settlers it was the possession of the land that counted.

This early date of the Ten Mile congregation is of moment because of the peculiar importance of Washington County in the religious development of America and the American West. It was in Washington County at the turn of the nineteenth century that Alexander Campbell, founder of the Disciples of Christ, lived and pioneered. It was here that he hammered into shape the convictions which became the basis of the movement he launched.

There are striking likenesses between the Brethren and the Disciples. These cannot be documented as to their source.

But Campbell's writings show that he was familiar with the Brethren. Language was no doubt a bar, but the influence of the Brethren upon Campbell was nevertheless profound. And through this influence the Brethren can be said in some degree to have entered into one of the most successful of indigenous American evangelistic movements.

# Chapter 13

# THE EIGHTEENTH AND TWENTIETH CENTURIES

We have been considering the Church of the colonial period. The Church of the eighteenth century was so different from that which we know in the twentieth that we need to give careful attention to the changes that took place between if we are to see the relationship of what is to what was. The nineteenth century was in a special sense the century of transitions.

The numbers we have noted in the colonial Church seem surprisingly small. There are, however, certain mitigating factors. One is that people then were sublimely indifferent to religious statistics. They were interested in truth, not in numbers. Another is that the total population was very limited. The first census, in the modern sense of the term, to be taken in any country was that of the American nation in 1790. The nation then had a total population of three million, nine hundred twenty-nine thousand, two hundred fourteen, only five per cent of whom were west of the Allegheny watershed. In Church history, general population trends have significance. But the principal point of difference between the eighteenth and the twentieth century that relates to Church statistics has to do with the way Church membership was regarded. The earlier century was dominated by the idea of a pure or regenerate Church membership, which necessarily made its number small.

All the non-State and non-Roman Churches had this restricted concept of membership. Even in Congregational New England, where infant baptism was general and the

South Waterloo Church, Iowa

Wichita, Kansas, Church

These church houses are illustrative of the twentieth-
century trend toward attractive up-to-date facilities.

Church was in partnership with the State, a definite experience of conversion was counted necessary to Church membership. Persons were admitted, upon relating their experience, by vote of the congregation. And the voting body was likely to be merciless in its judgment. The majority of the population in colonial America never had any real expectation of joining the Church. They knew they could not get in.

It is well to remember that while people generally did not join the Church, they did attend. In some colonies there were laws requiring attendance. Popular sentiment relaxed the rigid enforcement of these laws. But some people moved west to escape the supervision of the ministers. Release from constraint bred a moral and spiritual condition that was far from wholesome. Another factor on the coast was that many people lacked respectable clothing for Church attendance. These things made fertile soil for the Great Awakening in New England, which began in 1734. People remembered the more refined, moral ways of their parents and grandparents and responded to preachers like Jonathan Edwards by remorseful repentance. The Great Awakening of the eighteenth century was prophetic of the nineteenth. And so was the reaction that followed. It is estimated that when Washington became president only five or six persons in each hundred were formal communicants of the Church. Today fifty-one out of a hundred is the proportion.

It was the evangelical Wesleyan-Methodist emphasis reaching into the nineteenth century that changed the nature of Church membership in America. This was an altogether unintended by-product of the Methodist efforts. The circuit riders and evangelists stressed conversion and appealed for immediate acceptance of the love of a dying Savior. They gathered their converts into societies for spiritual nurture and protective fellowship. But they had to act as if they were a Church and soon had "bishops" throughout the colonies. The combination of efficient administration and soul-converting zeal proved amazingly effective.

The Methodist success stimulated many in the older Churches. In the case of the Brethren their methods were considerably adapted. The Brethren were not appreciably influenced until after the Civil War. In the division of 1881 the holding of evangelistic meetings was an issue. S. H. Bashor began to preach in 1874 and his later contemporary, I. J. Rosenberger, led the Brethren into the period of evangelism through "protracted meetings." This lasted until the second decade of the twentieth century.

It is claimed that ten thousand persons united with our Church under Bashor's preaching. But such men as he probably did little more than induce action by emotional means on the part of the Brethren's children, friends, and neighbors who were already more or less religiously educated and indoctrinated adherents of the Church. General Church membership statistics mounted rapidly. "The serious fact of course, is that so large an army should have changed the world so little."[1] So it was with the Brethren. Today only a small proportion of Christians attend Church services. The problem of inactive members is increasingly pressing.

The first clear indication of the inactive-member problem among the Brethren appears in the Annual Meeting minutes of 1849, Article 23: "What should be done with such members, as neglect attending our meetings for six or more months, and when the yearly visit is paid them, they seem or feel satisfied with the church, and when there is a love-feast, generally attend and commune?"[2] The answer merely suggests that the ministering brethren adhere to the advice in Hebrews 10:25.

As revivalism spread, many who had no Dunker background joined the Church, enticed into it on a wave of enthusiasm. They were not assimilated into the Church and it was

---

[1] F. Ernest Johnson, *Yearbook of American Churches; 1940.* Page 158.

[2] *Minutes of the Annual Meetings, Church of the Brethren, 1778 to 1909,* Brethren Publishing House, 1909. Page 108.

not long until they began to absent themselves from public worship and from love feasts. The Church found it had many members who were Christian and Dunker only in name. They became inactive members.

The Annual Meeting of 1858 dealt with the question of whether people should be asked to come forward after the sermon.[3]

In 1869, the Old Order Brethren (who had not yet broken off) objected to getting members by unwholesome emotional stress, feeling "that care should be taken that the understanding be enlightened, as well as the passions awakened . . . ."[4] Eleven years later they renewed the protest.[5] Viewed in the present light, it is tragic that the views of the Old Orders on this issue were not more respected.

Inactive membership came into Annual Meeting consideration again in 1870.[6] The pattern for handling the problem seems to have been that the negligent should be visited and reminded sharply of their duty.

In 1880 sterner measures were taken. The persistently erring were to be dealt with on grounds of disobedience. Dismissal may have been contemplated.[7]

Roland L. Howe's *The History of a Church* (*Dunker*), pages 432 and 433, gives the procedure for handling the matter in the First church, Philadelphia, our first urban center. Those absenting themselves for four weeks were to have an official visit. After four more weeks of neglect they were to have another. And if their attitude persisted till the next quarterly council, they were no longer to be counted as members.

Conference minutes indicate that preoccupation also was a factor in inactive participation in the Church. Membership in secret societies was counted an offender here.[8]

---

[3] *Ibid.* Page 175.
[4] *Ibid.* Page 276.
[5] *Ibid.* Page 382.
[6] *Ibid.* Page 288.
[7] *Ibid.* Page 374.
[8] *Ibid.* Page 299.

In 1925 the concern was raised that "quite a large percent of the small body of members, in easy reach of good working congregations became dissatisfied and indifferent to general church activities."[9]

There has been increasing tolerance of inactive members. The Church has largely lost its power to discipline members. Belonging to secret societies, participation in worldly interests, and materialism have increased. The voice of the Church has lost much of its authority.

In 1932 Annual Conference classified Church members as resident, nonresident, active, inactive, and absent.[10] This brought the matter to the attention of congregations anew and led many to deal with the problem. The action introduced a more uniform method of statistics of Church membership. But it did not show how to reduce the list of inactive members.

A 1936 minute brought some progress. It favored disfranchising members who had become inactive.[11] The Church was again taking unto itself the right of discipline and indicating that the manifold privileges of membership must be bought at a price. This step may lead to a stronger policy. Church membership has become cheap in many minds. Many people are only nominal Christians. Our obsession with numbers has bankrupted us spiritually. The Church is paying a high price for its past carelessness and, to be redeemed, must find means to convert the inactive and indifferent members who are misrepresenting it, and to raise the standards of membership to the point of sacrifice.

### NUMBER OF THE BRETHREN

On the background of the data and conditions presented above we can intelligently proceed to discuss the numbers of the Church membership. Here again we unavoidably draw upon Morgan Edwards. We have already quoted him as saying

---

[9] *Minutes of the Annual Conference, 1923-1944.* Brethren Publishing House. 1946. Page 33.
[10] *Ibid.* Pages 86 and 87.
[11] *Ibid.* Page 119.

of the Tunkers, "Their families are about four hundred and nineteen, which contain about two thousand and ninety-five souls allowing five to the family, whereof seven hundred and sixty-three persons are baptized and in communion." Later writers can do no better than mull over the Edwards data with a view to seeking new insights and adding very inexact guesses.

Dove gives an excellent statement when he says:

During the first half century of its existence (1708-1770) the Church of the Brethren was transplanted from its place of birth in the Rhine Valley in Germany, to the Penn Colony in America, and grew until there were about 800 members divided among about twenty congregations throughout eastern Pennsylvania, New Jersey, and Maryland. During the second half century (1770-1825) its borders were extended southward into Virginia, North Carolina, Tennessee, and Kentucky, and westward to the Mississippi Valley. The membership doubled in spite of the devastation of war, and Indian massacres on the frontier. During the third half century of its history (1825-1882) the western boundary was extended to the Pacific Coast and its members numbered about 58,000.[12]

In connection with this we may take also the summary of Gillin:

In 1770 there were fifteen congregations of Dunkers in Pennsylvania, with a membership of 763, one in New Jersey with 46 members, a total of 709 members in sixteen congregations. If the seventeen churches in Maryland and the other southern colonies had as high an average membership as these, which is hardly likely, since they were newer congregations, then in 1790 there were not more than 1462 members in the territory now included in the United States.

It would be interesting to know the number of Dunkers in different parts of the country during the period between the Revolutionary War and 1880, but there was no census of the Dunkers, until 1880, when Howard Miller prepared one.[13]

The first attempt at a comprehensive enumeration of the Church membership was made by Howard O. Miller and published under the title, *Record of the Faithful; For the Use of*

---

[12] Frederick Denton Dove, *Cultural Changes in the Church of the Brethren,* Brethren Publishing House, 1932. Page 57.

[13] John Lewis Gillin, *The Dunkers.* Page 200.

*the Brethren. Being a Statistical Record and a Complete Directory of the Brethren Church for the Years* 1881-1882.[14] After an extensive introduction the author says:

The membership will be given in detail first.

The State of New Jersey, complete ................................................ 302

The State of Pennsylvania is believed to be complete, numerically. The figures here given are not exact, however, as some of the Maryland churches extend into Pennsylvania. This Maryland membership is not counted in the Pennsylvania number. It will appear in its appropriate place. Pennsylvania has, upon this basis ................................................ 14,557

Ohio has presented many difficulties, but is believed to be exact as far as it goes. No account is taken of the divisions of the church, and some new churches, organized in 1882, have no numbers appended in the list, because they are evidently counted in with the old churches from which they were separated. Ohio is estimated at ................................................ 9,362

Maryland is complete, but some of its members are found in Pennsylvania. As they are not counted there, they appear in the Maryland number which amounts to ................................................ 2,604

Virginia shows, in the following figures, the membership of the State, and not of the Districts. Some of the Virginia District churches are in North Carolina. These do not appear here. The State of Virginia shows a membership of ................................................ 4,965

Tennessee District has some churches in Virginia and some in North Carolina. Only the State is given. In 1837, there were only eighty-one members in the State. Now there are, in Tennessee, ................................................ 1,088

In North Carolina, ................................................ 288

West Virginia has been very hard to determine exactly. A number of small churches are found in West Virginia belonging to and accounted for in (old) Virginia. In West Virginia, clearly accounted for, are ................................................ 1,587

Indiana has a large membership, and is believed to be practically complete. It has ................................................ 10,237

The State of Michigan has ................................................ 659

Illinois has been very well represented, and shows a membership of ................................................ 4,407

---

[14] Published at Lewisburgh, Pennsylvania, in 1882. See pages 65-67.

Iowa may have a few small churches omitted, and shows a membership of .......................................................................... 3,056

Minnesota has ............................................................................ 129

The Missouri churches are small and numerous. The State has .............................................................................................. 1,309

Arkansas is estimated as having, at most ............................ 20

Texas, ...................................................................................... 12

Kansas, in many cases, refused or neglected to answer inquiries. The number here given is very near exact, ................... 2,358

Nebraska, ................................................................................ 620

Colorado, ................................................................................ 80

California, ............................................................................... 211

Oregon, ................................................................................... 200

The totals are ........................................................................ 57,749

A few additions and changes have been made in the totals, varying very slightly from an accurate addition of the individual churches, and this has been done upon notification by the churches where the changes have taken place.

The Old Brethren aggregate very near ............................... 3,000

The writer is extremely reluctant to count these out. If it were done, the total membership would be ................................ 54,799

It is therefore safe to estimate the strength of the Brethren in the United States as (given) above(;) and for many years to come, at our present rate of growth, between "55,000 and 60,000" will be a truthful statement of our strength.

We would like to have information concerning the long chronological stretch from the American Revolution to 1882. But we are limited to some very uncertain conjectures. Nevertheless, we do have some scanty estimates. In the August 1858 issue of the *Gospel Visitor,* James Quinter wrote under the caption, "Who Are The Dunkards?" He answered a newspaper writer, James M. Swank, of the *Cambria Tribune,* Johnstown, Pennsylvania.

One of the statements of the reporter to which James Quinter takes exception is apparent from this reply.

The idea that we at the period of the American Revolution, eighty-two years ago, numbered more members than we do now, is not at all correct. And the inference that we are now rapidly declining, is no more so. At the time referred to, we were settled in some four or five states. Now, as Mr. Swank remarks, we "are scattered over eleven states in all," and he might have said over twelve or thirteen. Instead of having rapidly declined since the Revolution, we have rapidly increased, and where we then numbered hundreds, we probably now number thousands. . . . We recently attended a communion meeting six miles north of Johnstown, in the county in which Mr. Swank resides, at which there were no doubt upwards of two hundred members communed. . . . At our annual meeting in the State of Indiana, in May last, there were represented one hundred and twenty-six churches, and the representation was by no means full. The number of our churches was nothing like this at the Revolution.

We do not measure the moral power of the church by its numerical strength, nor do we think the truth is to be ascertained by the number of its adherents. But we think it would be a reproach to us as a Christian community, and a dishonor to the precious cause of Primitive Christianity which we advocate, should we suffer the withering power of declension to fall upon us.

This statement by the young editor is admirably supplemented and reinforced by the following:

During the ten years ending with the year 1860, the membership of the church undoubtedly had been growing numerically. But as the Brethren generally did not keep definite records of their numbers, we can only conjecture how numerous they were at any given period. An estimate which seems within reasonable bounds and which was published about 1870 says that in 1860 the Brethren were said to have about 200 congregations and 20,000 communicants.[15]

Taking this last-named figure as correct and comparing it with Howard Miller's concluding figure in 1882, we discover that in the twenty-two-year period, 1860-1882, the Church had tripled its size. This is the period of the most rapid growth the Church membership ever exhibited—both on a percentage basis and total numerical increase!

In 1890 the United States government census included a count of religious communicants. A mid-decade religious census was begun by the government in 1906. This was carried

---

[15] John Kimmel, "Chronicles of the Brethren. No. 9." Published in the *Vindicator*, July 1947.

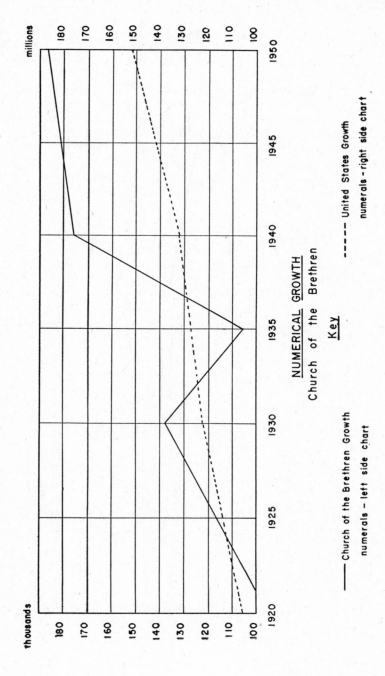

NUMERICAL GROWTH
Church of the Brethren

Key

——— Church of the Brethren Growth
numerals – left side chart

----- United States Growth
numerals – right side chart

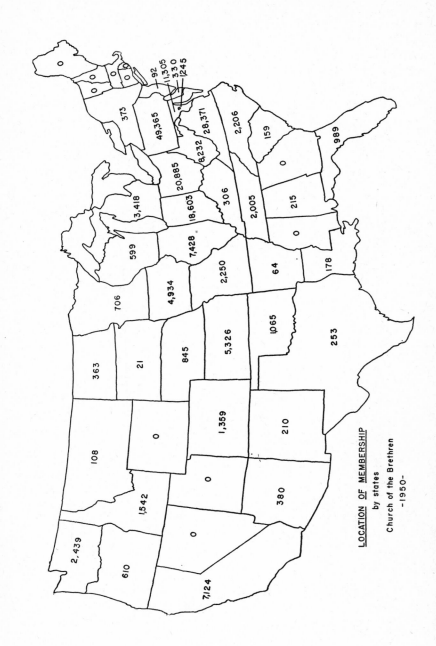

LOCATION OF MEMBERSHIP
by states
Church of the Brethren
-1950-

through in 1906, 1916, 1926, and 1936. The religious census of 1946 was never finished, because of the financial exigencies of World War II and the vagaries of government financing. So below we substitute the numbers given in the 1947 *Yearbook* as the statistics of the Church of the Brethren for 1946.

|  | 1890 | 1906 | 1916 | 1926 | 1936 | 1946 |
|---|---|---|---|---|---|---|
| Membership | 61,101[16] | 76,547 | 105,102 | 128,392 | 153,516 | 182,497 |
| Congregations | 720 | 815 | 997 | 1,030 | 1,143[17] | 1,018 |
| Ministers | 1,622 | 1,784 | 2,984 | 3,094 | 3,043 | 3,286[18] |

[16] It will be noticed that this is little different from the membership given by Howard Miller in 1882. But in 1890 the Census Bureau recognized the Old Order and Progressive branches.

[17] There is an error here. The *Yearbook* of 1937 gives 1,031 congregations. The census probably confused church houses with congregations.

[18] Includes twenty-eight nationals outside the United States or Canada.

# Chapter 14

## EXPANSION TO INDIANA

In the previous chapter we dealt with the numerical growth of the Brethren. A few sentences from Brumbaugh evaluate this growth:

The growth from 1724 to 1770 was good. The church prospered. Her elders were noble men. They wrought wisely and well. It was no small matter to travel long distances in a wilderness, preach in private houses, organize new congregations, and at the same time maintain a growing family in a new country. Add to this the fact that the Brethren were all Germans, that their message was only to Germans, that the population was dominantly English, and their success was wonderful. Surely the Lord was with them.[1]

When the Revolutionary War closed there may not have been more than one thousand members of the Church, and the majority of these lived in Pennsylvania.

We now return to the geographical expansion of the Church. This parallels closely the expansion of the American nation. The national growth is the background of the Church's growth.

If one were to look at a map of the United States upon which were marked all the churches of the Brethren, they would appear as a great, irregularly shaped fan spread across the central United States. The base or handle of the fan would be at Philadelphia and its hinterland, and the fan would reach its widest spread on the Pacific Coast. This means that New England and the South have practically no Brethren people in them. Some churches have grown up in the South recently

---

[1] M. G. Brumbaugh, *A History of the Brethren*. Page 33.

by fostered migration or colonization; there are none in New England.

*Pennsylvania.* Eastern Pennsylvania is the American homeland of the Brethren and the other groups of "plain people." The Church in Pennsylvania has grown until the *Yearbook* of 1950 lists one hundred ninety-six churches and forty-nine thousand, five hundred forty members — twenty-seven percent of the Brotherhood. The territory of Eastern Pennsylvania, in Brethren parlance, included all the colony in colonial times and in the mid-nineteenth century was designated as Pennsylvania east of the Susquehanna River; also New Jersey, New York and New England. However, the membership is largely confined to a few counties: Lancaster, Montgomery, Berks, Bucks, Dauphin, Lebanon, and Philadelphia. In 1911 the district was divided. Eight churches in and near Philadelphia and all the territory east of the Delaware River were organized into a district known as Southeastern Pennsylvania, New Jersey, and New York. Middle Pennsylvania originally was the country between the Susquehanna River and the Allegheny Mountains. In 1892 it was divided into the Middle and Southern Pennsylvania districts.

In the territory of Middle Pennsylvania there were probably six churches organized before 1800. Dry Valley (now the Lewistown church) is said to have begun as early as 1780. Ministers from Eastern Pennsylvania came to preach there. One of the earliest preachers was John Swigart from Berks County. He was the great-grandfather of Elders J. C. and W. J. Swigart. Abram Miller from Dauphin County was another early preacher. The Aughwick church was near here. Christian Long, its first minister, was elected in 1802. Lost Creek, in Juniata County, and Clover Creek, in Blair County, were organized about 1790.

Southern Pennsylvania includes the country between the Blue Ridge Mountains and the Susquehanna River. The churches are chiefly located in four counties: York, Adams,

Franklin, and Cumberland. We have already considered those churches which had colonial origin. Marsh Creek, in Adams County, was organized in 1811. David Pfoutz was active here, and elsewhere as well.

Western Pennsylvania is that part of the state lying west of the Allegheny Mountains — a vast inland empire. But the Church is concentrated in a few counties. It followed the "cluster" or "hiving" pattern which is characteristic in the Church's planting and spread. In the nineteenth century it was customary to speak of "the church in ———— County."

We have noted the early date of the Church in Washington County (1760). The Stony Creek church in Somerset County began as early as 1762 and had seventeen members in 1770. Somerset County conformed to the "county pattern" until 1849. The Yearly Meeting of 1849, through a special committee, divided the county into four organizations: Elk Lick, Berlin, Middle Creek, and Quemahoning. By 1877, Elk Lick had six hundred members and was itself divided into three parts: Elk Lick, Summit, and Meyersdale.

Farther north, close to Johnstown, Elder Peter Morgan settled in 1797. He came from Hagerstown, Maryland. Here began the very important Conemaugh congregation. Conemaugh included part of Somerset and all of Cambria and Indiana counties. Elder George Wolfe, Sr., settled here in 1787 and remained until he moved on west in 1800.

Western Pennsylvania remained frontier country from 1770 to 1825 and its written records are very scanty. It is from this area that several incidents involving Brethren and the Indians are related, and here the Brethren first began to preach in English. Among nineteenth-century preachers may be named Levi Roberts, a Welshman, and John Mineely, an Irishman.

*Maryland.* We have noted the pre-Revolutionary movement southward through Maryland and Virginia and the founding of the colonial congregations. In the early nineteenth century there were established, to the west of the colonial churches in Maryland, Manor (1800), Welsh Run (1810), Cherry Grove (1841), and Bear Creek (1846). The state was divided into two districts in 1867.

*Virginia.* We recall the activity of Elders Jacob Miller and William Smith in Franklin County and Elder John Garber in Rockingham County from colonial days. By 1794 the Brethren in Northern Virginia were numerous enough for an Annual Meeting to be held in the Shenandoah Valley. In 1797 one was held in Franklin County. In connection with the colonial churches we have sketched the main developments in Virginia. A quotation from Otho Winger will summarize the work in the state:

In the history of the Christian Church there are but few examples of greater sacrifice and courage than those of these pioneer Virginia preachers. Over the mountains and through the valleys for hundreds of miles they made their rounds to preach the Gospel. Some of them traveled thousands of miles in a single year. As a result of their labors the Brethren churches grew strong in faith and in numbers. The parent organizations were divided to form many new congregations. This missionary spirit became quite general. . . .

The church in Virginia has always been loyal to the general Brotherhood. This is evidenced by maintaining her doctrines under the most adverse and trying conditions. The attitude on slavery gave a most difficult and perplexing problem for these churches to solve, and to uphold the principles of peace under the fearful scourge of the war in the South was an ordeal that few could have withstood. The record of what the Virginia Brethren endured during the war is one of great heroism and Christian fidelity. It reached its climax in the martyrdom of one of the State's greatest leaders, Elder John Kline.[2]

*Tennessee.* Tennessee was virtually an extension of the Church in Virginia. There were a few members in Tennessee prior to 1800. In 1811 Elder Samuel Garber of Rockingham County, Virginia, visited and preached in Washington County, Tennessee, and organized the Knob Creek church—the mother

---

[2] Otho Winger, *History and Doctrines of the Church of the Brethren.* Pages 68 and 69.

church of Tennessee. Elder Garber lived three hundred miles distant but he visited the brethren at Knob Creek at least three times—in itself an immense labor. The second church was Cedar Grove in Hawkins County, organized in 1824. The third congregation was at Limestone in 1847. Quite an achievement was the erection of Limestone's meetinghouse, a large forty-by-sixty-foot building, in 1850. And it is interesting to contemplate that in 1860, as the North and the South were on the brink of the Civil War, the Yearly Meeting convened at Limestone.

*North Carolina.* North Carolina also was an extension of the Church in Virginia. The beginning in North Carolina is associated with the name of Jacob Faw. He heard of the Brethren in Franklin County and came to hear them preach. He was baptized and his home became an outpost. A church was organized and Jacob Faw was called to the ministry. The Church spread slowly, assisted by migrations from the North. Some very able Brethren, such as Elder John Hendricks, who pioneered in the work in Missouri and Illinois, have come from this state.

In 1919 Winger wrote of the region in a rather discouraging vein: "Emigration westward has weakened these churches. There are fewer than eight hundred in twenty-five congregations in the District, which includes South Carolina, Georgia, and Florida." But Florida and Georgia became a separate district in 1925. The *Yearbook* of 1950 gives North Carolina and South Carolina as having twenty-three churches and one thousand five hundred ninety-one members. The churches in South Carolina are the outgrowth of the work in North Carolina in the traditional manner, the Brethren spreading across the state line, oblivious of political lines.

*West Virginia.* West Virginia was not a separate state until the Civil War. The Church spread into what is now West Virginia from Virginia, Maryland, and Pennsylvania.

The oldest church with the exception of colonial Beaver Run, is the Sandy Creek church in Preston County, near the Pennsylvania line, which was established in 1825. The year after its organization Jacob M. Thomas was called to the ministry; he served for forty-five years. The Thomas family has been prominent in Brotherhood annals. In 1855 the German Settlement congregation, also in Preston County, was organized. From here have come the Fike and Abernathy families. Along the Virginia border the Virginia churches extended their care into the mountains and across the ranges. Notable among the "horseback preachers" were John Kline, Jacob Wine, and Jacob Miller.

*Kentucky.* Kentucky was in the line of westward migration, and so received the Brethren among its early settlers. Joseph Rodgers was the first man to preach the gospel within the borders of the state. It is said that about the year 1760 Elder Daniel Letterman and Casper Rowland, from Germantown, emigrated to the Carolinas, and there met with some members. Among them were John Hendricks, David Martin, Giles Chapman, and the aforementioned Joseph Rodgers. They moved northward into Kentucky.

The name of the great American hunter, pioneer, and explorer, Daniel Boone, is forever associated with Kentucky. The Boone family were from Berks County, Pennsylvania. The father, a Quaker, married a Pennsylvania Dutch woman of Brethren affiliation. Nine children, of whom Daniel is the best-known, came to the home. The majority of the children grew up to be Dunkers, among them Daniel, so tradition says, although no record of the baptism is extant.

The family started for Carolina in the spring of 1750, tarrying a year in the Shenandoah Valley, and arrived at Buffalo Lick on the north fork of the Yadkin River. In 1755 the young man served as teamster and blacksmith in a North Carolina company in Braddock's campaign. Here he

met John Finley, who fired his imagination with stories of
the vast lands of Kentucky. In 1767 he left his farm on the
Yadkin and with a couple of companions traveled far into
the unknown region. In May 1769 a small party moved to
what is now Estill County. They returned to Carolina but
came back to Kentucky to settle in 1771. At this time the land
titles over this entire area were in doubt. Today many Boones
are in the ranks of the Brethren membership and their family
traditions tell of Daniel and other branches of the family.

It may be noted that few American characters have been
more falsified by story writers. Far from being an enemy of
the Indians and an Indian killer, Boone worked for amity and
understanding between Indians and whites. The well-known
story of his being adopted into an Indian tribe attests his
friendly attitude to the Indians. Like many others, Boone never
seemed to doubt that it was the purpose of Providence to subdue the wilderness and exploit the resources of the vast
empire called North America.

The Boone family also illustrates another fact, not generally publicized. This is the interrelatedness of Dunker and
Quaker in the trek across America. The relationship of Dunker
and Mennonite is generally known and recognized. Usually
in the neighborhood of a Brethren church house stands a
Mennonite meetinghouse. Intermarriage has been frequent.
But the pattern of Quaker migration and interrelatedness of
influence has also followed the same general trend. At the one
hundred seventy-fifth anniversary of Pipe Creek (Maryland)
the name of an ancestor of the Quaker president, Herbert
Hoover, was found on the deeds of the land on which the
meetinghouse stands. This Quaker family too trekked from
eastern Pennsylvania, through Maryland and the Carolinas, to
the great prairie lands of Iowa.

But in spite of our early association with Kentucky, the
name of the state remains but a bitter memory for the Brethren. The one-time promising beginning was wiped out (for

the frontier has its losses and defeats). In the discussion of the Far Western Brethren we shall return again to the subject of Kentucky. Today several very small churches in the edges of the state under the care of ministers of Tennessee and Southern Ohio are the only stake of the Brethren in Kentucky.

*Ohio.* Ohio is in point of Brethren membership the third state. Its three districts contain one ninth of the total membership, or twenty-one thousand four hundred twenty-two members in its one hundred sixteen churches (1950).

The Brethren came by two different routes. They floated down the Ohio River in flatboats or came overland by wagon via Pittsburgh, which in the first quarter of the nineteenth century was thought of as a point of departure for "the West."

The oldest churches were organized near the Ohio River, in the counties east of Cincinnati. There were at one time ten churches in this area. The first minister, John Countryman, came to Adams County in 1793. Stone Lick was the first church organized in Ohio, with David Stouder as minister and elder. The Highland church, in which lived Elder Thomas Major and his wife, was here. Sarah Major was regarded as a preacher, in a day in which the Brethren did not permit women to be preachers. Landon West long served these southeastern Ohio churches.

Elder Jacob Miller from Virginia moved into the Miami Valley in 1800. Elder David Bowman, Sr., was another early arrival. In 1805 the Miami church was organized. In 1812 this was divided into four parts: Lower Miami, Bear Creek, Wolf Creek, and Stillwater. By 1850 there were fifteen churches in this area of Ohio. These churches of Southern Ohio have had such leadership as Peter Nead, Jacob Garber, H. D. Davy, J. C. Bright, Jesse Stutsman, and W. K. Simmons.

About the same time that the Brethren were coming into Ohio by the Ohio River and through Cincinnati, they were also entering through the Pittsburgh gateway. Elder John

Gans moved into Stark County in 1804. Shortly after his arrival the Nimishillen congregation was organized. In 1822 the first Yearly Meeting west of the Allegheny Mountains was held within this congregation. Mill Creek, later called Mahoning, near the Pennsylvania state line, was organized in 1815. Shortly after 1815, George Hoke was elected to the ministry. He soon became a leader of the Brotherhood, and the designation, "old brother George Hoke," was a title of respect and power throughout the nineteenth century. It was in Mahoning that Henry Kurtz lived and served as bishop for many years. Here he began to publish the *Gospel Visitor*—a harbinger of a new church life.

Northwestern Ohio was the Great Black Swamp country and was not settled as early as some of the territory that lay farther westward. The first three churches were Logan (1827), Seneca (1828), and Sugar Creek (1833). Logan and Sugar Creek were organized by Elder Abraham Miller from Virginia.

It is somewhat astonishing to contemplate today that the hoofbeats of Elder John Kline's horse have echoed and re-echoed over the primitive roads of northwestern Ohio and northern Indiana as he sought to bring spiritual strength to those who were at the same time battling the world, the devil, and the great continental wilderness.

*Indiana.* No one ever lived who was better acquainted with the Brethren in Indiana than Otho Winger was. Writing about 1919 and basing his statistics on the Census Report of 1916 he says:

The first congregation in the State was the Four Mile in Wayne and Union Counties. Elder Jacob Miller of the Miami Valley, Ohio, did the first preaching in the State. Four Mile was organized in 1809 by Elders Jacob Miller and John Hart. At that time Daniel Miller and John Moyer were called to the ministry. The first meetinghouse was erected on Four Mile Creek, two miles north of College Corner, about 1840. The second congregation was Nettle Creek, in Wayne and Henry Counties. It was organized in 1820 by Elders David and Aaron Miller, sons of Elder Jacob Miller, the pioneer preacher. The Nettle Creek meetinghouse, erected in 1845, was the second to be built in the State. At this house was held the Annual Meeting of 1864, when John Kline was moderator for the last time.

These two congregations became mother churches for a number of other churches in the State. From Four Mile some members moved to Montgomery County, where, under the preaching of Elder William Smith of Ohio, they organized the Racoon church, the third congregation in the State. From Nettle Creek the Miller brothers moved to South Bend in 1830 and began the work there. Pyrmont was settled in 1829 under the leadership of Elder John Metzger. Bachelor's Run, in Carroll County, was organized in 1829 by Elder Peter Eyman, who later left the church and organized the New Tunkers. In 1830 Elder Daniel Cripe, the elder of the Wolf Creek church in Ohio, emigrated to Elkhart County and began the work in that county, which today has more Brethren congregations than any other county in the State. From the original Elkhart church territory there have been organized sixteen congregations, with a membership of more than 2,500. Mexico, Manchester, Mississinewa, Salimony and Somerset were other parent organizations before 1850.

By 1860 there had developed two State Districts, a Northern and a Southern, with District Meetings of their own. October 25, 1866, at a State meeting at Andrews, the State was divided into three districts, Northern, Middle and Southern. At that time there were fifty-five congregations. In 1916 there were one hundred and twenty-five congregations, with over twelve thousand membership. But the membership and the territory are not equally divided. The Southern District has two-thirds of the territory of the State, but only about one-fifth of the membership. The largest congregation in the State is North Manchester.[3]

To this need but be added that the *Yearbook* of 1950 shows one hundred eleven churches with a listed membership of eighteen thousand three hundred ninety-seven or just about ten percent of the entire membership of the Brotherhood.

---

[3] Otho Winger, *History and Doctrines of the Church of the Brethren.* Pages 77-78.

# Chapter 15

## ILLINOIS TO THE WEST COAST

We continue to follow the course of the Brethren pioneers as they go northward and westward.

*Illinois.* The Brethren pressed into Illinois from the south. Elder George Wolfe, Sr., had moved to Kentucky from Fayette County (George's Creek) in Pennsylvania. His two sons, George and Jacob, moved farther west into Union County, Illinois. On a preaching trip Elder Wolfe sickened while preaching at Kaskaskia, Illinois, died, and was buried there. In 1812 his two sons, their wives, and eight other persons were baptized by Elder John Hendricks of Kentucky. In the organization of the twelve into a congregation, George Wolfe, Jr., was chosen as the minister, and Jacob Wolfe and George Davis, deacons. In 1813 Elder John Hendricks died, and George Wolfe was ordained as elder of the group. In 1831 the Union County members moved practically in a body to Adams County to a place soon afterward named Liberty. The Liberty church is still in existence—the oldest Brethren congregation in Illinois, since the organization itself moved.

In 1828 there was a church established in Macoupin County, called Pleasant Hill, the forerunner of the present Girard church. The Sugar Creek church, in Sangamon County, south of Springfield, was organized in 1830. At one time Sugar Creek was called Otter Creek. It was in this church that Daniel Vaniman was called to the ministry in 1865. The original Sugar Creek is today divided into half a dozen churches. We must name two more Southern Illinois churches of fame, which have been the homes of well-known leaders.

Cerro Gordo, founded in 1857, was the home for many years of the beloved Elder John Metzger ("Uncle Johnny"). Panther Creek, the home of Elder James R. Gish, was organized in 1852.

Northern Illinois was settled independently of Southern Illinois by direct migration from the East. The first church was established in the summer of 1842 at Arnold's Grove, near Mt. Carroll, by a small party from Franklin County, Pennsylvania. At that time there were nineteen members, who lived in both Carroll and Ogle counties. Arnold's Grove later divided into two churches but these became extinct. In fact, as we move further into the annals of the nineteenth century some un-noticed changes were coming. The information about Arnold's Grove is fairly abundant and possesses a representative charac-ter, and so we quote.

One of the early ministers was Christian Long, who lived in Arnold's Grove from 1852 to 1870. Writing in the *Brethren at Work* for July 16, 1877, Christian Long says:

## THE CHURCH IN CARROLL CO., ILLINOIS
### AS IT WAS AND AS IT IS.

In the Spring of 1852 we moved to Mt. Carroll, Ill., and found about twenty members in the county. Among them was brother Henry Strickler, Sen., the first minister in the county. Had a school-house 14 x 18 to hold meeting in; we could all get in nicely. In the summer of '52 we added about forty by baptism, besides a number who moved among us. In '54 we built a meeting-house at Arnold's Grove; had a choice for a minister and the lot fell on brother David Emmert, we soon had another choice the lot falling on brother Michael Sisler. The church increased moderately till the winter of '57, I think it was, when we baptized about ninety-six inside of two months. Soon after that brother Henry Myers, with a good many others, settled at what is called Dutch Town, brother David Rittenhouse at Hickory Grove and brother John Sprogle at Cherry Grove. The church now numbering over four hundred we thought it good to move for a divide; so, I think it was in '61, we divided into four congregations, Cherry Grove in charge of J. Sprogle and M. Bolinger, Hickory Grove in charge of David Rittenhouse,

Dutch Town in charge of Henry Myers and Arnold's Grove was left
to the rest of us. In the divide we agreed to assist mutually to build
meeting-houses in each district, which was soon done. Each district
then chose its own officers. Some three years ago the brethren built a
new meeting-house at Shannon, also made a new organization called
the Shannon church; also built a new meeting-house at Lanark. Quite
an interesting paper started in Lanark, called the *Brethren at Work,*
and from its present platform and contents we think it may be, and is
now, a useful medium and has the right name. The brethren in the
Arnold's Grove church also recently purchased a substantial house in
Mt. Carroll, where they now have meetings regularly. The churches in
Carroll county have been steadily increasing in number, notwithstanding
the many that have moved away to other places. We remember of giving
56 certificates of membership at Arnold's Grove alone in one year.
Would still number about six hundred in the county. The start of the
Brethren in Grundy and Dallas counties, Iowa, Falls City, Neb., and
Bourbon county, Kansas, was from Carroll county, Ill. The different
organizations stand blest at present with ministers as follows: Hickory
Grove, D. Rittenhouse, George Zollers and Jesse Heckler. Dutch Town,
J. S. Hauger, Martin Meyer, D. Miller, Michael Kimmel, Tobias Myers
and Wm. Provont. Arnold's Grove, J. J. Emmert, Joseph Stitzel and
Jacob Shirk. Cherry Grove, Michael Bolinger, Henry Martin, J. H.
Moore, David Puterbaugh and S. J. Peck. Shannon, Lemuel Hillery,
Solomon Mattes and F. McCune.

Carroll county, Ill., being my field of labor for nearly eighteen years,
I felt like reviewing its progress as far as I know it.

The evidences of this valuable review are numerous.
Communication between parts of expanding America was
becoming more speedy and easy. Mobility of population was
greatly increased. Economic opportunities seemed more
abundant. The older centers had to endure a drain on their
strength, with a result that the rate of congregational mortality increased. The remarkable thing about Brethren expansion is the large number of the earliest congregations that
exist today. But the farther into the West the Church moved,
the more uncertain the life expectancy of new congregations
became. The arrival of the railroad changed the character of
the Western settlement.

Let us complete our mention of Arnold's Grove. It could not be summed up better than John Heckman has told it:

The last love feast in historic Arnold's Grove was held on May 28, 1902. In 1908 it was voted to make two organizations, and on January 13, 1909, the town group was organized as the Mt. Carroll congregation with J. G. Royer as elder. Alice Garber became mission worker, the district mission board gave financial aid, pastors served for several years, but the work did not prosper. Arnold's Grove transferred its property to the district mission board. Later the house was sold for four hundred fifty dollars. The Mt. Carroll property was likewise deeded to the district board and later sold for eighteen hundred dollars. On January 14, 1932, at the last business meeting, directed by O. D. Buck and J. H. Mathis, the congregation was disorganized and letters were issued to the nineteen remaining members.[1]

What an anticlimax to Christian Long's thrilling, epic-like narrative. But the historian must chronicle the losses, tragedies, wastes, and defeats as well as the victories.

The twentieth century brought the age of industrialism in earnest, with its shifts of population, consolidation of farms, and greater mobility of the automobile era. And we need to add that the greater absorption in material values and the scattering of the family clans abroad have all too frequently made the story of Arnold's Grove a representative one. No major metamorphosis of human society is possible without waste.

The second church in Northern Illinois, Rock River (later Franklin Grove), was formed in 1845. It was formed of thirteen charter members who had come from Washington County, Maryland. In 1842 Elder Joseph Emmert and his son-in-law, Christian Lahman, came to this area of cheap land and then returned with their families in covered wagons in 1843. Several friends had joined them by the time of the organization.

The third church was West Branch, formally organized in 1846 in Ogle County. The members also came from Washing-

---

[1] Heckman and Miller, *Brethren in Northern Illinois and Wisconsin.* Page 19.

ton County, Maryland. The first member was John Fridley, who came as early as 1836 and bought a claim between what are now Oregon and Mount Morris. A love feast was held in John Price's barn in the summer of 1845. A second love feast the next summer at the same place was the occasion of the organization.

Ere long the growing congregation felt the need of a meeting-house. The greater part of the congregation being in the Maryland neighborhood, the house was located in that section. In 1848 they erected a house about thirty-six by forty feet, one story with an attic that furnished ample room for sleeping quarters for those who came to the love feasts and found the distance home too great after the evening services. The main floor furnished the audience room and a kitchen. There was an entrance from the east to the kitchen and two to the audience room, one for the men and one for the women, for, of course in those days there was no mixed seating.

Simple handmade furniture sufficed for this simple house and these simple people whose tastes had not yet run to extremes. Stored away until love feast occasions were the tables, enough of them to meet the needs of the congregation, all except the one behind which sat the ministers in seniority order, and in front of which sat the deacons also in seniority order. Following the old rule the deacons read the Scriptures at the regular services.

In the southeast corner of the audience room were the winding stairs to the attic with its straw ticks waiting for the overnight guests. In the kitchen were the cupboards for the tableware and linen, while the open fireplace furnished ample facilities for cooking the meals for love feast and district meeting. As the old schoolhouse had provided the first place for worship so now in turn this new church reciprocated by allowing it to be used as a schoolhouse in which John Burner taught readin', 'ritin' and 'rithmetic while a new schoolhouse was being built.[2]

Yellow Creek was organized in 1848. Two small groups of members, from Ohio and from Pennsylvania, began to settle in Stephenson County as early as 1843. At the organization in 1848 there were thirty members and two ministers. The ministers were John Lauver, a German preacher from Pennsylvania, and Daniel Fry, who moved thither from the Nimi-

---

[2] *Ibid.* Pages 27 and 28.

shillen congregation, Ohio. This is the Elder Fry who in old age assisted in starting the Danish mission. The first ten years there was no meetinghouse. In 1855, fifteen members came from the Aughwick congregation, Huntingdon County, Pennsylvania. Yellow Creek took the lead and the four churches of Northern Illinois called for the Yearly Meeting of 1856.

It was a tremendous undertaking to entertain the Yearly Meeting of 1856 in the remote West of Illinois. The meeting had never before been held so far west. The people rode from Chicago on the new Illinois Central Railroad to Lena, where they were met in buggies and wagons. The Meeting was held in the house and barn of Michael Reber. Lodging and meals were, according to the prevalent practice, free. The old records show that the total cost of the meeting was eight hundred eighty-one dollars and fifty-eight cents and that the four churches had a balance of one hundred eighty-three dollars left. Of course this was achieved by donations of labor and provisions.

Further organizations were Hickory Grove (1858), and, the same year, Pine Creek and Milledgeville (Dutchtown). Between 1858 and 1860, Bethel (or Naperville) in DuPage County was begun. Batavia and, in a certain sense, Chicago, were outgrowths of Naperville. The year 1859 saw Cherry Grove set off from Arnold's Grove and Waddams Grove (Lena) set off from Yellow Creek.

The *Yearbook* of 1950 reports twenty-seven churches with four thousand nine hundred forty-four members for the District of Northern Illinois and Wisconsin.

*Wisconsin.* The Wisconsin congregations never have achieved a genuine independence but always have lived under the shadow of the Northern Illinois churches and have been dependent upon them. The first of the Brethren to come to Wisconsin was Anthony Huddleson, in 1835. The first church was Ash Ridge, organized in 1854 by George W. Studebaker

from the Mississinewa congregation in Indiana. There were
at that time thirty members in Ash Ridge, and, eighty miles
to the south of them, was Yellow Creek, one of the four sturdy
Illinois congregations. True to Brethren usage, Enoch Eby,
Daniel Fry, and Allen Boyer from Yellow Creek came by
horse or other private means through the woods, across
streams, and over hills to assist these Brethren. But in 1860
it is recorded that there were only twenty-eight members in
Ash Ridge.

The free ministry long prevailed in Wisconsin. For many
years the ministers from Illinois did much preaching, sometimes receiving pay for expenses but often at their own expense.
Later the mission board bore the expense and also introduced
the pastoral system. There is a record of fifteen congregations
organized, besides numerous preaching points; seven small
churches survive. The churches report six hundred sixty-two
members in 1950. Wisconsin reflects the increased congregational mortality of the more commercialized settlement and
land exploitation.

*Michigan.* The story of Michigan has some points of
likeness to the story of Wisconsin. In pursuing the simile of
a fan we can say that Michigan and Wisconsin represent the
northernmost rib of the spreading continental fan. Settlement
on the part of the Brethren came late. These northern states
were first settled by the New England element and possess
a certain New England character sometimes overlooked
because of recent European immigration and the rapid developments of industrialism. The Pennsylvania migration
touched the northernmost tier of American states lightly.
Hence the Brethren in these states appear more sharply as an
alien cultural group.

In 1864 Elder John Wise of Washington County, Pennsylvania, traveled through central Michigan and found a few
scattered members. The first churches were Thornapple,

organized in 1868; Woodland, 1874; Sunfield, 1877; and New Haven, 1878. In more recent years land developments planted churches farther north. Since about 1910 migration into the expanding industrial cities of Michigan has planted a number of congregations in the cities of Michigan.

The District of Michigan was organized in 1874. The southernmost counties have always been treated as parts of Northern Indiana or Northwestern Ohio. One wonders whether the autonomy of the region may be a part of the explanation as to the differing growth in Wisconsin and Michigan. The *Yearbook* of 1950 reports twenty-five churches and three thousand three hundred seven members.

*Missouri.* The Church was established in Missouri before it was found in the Indiana-Illinois area. As early as 1795 there was a congregation in Cape Girardeau County. Among the early members were Daniel Clingensmith from Pennsylvania and Peter Baker, John Miller, and Joseph Niswonger from North Carolina. It is conjectured that these earliest members came up the Mississippi through New Orleans. Elder John Hendricks from Kentucky found them and visited them. In 1824 there were fifty members of the Cape Girardeau brotherhood. But the congregation died out and some of the members joined the beginnings in Southern Illinois. The Church was re-established in the fifties, there being a church in Clinton County in 1854, presided over by Elder William Gish. A metal memorial plate has been placed at Plattsburg announcing Plattsburg as the "mother church" west of the Mississippi. In this church, in 1859, J. H. Moore was baptized. During the sixties a number of churches were organized, the largest being Mineral Creek, organized in 1869. In 1950 the twenty-eight churches report two thousand, two hundred seventy-two members distributed over the state and in the three districts. Southern Missouri includes Arkansas, which has but a single small church.

*Iowa.* While we are considering the Brethren's crossing the Mississippi we must chronicle their entry into Iowa. Here again we meet Elder George Wolfe of Southern Illinois, who assisted the organization at Libertyville, Jefferson County, in 1844. How this can be reconciled with the claim of Plattsburg, in view of the lapse of the earlier Cape Girardeau organization, is not apparent. Iowa was from 1850 the recipient of a number of very stable members who came from the East and settled and were satisfied with the rich soil they found.

In Southern Iowa, where Libertyville was the first church, organizations followed at Mt. Etna, Adams County, 1851; Fairview, Appanoose County, 1853; Monroe County, 1854; and the English River church, in 1855. The Brethren at Libertyville built a meetinghouse in 1858, the first in the state.

In Middle Iowa, Cedar Grove in Cedar County was organized in 1852. In 1856 three new organizations were effected: Indian Creek, Dry Creek, and Iowa River. At Dry Creek the second meetinghouse within the state was built, in 1858. It was at the Dry Creek house that the famous Quinter-McConnell debate occurred in 1867. And it was at this house that the first Annual Meeting west of the Mississippi was held in the year 1870.

In Northern Iowa the famous South Waterloo settlement began in Black Hawk County and a church was organized in 1856. A house was built in 1868. Few congregations have been more celebrated than this South Waterloo church.

*Minnesota.* The few scattered members in Minnesota have always been grouped with the northern Iowa churches. Howard Miller lists three churches with one hundred twenty-nine members in 1882. These came to be known as Root River and Winona, both of which dated from 1858; the third was a now-extinct church in Rice County. In 1950 there were seven churches in Minnesota, including a mission church in Minneapolis. The total membership is six hundred eighty-three.

*Oregon.* Hitherto we have followed a story of expansion which was largely from one contiguous area to another. The first members to locate on the Pacific Coast came to Oregon from Indiana in 1850. In 1853 eighteen more followed.

The *Gospel Visitor* was begun in April 1851; through its columns we gain glimpses of early beginnings on the Pacific Coast which also are invaluable documentation of the church life of an earlier day. In the July 1853 issue we read this from the editor:

We rejoice to learn that the *Gospel Visitor* is welcome in your remote parts, and we should like to know as much as possible of your interesting country. There are some friends and brethren, here in the East, who are particularly interested & desirous, to be informed about what prospect there is or would be, when the Gospel would be preached in its purity and simplicity with you? Whether there are any preachers among you? And if not, whether there is a desire for them, &c., &c. It depends upon you, under God, upon your faithfulness, upon your prayer and your preaching by your lives, whether a church shall be planted in your wilderness, and when planted, whether it shall increase and prosper. Think, dear brethren, of your high calling, and be assured that we shall rejoice to hear of your prosperity, and sympathize with you in all your trials and difficulties.

In the December 1853 issue of the *Visitor* appeared a letter from Jacob Wigle, which we print together with a portion of the letter of the editor, Elder Henry Kurtz.

Calapooia, Linn. Co., Oregon Terr.

August 8th, 1853

Dear brother in the Lord. I have thought it necessary, to drop you a few lines for the *Visitor,* rather as a short history of my life. . . .

George Wolf is my mother's brother; so I was brought up under the protection of the Gospel, and in an early day of my life I thought it fit, to join myself to the body. . . .

But in the spring 1852, on account of circumstances taken place, I and two of my brothers set out for Oregon Territory. I was told before I started by father Wolf, that our crossing the plains was a denial of the faith, because we would have to travel under military form. Which we did not do; for we found no need of it, but the Indians were no hindrance to us, and rather were entirely friendly to us.

Through much affliction we all got through, and once more restored to good health, and hoping that these few lines may reach you and find you all well. Now, beloved brother, if I could place my body with my mind, I would be often with the brethren; as reflection often runs over my mind of the sweet hours of admonishing, that I have spent with my brethren in the different branches of God's vineyard.

But I can blame no one with my separate condition from the body but myself. I only set out for the purpose of finding a milder climate, which I have found, . . . But this does not satisfy my desire. . . .

We are 7 in number, 3 brothers and 4 sisters, there were 3 more crossed the plains, but settled about one hundred miles from us. Now we have no one among us with any church-office but myself. The church appointed me in the office of a Deacon. . . .

And we also want the body of the church to take our case into consideration, and let us know, what we had better do; whether we had better lay still, or wait for help. . . .

As my whole desire and prayer is for the welfare of the church, and I rather think, if we were in an organized condition, there might be some growth amongst us. . . .

So nothing more at present, but remaining your lonely brother and may the grace of God abide with you is my prayer. Amen.

Jacob W. Wigle.

## The reply followed:

. . . Our deacons all are charged, that in case no preacher should be able to attend a meeting, it is their duty, to open the meeting by giving liberty for naming a hymn to be sung to the praise of God, to give out the hymn, and after singing to exhort to prayer, and after prayer to give liberty for a chapter to be named, and to read the same. And after reading the word is done, he may also exhort, as he may be enabled by grace. But as preaching is not his proper office, the advice of the brethren to deacons was always, not to rise up in order to speak to the congregation, but to keep their seats while exhorting. Finally it is their duty also to close the meeting in the same order, as it was opened, and to give out the next meeting. . . .

Now, beloved, receive these few hints in love, as we have given them, and be assured, that we feel a deep interest in your condition. If we live, we will try to present your case before the next Yearly Meeting, and are fully persuaded, that there is a way provided even for you, if you are truly humble and sincere, that you may go on rejoicing, and prosper, so that the Gospel in its simplicity may be preached, and churches be established, and souls saved even from the Rocky Mountains to the coast of the Pacific, to the honor and glory of our God and Savior Jesus Christ. . . .

As to other members in your Territory, we can give you the name of one brother, who is also a subscriber to the Visitor. His name and address is David Peebler, Salem, Marion Co., Oregon Terr. . . .[3]

Interest is added to this correspondence because a member of the famous Wolfe family is involved. The story of the Wolfe family vividly illustrates how vast an expansion of the Church had occurred in how short a time. Elder George Wolfe, Jr., had been a pioneer in the Illinois country—a contemporary and neighbor of young Abraham Lincoln, who must have seen him and had doubtless heard him preach. His father, George, Sr., had come from Fayette County, Pennsylvania. Jacob Wigle, the nephew of Elder George, Jr., settled as a pioneer in Oregon; another nephew, also known as George, Jr., traveled from Hancock County, Illinois, via Panama, landing December 16, 1856. Two years later a church was organized in California. It was formed in Santa Clara County and later moved to the San Joaquin Valley. What an achievement! Three generations, and under the informal, undirected migration connected with America's expansion the Brethren had spanned the continent. In the 1850's the country between Missouri and Iowa and the Rocky Mountains was thought of as largely uninhabitable and at least semi-desert.

There has been a disposition to speak slightingly of the period of Brethren history from the American Revolution to the mid-nineteenth century. It was the "wilderness" period, some have said. There has been a tendency to apologize for the period, and to regard the greater urbanity and sophistication of the grandchildren of the period as indications of an improvement. We are confronted with the fact that the foundations of the existent church were laid during that period. It was the congregations planted then that have

---

[3] The *Monthly Gospel Visitor,* December 1853. Page 165.

increased by division and extension; the membership on that soil has multiplied. The church of 1950 rests upon foundations that were substantially laid by 1850!

*Observations.* As one looks back upon the colonial and expansion periods of the growth of the Church there emerge two principles that deserve consideration. The first is that the Church must be located in the midst of the people. This seems so obvious and simple that it could be overlooked. The success in the colonial German population began by the observance of this simple fact. And success on the Western frontier came about because the Church was carried with the early settlers; sometimes a minister was in the vanguard of the settlers.

The second principle is that there must be a self-sacrificing and respected ministry who stay with the people. Under the free-ministry plan that then operated among the Brethren the congregation elected a man who lived among them more or less permanently. They chose one of the more stable brethren, a man already known and respected. His sacrificial quality was attested by his own generosity and by the fact that he took up the ministry without prospect of pay. Writing of the old Yellow Creek church, Illinois, Elder John Heckman observed pointedly, "The seventy-six years of service of four elders stands in bold relief against eight pastors in twenty-four years."

# Chapter 16

# PLANTING THE CHURCH AFTER 1850

We follow the expansion of the church through the Central West and adjoining area after 1850, and then note the colonization procedure in North Dakota, the Northwest, California, and Florida.

*Kansas.* The great rush to settle Kansas came after the great compromise of 1850 had been reached in Congress. The Brethren joined the rush and before 1860 there were three churches in Kansas: Cottonwood, Lyon County, 1856; Washington Creek, Douglas County, 1858; and Wolf River, 1859.

With the 1860's came crop failure and drouth as well as the Civil War. The peaceful settlers, such as the Brethren, were at the mercy of guerilla bands. Elder Abraham Rothrock was shot and left for dead as punishment for his known anti-slavery views. He, however, revived and recovered. In the far-reaching relief which was carried on in Kansas and other parts of the drouth-stricken West there was a distinct foreshadowing of the more recent Brethren relief work.

During the seventies, migration to Kansas increased greatly. Shortly after 1870 the state was formed into a district and in 1880 it was made into two districts. By 1891 it was divided into four districts. Since the age of automobiles has come one wonders whether some of our districts are not too small. The growth in Kansas has been very slow during recent years, although the Church may be regarded as well established in the state.

*Nebraska.* The Brethren entered Nebraska in the same

movement of population that pioneered Kansas. The Bell
Creek church in Dodge County was organized in 1866. The
Bethel Creek and Beatrice (today there are a Beatrice and a
South Beatrice) church was organized in 1875. The vicissi-
tudes of the West have been hard on the church in Nebraska.

*Colorado.* Howard Miller in 1882 listed one church in
Boulder County, with eighty members. In 1895 D. M. Click, a
minister, located at Grand Valley near Grand Junction. The
First Grand Valley church was begun in 1897. Western Colorado and the churches in eastern Colorado which had been
attached to Kansas were combined into the District of Colorado
in 1939.

*Oklahoma.* Oklahoma was entered by the Brethren in 1891
when Elder Jacob Appleman settled near Clarkson. The Para-
dise Prairie church was organized with Elder Appleman in
charge. At first it was regarded as part of Kansas. In 1897 the
District of Oklahoma was formed. The Panhandle of Texas
and most of New Mexico have been regarded as part of this
district.

*Texas and Louisiana.* Our smallest district is Texas and
Louisiana. In 1890 Elder Jacob Berkey preached in Texas. The
Louisiana churches belong to the "fostered" immigration type
of churches, i. e., they came into being through the attempt to
establish a church in connection with the promotion of land
sales.

*North Dakota and the Northwest.* The gallant little District of North Dakota and Eastern Montana came into being in
similar fashion. When government land was thrown open to
settlement, the railroads played their part in encouraging colonization. The story can hardly be told better than by Gladdys
Muir in her careful book, *Settlement of the Brethren on the
Pacific Slope.*

 . . . Brethren colonization in North Dakota was largely the result
of the activity of the Great Northern [Railroad] and its immigration

agent—Max Bass. Mr. Bass had had some experience in colonizing Amish Mennonites and found that their natural tendency to move in groups made work among them very profitable. The United States Land Commissioner at Cando, F. L. Thompson, suggested to Bass that the "Dunkers" showed similar tendencies. So he visited the Annual Conference held at Muncie, Indiana, in 1893, and succeeded in interesting two Brethren in Dakota: Elder A. B. Peters, and T. J. Beckwith, a deacon. Peters had been left bankrupt by the panic of that year and was naturally interested in a plan that promised to be a way out of disaster. After some correspondence, Bass offered Peters a free trip to Dakota for the purpose of investigation. The latter suggested that since he himself did not have a great deal of prestige it might be well if the Great Northern would permit him to select other Brethren of influence to accompany him. This was done. All were furnished with passes. The committee made a trip to Dakota, looked over the homestead land available, and examined samples of grain, potatoes, cabbage, carrots, etc., which they later took as exhibits back home with them. On their return to Indiana meetings were called of friends and neighbors, and soon others became interested in Dakota. Within ten days a second group of twenty-three was taken by Peters to Dakota, and nearly all of them filed claims for homesteads. Later a third group of fifty filed claims. During the winter no more groups were taken north, but Peters continued his solicitations, and in the spring of 1894 a colony of three hundred and twenty persons, largely Brethren, was conducted to Cando, North Dakota. Several freight trains were required to carry the household goods. At the Annual Conference, later in the spring, Peters succeeded in interesting a great many more Brethren. In the spring of 1895 he secured about four hundred and twenty colonists. From this time until 1900, Peters continued to take groups to Dakota. He solicited friends and Brethren throughout northern Indiana and Ohio, making personal visits and speaking at public meetings with Mr. Bass. About three thousand went to Dakota in 1900. The result was that a large Brethren colony developed at Cando, North Dakota, almost overnight. Soon Brethren were settled all along the main line of the Great Northern as far as Williston.

The success of this experiment naturally encouraged the Great Northern to urge Brethren colonization along its lines in Montana, Idaho, and Washington. . . . To further assist them the Great Northern employed in 1896, as Traveling Passenger Agent, George McDonaugh, . . . In 1898 Bass inserted an advertisement in the *Gospel Messenger*, stating that a new "missionary field" was now open, and invited the attention of *Messenger* readers to the Milk River Valley of Montana. The church in North Dakota was already firmly established, he said, and Montana was the next state inviting attention.

About this time it became evident that the Great Northern had a serious competitor in the Northwest, the Oregon Short Line, a branch of the Harriman system. This railroad by its advertising was diverting the attention of the Brethren to southern Idaho. Brethren were even leaving North Dakota to go to southern Idaho. ...

.  .  .  .  .  .

The Oregon Short Line, the railroad which was causing Max Bass so much anxiety, was now strongly urging the Brethren to establish colonies along its line in southern Idaho. This line employed a member of the Brethren, Samuel Bock of Ohio, as its colonization agent. He worked for the Oregon Short Line from 1898 until 1911, making Nampa, Idaho, the chief center of his efforts. A glance at the advertising of the Oregon Short Line shows that Brethren were now being shown the agricultural possibilities of Boise, Nampa, and Payette valleys. Testimonials of Brethren who were early comers to these localities were printed to give the Brethren greater confidence in the region. ...[1]

Another railroad to enter the competition was the Northern Pacific. The following advertisement was inserted in the *Brethren Family Almanac* by that road in order to attract Brethren settlers to the Northwest.

PROSPERITY
Attends the
BRETHREN COLONIES
on the
NORTHERN PACIFIC
... IN ...

CENTRAL NORTH DAKOTA
Where crops have been good and land has trebled in value.

THE NEZ PERCES COUNTRY IN NORTHERN IDAHO
The banner wheat and stock-raising section of the Pacific Northwest.

THE YAKIMA VALLEY
Where the Brethren have a strong congregation and a church

---

[1] Gladdys E. Muir, *Settlement of the Brethren on the Pacific Slope.* Pages 156-160.

house of their own at Sunnyside, the town in which immorality and vice can never gain a footing, where land sown to Alfalfa yields an income of over $50.00 per acre each year, and Fruit Orchards bring their owners a yearly revenue of from $50.00 to $250.00 per acre, according to the age of the trees. Elder D. B. Eby calls it the GOSHEN of the Northwest. Kennewick, the Gateway of the Valley, is fast developing. Land there can be purchased at Lower Prices than any other Irrigated Land in Central Washington, but will advance rapidly. *Berries ripen here earlier* than in any other part.

THE FERTILE VALLEYS OF WESTERN WASHINGTON
Where Grain, Stock and Fruit Flourish and Climate is tempered by the Breezes from the Pacific Ocean; where Lumbering, Mining and Fishing offer boundless opportunities for remunerative labor, and the profitable investment of capital.
For particulars about *Government Land,* and *Unoccupied Land* owned by *Private Parties* or *Companies,* suitable for *Single Farms* or *Colonies,* and for maps and printed matter descriptive of NORTHERN PACIFIC RAILWAY LANDS, and for information regarding *Industrial* and *Business Openings* along the line of the NORTHERN PACIFIC RAILWAY, write to

C. W. Mott,
General Emigration Agent
Northern Pacific Ry.
ST. PAUL, MINN.[2]

Across the border in Canada, the Canadian Pacific Railroad also had land to sell and was interested in getting Brethren colonies to settle either on its land or on homestead land that was still available. Its land agent, R. R. Stoner, located at St. Paul, Minnesota, began an advertising campaign in the *Inglenook* about 1902. Special excursions to Canada were offered at very low rates, and Brethren were urged to take advantage of them. The railroad succeeded in interesting David Hollinger, an influential elder of Ohio, in the region. He bought land there himself and later became associated with the Stoner Company. Many more parties of Brethren were taken to visit the land. The result was that in a short time thousands of acres of Canadian Pacific land were occupied by the Brethren.[3]

In the *Missionary Visitor* of February 1906 there is an

[2] *Brethren Family Almanac,* 1904.
[3] Muir, *op. cit.* Page 162.

editorial which exhibits much of the thinking of that time.

The railroads, though soulless corporations, are being used wonderfully by the Lord for the spread of the church. Even though it be true that the agents for the railroads have been active in urging people to go and see and believe and settle, from sinister motives, that does not keep God and His real children from taking advantage of these opportunities for the glory of His name. And, perhaps, when the books are opened on the other shore it will be revealed that the agent who reported the country to the people possessed no more selfishness than many in the church, who eagerly took advantage of the "bargains" for their own personal good. At least it would be well for him, who is clear of the sin of selfishness in all this emigration business, to cast the first stone at the ones who have made it possible to have the good homes and prosperous congregations in these goodly lands.

It would, in the mind of the editor, be perfectly unjust, in this review of the progress of the church, to pass by and not recognize these agencies properly. For whatever have been their motives their efforts have resulted in much good. And whether the members scattered over this Great West realize it or not, they bend their knees in worship where they do and enjoy the favors which are theirs, largely through those agencies. Indeed, all through the west and northwest are God-fearing men and women who hold dear in memory's casket such names as Bro. Geo. L. McDonaugh, of the Union Pacific railroad, one of the oldest colonizers among the Brethren; Mr. Max Bass, of the Great Northern railway; Mr. C. W. Mott, of the Northern Pacific railway; Bro. S. Bock, of the Oregon Short Line. . . .

Today these roads may be reaping rich returns financially for their aggressive work. Well and good. These arteries of our nation have made it possible for the hands of the church to operate where, had they not gone, the church could not be now.

The Brethren Publishing House began a general magazine in 1897 which was published under the name, the *Pilot*, until 1900, when it became the *Inglenook;* it was published until 1913. The files of this publication exhibit lush land advertising aimed to build the Church while the individual Brethren became prosperous, for in 1897 the Annual Conference had indirectly advised that land advertising be excluded from the *Gospel Messenger*.

In the various parts of the vast West there were isolated

families and many were the calls "to come over into Macedonia and help." Miss Gladdys Muir, the authority on Brethren colonization, makes this observation: "None of these calls, however, resulted in the development of new churches. A missionary call, even though accompanied by material attractions, if not reinforced by realtors' circulars and railroad literature, seems to have been difficult to hear."[4]

*California.* We have previously spoken of the early entry of the Brethren into California. The Church grew very slowly and was entangled in the trouble of the Far Western Brethren. The discussion had persisted even after the two parties had been officially reconciled. This is the reason that when the "Progressive" rift came in 1881-1882 a general schism occurred.

. . . The leader of the Progressive movement, H. R. Holsinger, visited the California church and was favorably received. This caused alarm among the Oregon churches, which . . . asked the Annual Conference "to look after those Brethren." The result was the sending of a final committee to the Church of California in 1884. This committee found the church "ignoring the counsels and advice of our General Conference" and recommended that, since several committees had been sent to the California church and had been ineffective, the brotherhood should withdraw fellowship from all who would not respect nor hear the counsel of the church. The result was that the Church of California and Chaparral became Progressive churches. The Stanislaus church had already been disorganized. A few who were dissatisfied with the outcome now began to emigrate to southern California, helping to form the nucleus of a colony of Brethren at Covina, out of which was to come the mother church in the south—the "Church of Southern California."[5]

It is thus from this beginning near Covina, from 1885 to 1889, that the present Church in California dates.

There were, in 1889, only two churches in southern California, the Covina and Conejo congregations. The Covina congregation was prospering. A Covina church council, reported in the *Southern Californian* for October 9, 1890, was attended by Brethren from Los Angeles, Tehunga, Glendora, Eswena, Spadra, and Lordsburg. The other con-

---

[4] Muir, *op. cit.* Page 211.

[5] Muir, *op. cit.* Page 87.

gregation, Conejo, had not thrived so well: the Brethren here were located at quite a distance from the railroad; then, too, they could only engage in dry farming. Work of other sorts was scarce, and thus they had to leave home if they desired employment. The result was that the Brethren soon began to move away. The District Meeting of 1894 discouraged the idea of disorganizing, but it was in vain. Eventually nearly all of the Conejo Brethren moved to other places, and in 1901 the church was officially disorganized.

However, the center of interest naturally lies with the new congregations established during this period. They were, in the order of organization: Lordsburg, Tropico, Glendale, Egan, and Inglewood. Two of these, Lordsburg and Tropico, were offshoots of the Covina church. The Covina church also held meetings at Glendora during the greater part of this period, but the latter congregation was not formally organized until 1902. A Brethren colony was also established in northern California at Merced, and a church organized there. . . .[6]

But there was an increasing questioning of the colonizing schemes. In 1904 J. H. Moore, editor of the *Messenger,* dared to question the whole idea. From the reported discussion we quote again from Muir a few lines which show the status of the Church and of thought in 1904.

. . . George L. McDonaugh, staunch friend of colonization, also came to the rescue, bringing forward the results of his experience to back up the theory. He reminded his readers that at the beginning of 1889 Covina was the only church in southern California; but that since that time fifteen more congregations had been formed, built up largely by colonization. If eastern readers could only attend the meetings in these fifteen churches, he felt sure they would all become converts to the policy of colonization. "Colonization builds up the church," he said, "and assists in the spreading of the Gospel in all its purity."

Some of the easterners, however, who had been in California, were not so favorably impressed. I. J. Rosenberger, who visited the Brethren here in 1904, wrote:

"The churches in California have been built up to the point of organization by immigration . . . but to me it seems unfortunate that so many ministers have located in each congregation. The churches I visited have from six to twelve preachers, and about half of these are elders. Then add to these the number of tourist preachers . . . and you

_____
[6] Muir, *op. cit.* Pages 116 and 117.

have a state of things that does not demand encouragement. While climate and soil deserve consideration in selecting a home, surely the needs in the Master's cause should have some weight in locating in our Master's vineyard.[7]

By 1918 the land era was practically over.

*Florida.* May we turn our attention to another point of the compass. The development of Florida was as a repetition of the pioneer expansion, born out of due season. Mary Margaret Parker, writing in 1941, has pertinently sketched the main lines of Florida development.

The thrust of the church into Florida may be regarded as a part of the general southern migration which began about 1880 and received strong impetus following the World War in the period known as "the boom." Between 1920 and 1930 the population of Florida increased 51.6 per cent. Among these south bound migrants were found an increasing number of Brethren. . . . Records indicate, however, that there was a Brethren family in the state as early as 1873.

The three churches established during the period from 1885 to 1900 did not survive, due partially, no doubt, to the devastating effect on many people of the freeze of 1895. For about ten years following, we find a lull in activity until 1912 when organization of the Tampa church was the first of a series of five in four years. The first Brethren were in Sebring in 1916: Eli Cottrell, Indiana, J. H. Garst, Virginia, J. H. Moore, Illinois, and A. M. Stout.

With the exception of a short-lived organization at Chosen in 1922 there was another slump in activity during the United States' participation in the Great War. In 1925, however, three churches were organized in as many months and a fourth one followed later in 1929. Of these, two are now alive and well. The other two await the touch of a consecrated pastor to restore them to life.

The period since 1935 has been concerned more with stabilizing the present organizations than with encouraging new ones. It is, of course, natural and to be expected that the death rate of congregations should be high in a pioneer area where the population is constantly shifting, but as long as the birth rate remains correspondingly high, there is not great cause for alarm. There comes a time, however, when to be effective, the church must sink her roots deep into the soil and become a vital part of the community, controlled and supported by the native people whom it

---

[7] Muir, *op. cit.* Page 171.

seeks to serve. Okeechobee is probably the most outstanding example at the present of rapid progress made in this direction.[8]

There have been omissions in the telling of this story. But we have sought to make intelligible why and how the Brethren find themselves at the midpoint of the twentieth century scattered abroad in one thousand twenty-five congregations. The five regional maps show the geographic distribution of these congregations at this time, each dot representing one congregation.

The expanding American society was the milieu in which this company of religious idealists found themselves earning a livelihood and rearing their families. The American development is the curtain backdrop against which the Church's development needs to be viewed.

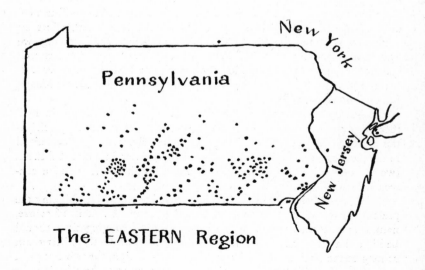

The EASTERN Region

---

[8] *A History of the Church of the Brethren in Florida*, a thesis in the Bethany Biblical Seminary library. Pages 1-5.

The
SOUTHEASTERN
Region

The CENTRAL Region

The
WESTERN
Region

The PACIFIC
COAST Region

## Chapter 17

## RURAL BACKGROUND DISTURBED

We have sketched the geographical expansion of the Church from Germantown to California and seen the fan-spread of the Brethren from North Dakota and Canada to Florida. Great changes were wrought in both the country and the Church in the process of that coverage. It will now be our task to note some of the most significant of these changes. First, we seek the setting for them.

From 1800 to 1900 occurred the great geographical transformation of America. By 1910 the end of the frontier period was reached; there was no more free land. But meantime a still more significant project was underway: the change from a rural to an urban manner of living, from an agricultural to an industrial economy. The industrialization of America got well underway by about 1850. This date virtually coincides with the turning point in Brethren history, which was the issuing in April 1851 by Elder Henry Kurtz of the first number of the *Gospel Visitor*. The *Visitor* not only utilized one of the most important devices of technology—the printing press—in the service of the Church; it became at the same time a symbol of the spread of industrialism.

It is true that Brethren in Germantown in the eighteenth century had operated a printing business long before the time of Henry Kurtz. But while they carried their occupation in a profoundly religious spirit, they thought of themselves as serving the Germans in America rather than any particular Church. The Germantown people were a small minority of urban dwellers in the midst of a rural society. But the movement of 1851 was different. Then the character of the entire society of which the Brethren were a part began to change.

Title Page of a Sauer Bible

And Elder Kurtz began to publish the *Gospel Visitor* for the Brethren, as such.

Christopher Sauer was not an exemplar of the social period of which he was a part. On the contrary, he was a religious radical, a nonconformist and a nonresistant who forfeited his vast fortune and stood ready to forfeit his life rather than deny his faith. This is the religious import of his story. One wonders how many spiritual descendants he has in our century.

The burden upon the hearts of the Sauers, father and son, was to put Bibles within reach of the German colonists. Bibles imported from Europe sold for five pounds sterling—at least a hundred dollars in our currency. The younger Sauer printed and sold Bibles for eighteen shillings—about eighteen dollars. And he was embarrassed by the size of his profits. In spite of his spiritual sensitivity Christopher Sauer, Jr., became one of early America's rich men. The Revolutionary government decided to make an example of this rich old publisher, who was really a symbol of Tory Loyalism.

We return to the changes wrought in America in the nineteenth century. While in 1790 only three percent of the nation's population lived in America's six cities of eight thousand or more people, by 1860 one person in six, or sixteen and two-thirds percent, lived in cities. By 1950 hardly more than one in six resided on farms and were bona fide farmers. There was change in economy, change in interest, change in direction, change in the whole manner of living, penetrating even into remote areas. The change was felt keenly by 1880. Brethren were not exempt from it. It is significant that the major crisis in the history of Dunkerism culminated in 1881-1883. The Brethren fell into a three-way division. The three resultant groups represented three predominant attitudes toward the rising American industrialism.

One was the emphatic rejection of the new techniques, modes, and manners of the era, insofar as the Church and the direct service of God were concerned. This led to the "Old Order" organization.

The other extreme was an enthusiastic adoption of the new techniques and the cry for change and progress; hence the "Progressive Brethren."

The majority party came to be called "conservatives," although one wonders whether "moderates" or "middle-of-the-roaders" would not have been a more accurate designation. This group had the advantage of numbers, with both the inertia and the strength that numbers give. And it had the weakness of a poorly defined position. Many had not thought on the issue at all, and merely stayed with the majority party. The moderate always has a certain advantage in having ele-- ments of truth from all views of the subject. But he is likely to lack zeal and become only lukewarm.

We return to the contrasting rural and urban types of life. There is a widespread but erroneous impression that city life is superior to that of the countryside. Cities were perhaps first built for security. Behind city walls men sought safety from their enemies. The gregariousness of men was another attraction to the city. The comforts and conveniences were additional factors that held men to cities. These advantages are not apparent in our modern life. The city is not an especially safe place. It is a lonesome place. And modern conveniences have brought city comforts to the countryside.

The farmhouse in the open country is characteristically American. Over much of the world the small village or hamlet has been the form of country life. Those desiring to pursue the many interesting phases of country life are referred especially to the book, *Rural Life in the United States,* published by Alfred A. Knopf, New York, in 1949. It is the work of eight authors from the United States Department of Agriculture.

There are various systems of economy. E. O. Baker in his *Agriculture in Modern Life* makes a good analysis of them. He points out that the familistic system is characteristic of agriculture in the United States. The individualistic is that of independent artisans and small tradesmen. The capitalistic is characteristic of a manufacturing and commercial society. In addition, there are the co-operative and the socialistic. There will be need for this classification in our further story.

We need to lift up several contrasting characteristics of rural people as opposed to urban. To the city dweller, the ruralite seems naive. The person in the country tends to accept the natural as right and good. He has a large family. He finds it easy to believe that God will provide. A hearty acceptance of life and the universe tends to run through all of rural life and thought. On the traditional Christian background it tends to produce childlike faith and an easy acceptance of formal religion as literal truth.

His city cousin is sophisticated. Living in close quarters, he looks upon the large family of his rural relative as a kind of affliction. He gets his supplies with cash from the grocery, and his faith in God's provision is likely to be little more than a theological proposition. The urbanite is self-conscious and critical, and tends to be more fearful. To cover inner fears and timidity, he puts on a bold front of self-assertion and seems proud, aloof, and "hard-boiled."

Second, country people tend to be provincial; city people, cosmopolitan. Though it is true now that "Americans have wheels under them" in the country as well as the city, provincialism is persistent. The urbanites' acquaintance with the world is broader, but is thereby more superficial. He prides himself on his breadth, but his convictions are not intense. The difference between the provincial and the cosmopolitan becomes clearly apparent in personal habits and living—in dress, food, housing and language.

Third, the rural environment is comparatively simple; the urban, complex. People in the country have big houses. Food is cheap. Hospitality thrives. In the city housing is limited. Food must be bought. Hospitality lags. No complaint against a city congregation is more common than that the members are not sociable. The very press of city life compels people to have a certain aloofness. Without it there would be no privacy.

The urbanite spends freely. The farmer is frugal. To him money is for uncommon necessities, luxuries, and savings. A plain brother gave testimony before he died that he had tried to avoid all foolishness and had never wasted money, excepting one time when he went to a sale he spent fifteen cents for his dinner.

Fourth, the people of a rural community find life a network of personal relationships, while in the city life tends to be impersonal. The average rural community tends to become a neighborhood of relatives. This is illustrated by the typical rural Brethren congregation. The intimacy of the rural community irks the more independent, and the closeness of association may produce friction. Yet there is security in intimate association which is seldom found in the city. Loneliness is the malady of the city.

All this is a way of saying that rural life tends to be of the familistic pattern, while in the urban center life tends strongly to be of the individualistic type.

A general statement may be made covering Brethren history of the past century. It is the story of a religious fraternity which had become accustomed to working in an agricultural society finding itself in the midst of that society's transformation into an urban industrial order. It is the struggle with the environing "great society" as it ceased to be predominantly naive, provincial, simple, and personal and became increasingly sophisticated, cosmopolitan, complex, and impersonal. From a religious viewpoint it is a development of increasing difficulty and strain. For the socio-psychical (or psycho-social) traits of a rural society which we have here selected are closer to traditional Christian viewpoints and virtues than the characteristic traits of urban life.

It would be too sweeping to say that the traits which we have associated with rural life cannot exist in an urban center. But it is safe to say that if these qualities do persist it will be only by deliberately cultivating them. And without these qualities and virtues one does not see how we may have a New Testament Church. For these traits are the characteristics of rural, i. e., familistic society. And a New Testament figure of the Church is that it is a family, the family of the Father (Matthew 23:8-10) or the "household of the faith" (Galatians 6:10).

# Chapter 18

# INDUSTRIALISM REACHES THE BRETHREN

Brethren history, in a changing century, must be viewed as a development or a struggle with the changing social milieu. Many aspects of this transition might well be examined, but we shall choose a few only as illustrations.

Let the first be the carpet question.[1] The first query about carpets came to the Yearly Meeting of 1827.

[1827] Art. 8: How is it considered to lay carpets in (our) houses? [Answer:] It was considered that it belongs to the grandeur (highness) of this world, and that it will not become a follower of Jesus to garnish his house in this manner, but rather that he should adorn his house as may be consistent with lowliness.

Queries concerning carpets again appeared in the minutes of 1846 and 1853. Note how the references group themselves about our pivotal date, 1851.

[1846] Art. 10: About pride, in its various forms, which is creeping into the church, [answer] It is thought highly necessary that the Yearly Meeting instruct and urge it upon all the overseers of the churches to see especially to that matter, and protest strongly against all manner of superfluity and vanity, such as building fine houses, and having paintings, carpetings, and costly furniture, etc., together with the adorning of the body too much after the fashion of the world. We believe that we should deny ourselves, and abstain from these things, especially the laborers in the Word, who are called to be ensamples to the flock.

[1853] Art. 23: Does the answer to the tenth query, as it stands on the minutes of 1846, only forbid the grandeur of paintings and carpets, or does it forbid them altogether? [Answer:] We consider the advice of our Brethren in 1846 sufficiently clear.

---

[1] *Minutes of the Annual Meetings, Church of the Brethren, 1778 to 1909.*

Nothing more is heard of carpets until 1878.

[1878] X: Will this District Meeting petition the Annual Meeting of 1878 to reconsider Art. 8, of Annual Meeting of 1827, and Art. 11, of the Annual Meeting of 1828, and give us a more definite answer, or show by the Gospel that if we have plain carpets on our floors, it will lead to elevation (pride)? Answer: We consider the above queries, and decide that plain carpets have no tendency to pride and elevation, and they may be enjoyed by us; but fine and fancy carpets are not consistent with our humble profession, and should not be in our houses.

From 1827 to 1878 is fifty-one years—from "it will not become a follower of Jesus" to "plain carpets . . . may be enjoyed by us." Now, what happened in those fifty-one years?

Carpet is such a commonplace article today that we get something of a shock to read of its recent origin. Carpet came from the Orient and was first used not on floors but to cover tables or beds in ladies' boudoirs. It was first made in continental Europe in 1607, in England in 1735, in America in 1791. There were several small American carpet factories before 1841. The maximum production was eight yards a day on the hand loom. Then in 1841 a power loom was invented that soon was making twenty-five to twenty-seven yards daily—and then sixty-five yards. In 1849, one hundred sixteen establishments were making $5,400,000 worth of carpets and rugs. This has risen sharply in the years since. The agricultural economy of scarcity gave way before the increasing abundance of the industrial era. Carpets became cheaper and cheaper. Then there came a day when it seemed senseless formalism to continue to forbid the use of them.

Our country came into a money-based economy. The output of mill, factory, laboratory, and mechanized farm fills warehouses, and unemployment results unless the goods can be sold. The goods are desired on every hand. There must be profits in order to secure them. Farming, under this pressure, became a way to make profits instead of a way of life. The "graceful life," the "good life," has come to be regarded as dependent on the abundance of possessions.

The wealth of the American nation increased enormously. From a population of four millions with a wealth of $750,000,-000 in 1791, the increase to 1850 was a population of twenty-three and two-tenths millions and a wealth of $7,164,000,000. The figures in 1880 had reached fifty and two-tenths millions with $43,642,000,000 of wealth, and in 1937 the stupendous figures of one hundred twenty-eight and eight-tenths millions with $321,792,000,000 of wealth.

This has created enormous complexities for the Brethren and the whole Christian Church. The Brethren had no way to deal with increasing pressure for consumption than to give negative advice, to decry the increasing expenditure and "waste," and to commend the simpler ways of the traditional agricultural society. The Annual Meeting never dealt with the problem in its entirety. The genius of Dunkerism is practical; we are prone to proceed from one immediate problem to another, not always seeing relationships.

Religion is life. And so the Yearly Meeting dealt with all manner of the minutiae of life: carpets, wallpaper, lace curtains, pictures, musical instruments, sleigh bells, and, above all, personal adornment and dress. If religion insists on being practical and dealing with life, there is no possibility of avoiding the discussion of these things. They are the common details of life.

A Church nourished in an economy of scarcity and familiar with the mores of an agricultural society could readily give advice "to abstain" and "to deny" oneself. But the advice given was so largely negative and the pressure of industrialism so steady that the Church from 1851 to 1926 appeared to be fighting a losing and retreating action.

In 1926 a small schism (the Dunker Brethren) registered a protest against a too-rapid adjustment to industrial society. The problems still press upon us in varying forms and degrees. We are groping for positive solutions. But we must say this for our forefathers: they found their negative words in the vocabulary of the New Testament.

There are other aspects of the industrial transformation of the Western world besides the transition from an economy of scarcity to one of abundance. The way the Brethren dealt with lightning rods illustrates one of the other aspects.

It was argued that lightning rods offered a conductor to receive and "drain off" the potential of accumulated electric charge. Their extensive manufacture and sale did not come until the middle of the nineteenth century, and then in 1851—right on the dot! — came the first query to Yearly Meeting.[2]

[1851] Art. 7: Should brethren have the privilege to put up light-ning-rods? [Answer:] Considered, that we would not advise brethren to do so; nor would we say to those who have them, to take them down; but advise all our dear brethren to bear with each other in such matters, and try to put their chief trust in God.

One cannot help but be impressed with the sound sense and restraint of this and much else in the minutes. Our early Brethren were not fanatical. The minutes are as remarkable for what they do not say as for what they say.

The developing art of salesmanship continued to press lightning rods upon the Brethren in the 1850's and the 1860's. Queries kept coming to the Yearly Meeting — in 1856, 1864, and 1865. Finally, in 1866, came the following:

[1866] Art. 20: Inasmuch as the subject of lightning-rods has been before the Annual Council, and brethren have only been advised to bear with one another, which we consider is no decision at all; for, if right, why not recommend it to all, and if wrong, why tolerate it at all? [Answer:] As we have no command to erect or forbid lightning-rods, we would not advise brethren to put up such rods, but the Brethren should bear with one another in love in such matters. (Minutes of 1851, art. 7, and of 1856, art. 25.)

This was the last query ever presented to Yearly Meeting on lightning rods. We are dealing here with the natural conservatism of the rural mind. Sociological observers have long

---

[2] *Op. cit.*

noted the reluctance of tillers of the soil to accept new devices and new tools. The older ways are safe and tried. Why waste much-needed money on the new and untried? When slick-looking salesmen from the cities sold lightning rods to some Brethren, it disturbed the others. Were they being swindled? Was the new device, indeed, a scheme to outwit Providence? Suppose it was God's purpose to burn your barn with lightning? At least, the rods were new-fangled gadgets and hence questionable.

The natural conservatism of the rural mind has been sorely tried many times in the era of industrialism. Industrialism has literally flooded the world with gadgets, contrivances, machines, new devices, and new processes. That is why the Brethren have reluctantly consented to bells on horses, and why the Old Order Brethren have so earnestly and often discussed telephones, automobiles, and radios.

The writer in his boyhood listened to much ridiculing of a former generation concerning their slowness in appreciating lightning rods. It was said by many of those around him that we ought always to accept the findings of "science." But reference to a modern encyclopedia will show that insurance companies have made no difference in rates on buildings "protected" by rods and that the lightning-rod business is now virtually extinct. There is something to be said for the natural conservatism of the rural mind!

There is another element in the industrialization of American society which has borne upon the Brethren. It is the combination of natural rural conservatism with an aversion to personal vanity and ostentatious display. Both are illustrated from the Annual Conference minutes in regard to "likenesses" or photographs. After the perfecting of the doguerreotype in 1839, the matter became of concern to Brethren.[3]

The first Yearly Meeting minute on "likenesses" was in 1849: "Art. 18. Whether Brethren can be allowed to have their

---

[3] *Op. cit.*

likeness or profile taken. [Answer:] Considered, it is not advisable."

Again the matter came up in 1857, 1858, 1867, and 1869. The answer in 1869 was: "We consider it not right for members to have their likenesses taken, and if they have done so, they should be admonished to put them away."

It is apparent that there was a definite reluctance to make this an excommunicable offense. The designation "sin" has been avoided throughout, and it has been treated as a foolish foible which mature Brethren should avoid. Again in 1872 the matter came up.

[1872] Art. 10. Does this District understand the Annual Meeting to mean that we should dispose of our likenesses entirely when it advises us to put them away? (See Minutes of 1869, art. 21). Answer: This Annual Meeting understands the phrase "put them away" to mean to put them out of public sight.

Here, twenty-three years after picture-taking was first discussed, the Yearly Meeting said in effect, "Don't make a foolish display of yourself."

Various phases of the matter were brought up again in 1892, 1894, 1895, and 1903. On the last query, a committee was appointed. It brought back a report the next year, but the following answer was approved:

Answer: While not unmindful of the good intentions of the Conferences passing the decisions regarding likenesses, we now decide to repeal these decisions, and at the same time enter our protest against the extravagant use of money for photographs.

The earlier decisions had protested against vanity; this one protests against waste. But all America was being brought up to such an excessive scale of expenditures that the waste of a previous generation no longer seemed like waste.

The natural caution concerning the new and the dislike of the ostentatious dealt not only with picture-taking but with dress. Other new social practices and institutions came in for scrutiny: examples — life insurance, interest, the sale of stocks and bonds, high schools, colleges, Sunday schools, and salaried religious workers. The Brethren opposed most of them. The discussions were practical and emotional rather than intellectual. Sometimes prejudice prevailed. But the advocates of changes were often naively childish in their optimism about the trends of society.

We select interest and insurance for consideration in the concluding part of this chapter.

The taking of interest was frowned upon by Plato, Aristotle, and the Hebrew law. For centuries the Christian conscience forbade it. Only with the rise of the age of commercialism was the taking of interest really permitted. John Calvin was a pioneer in justifying it. The discussions have now centered upon usury, or excessive interest. Interest itself has become commonplace as a way of financing.

There were minutes against taking interest in 1783, 1822, 1837, 1845, 1856, 1862, 1863, 1872, and 1873. A couple of examples will be quoted:[4]

[1822] Art. 12. Whether it be right for a follower of Jesus to take interest. [Answer:] Considered, that neither the law nor the gospel gives us such privilege, and that it should not be among the membership.

[1837] Art. 9. How is it considered if members take more than lawful interest? [Answer:] Considered, that it ought to be by no means; and if a brother should do so, he ought to be visited, and if he would not take advice, we could not be satisfied with him.

Note that "taking interest" has given way to "taking more than lawful interest." Even then there was difficulty in getting action, as the queries of 1872 and 1873 attest.

Concern about insurance is a more recent item. Insurance is one of the key institutions of our modern capitalistic order. It was greatly extended in the latter half of the nineteenth century.

The question of insuring property against fire reached the Brethren's Yearly Meeting in 1847. (Everything seems to

---

[4] *Op. cit.*

cluster around 1851.) The idea of pooling property losses is not too difficult to grasp and appeals to the cautious side of our nature. The Yearly Meeting had to discuss it in 1847, 1848, 1856, 1865, 1869, 1870, 1871, 1875, and 1879. The attitude adopted was analogous to that on the lightning-rod question. The Annual Meeting never endorsed and never condemned fire insurance. When a German Baptist Fire Insurance Company came into existence, it gave rise to a query:

[1879] XV: Is it considered right and according to the Gospel and the old-established order of the Brethren, to organize a mutual fire insurance company? Answer: It is neither contrary to the Gospel nor the principles of the Brethren, provided the charter, if there is one, does not require the brethren to compromise any of our principles.

But life insurance was a much more difficult question. Life insurance reached the Brethren in the 1870's.[5] A query in 1871 had dealt with livestock insurance. In 1873 one came directly upon life insurance.

[1873] Article 1. Is it consistent for brethren to have their lives insured: and how shall we proceed with those brethren who have their lives insured? Answer: It is inconsistent for brethren to do so.

Not all were obedient.

[1882] XXIX: As the Annual Meeting has decided that it is inconsistent for members to have their lives insured, (Annual Meeting 1873, page 329, art. 1st) what is to be done with a brother who has his life insured, especially ministers and ordained elders who persist in so doing? Answer: Those who do so shall be dealt with as transgressors.

Still the problem persisted. It was dealt with in 1883, 1886, 1896, 1902, and 1903. In 1883, different views on insurance were admitted and further action was deferred. In 1886 the giving up of life insurance was made a requirement for membership. In 1903 an investigating committee's moderate report was rejected, but the discussion on the Conference floor is, from our point of view, an ample documentation of the thesis of this chapter, namely, that Brethren are caught

---

[5] *Op. cit.*

in the meshes of a major social transformation. A final insurance item is a request in 1939 for a Brethren Insurance Cooperative. It was decided to take no action. Now we have ministerial annuities and pensions and are in the process of getting limited group insurance for ministers.

Caution is in place, for in the era of industrialism he who is involved with corporations is likely to be brought into personal contact with the law or he draws directly upon the law. The law and its works of lawyers and courts are suspect. They are of the State. And the less one has to do with the State, ordinarily, the better it is, for the State may spell military service or the use of force in other ways. That is the characteristic Brethren view.

But here we are in 1950. The institutions of interest and insurance are twin pillars of our contemporary economic society. They verily sustain the keystone of capitalistic society —the productivity of capital. What is the meaning of the long and seemingly losing struggle against interest and life insurance? Does it mean that Brethren are nonconformists in our economic order?

In many quarters of the Protestant world there is eagerness to throw the Church behind the capitalistic order and to say, "This way the Kingdom lies." But the Brethren have been reluctant. The Brethren recognize that they are in the world but not of it. They are champions of no economico-politico-social order. The Kingdom will come—from God. They assert nothing more.

## Chapter 19

## ANNUAL MEETING AND CHURCH POLITY
## TO 1848

We interrupt the story of the Church's struggle with and in the milieu of its environing society to discuss the governmental development and church polity of the Brethren.

Today we have conventionalized denominationalism covering Christendom. It requires for us the most heroic effort of imagination to picture the religious conditions of the world in 1708. After the peace of Westphalia (1648) it became apparent that the medieval unity of Church and State was not going to return. In 1708 those who could not accept either Rome or the State Church could only say, "As for us and our families, we will serve the truth." They could not have envisioned our denominational order.

The Brethren started out to live according to the New Testament. But they had no well-worked-out views of what this would mean with respect to Church government. In fact, they were so little conscious of being a Church in the institutional sense that Alexander Mack in his original German writings preferred the word *Gemeinde* to *Kirche*. The emphasis was upon fellowship, the family of faith, upon the observance of brotherhood. Such officials as they had, they adopted imitatively from the New Testament. Their likeness to the Anabaptists (i.e., the Mennonites) in government leaves unresolved only the question as to whether they learned from them consciously or unconsciously. Yet, with all the simplicity, there was a stringency about the discipline that is startling.

They practiced "avoidance," that dread excommunication which barred from ordinary social intercourse as well as from the Lord's table.

Dunker polity may be said to have begun with the Annual Meeting, which was called in German the Great Meeting or Assembly or the Great Council, and in English, for a long time, the Yearly Meeting. We trace this meeting back to 1742.

There has been a wrong impression about the origin of Annual Meeting. The occasion that first called for a Great Meeting seems to have been the synods of Count Zinzendorf, but M. G. Brumbaugh wrongly leaves the impression that our Yearly Meeting was derived from those synods. The Yearly Meeting of the Brethren was the great "town meeting" of the fraternity. It was face-to-face democracy. It was the primary group association, and its pattern is to be found in the Quaker Yearly Meeting, not in the synods of Zinzendorf.

Let us take a look at the synods of Zinzendorf, which occasioned our first Great Assembly.

Zinzendorf arrived at Bethlehem, Pennsylvania, on December 24, 1741. He came to this country with the ideal of a united Church of all Germans in the New World. He intended that his united German Church should evangelize the Indians.

Three joint "synods" were held to launch his project. These he characterized as a spontaneous uprising of the Germans.[1] A number of Brethren attended the third synod at Oley. A missionary to the Indians was ordained there, and three converts were baptized by sprinkling. Three groups immediately withdrew, and a fourth, the Tunkers, withdrew ultimately and set up their own Annual Meeting.

George Adam Martin was sent by Martin Urner, elder of Coventry, to attend these interdenominational conferences. He arrived at the third synod in February 1742. Of it he later said: "The Count himself was present, and for three days I heard queer and wonderful things there. After my

[1] M. G. Brumbaugh, *A History of the Brethren*. Page 175 f.

return home I went to my superintendent and said that I looked upon the Count's conferences as snares, for the purpose of bringing simple-minded and inexperienced converts back to infant-baptism and church-going and of erecting the old Babel again. We consulted with each other what to do and agreed to get ahead of the danger, as Baptists had already been smitten with this vain doctrine, and to hold a yearly conference, or as we called it, a Great Assembly, and fixed at once the time and place. This is the beginning and foundation of the Great Assemblies of the Baptists."[2]

One of the things that appears in this account is an ingrained fear of a State Church on the part of these early Brethren. Some of their grandchildren who never have seen a State Church might well ponder this story.

The Dunkers met the situation by a direct appeal to the conscience and reason of the rank and file of the Church. The appeal was on the basis of their own tradition, their experience, and their understanding of the Scriptures. Their procedure, as indicated above, was the calling of a meeting. Their pattern for this came from the Quakers. Even a cursory view of the Quaker meetings reveals the relationship.

Henry Kurtz[3] quotes at length Quaker writers on their procedure. Significant points that he lifts up are: the Quaker Yearly Meeting originated in London in 1666; it is held in Whitsun-week each year; deputies are chosen in each Monthly Meeting to represent it in the Quarterly Meetings, and in Quarterly Meetings to represent in Yearly Meetings; these deputies bear partial answers to queries relating to the governing of the Society; these answers are put together and decisions are made by weight of religious character; no voting is done; there is no ostensible president or head; there are no opposing leaders; there is no ostensible majority or minority; there are no divisions; settlement is made in brotherly love.

---

[2] See Appendix I.
[3] Article, "Yearly Meeting," *Brethren's Encyclopedia, First Part.* Page 197 f.

Elder Kurtz regards these Quaker Yearly Meetings as exemplars for the Brethren. In their light and in the light of Acts 15 he suggests seven principles for our meetings: (1) simplicity, (2) liberty, (3) order, (4) subordination of our reason to the Word of God, (5) due regard to the conclusions of former Yearly Meetings, (6) a sincere love of the Brethren, and (7) a constant aim for union in the Body of Christ.

Our knowledge of early Annual Meetings is very limited. We have no minutes prior to 1778. It is not certain that there was a clerk or a written record earlier. There must have been some moderatorship. In the "Great Assembly" of 1742, Martin Urner surely was the leader. The moderatorship of the Brethren Yearly Meeting seems to have evolved from the eldership of the church entertaining the meeting. This was a divergence from the Quaker pattern. In the common parliamentary procedure of the seventeenth century the clerk performed many of the duties that a moderator now performs.

Among the Brethren, the New Testament office of elder or bishop was pre-eminent. It fitted the needs of the situation. The bishop was a father to the brotherhood around him.

As the moderatorship arose out of the eldership of the church entertaining the meeting, so the Standing Committee evolved from the elders present, who planned and directed the meeting. Here also was divergence from the Quaker pattern, which set up two standing committees. The Quaker meeting of elders, however, may well have been the pattern for the Brethren elders' meeting.

Pentecost was the time of the Yearly Meetings. Some have mistaken a minute from 1832 to indicate otherwise. The statement reads: "Art. 8. Change of the time of Yearly Meeting. Meeting to convene on Pentecost with a public meeting and love-feast. Monday and Tuesday, council meeting."

A sketchy note like this from the time when records were

just beginning to be kept must not be allowed to discredit later and more adequate statements.

The minutes are explicit in 1841, when Henry Kurtz took the clerkship:

Art. 3. How is it considered, to make a better arrangement in holding annual meetings according to the pattern of the apostles? (Acts 15.)

The unanimous counsel of this meeting and desire of the old brethren is, to follow the track of the apostles as closely as possible. Therefore the council-meeting ought to consist of the elders and all the members of that church which receives the meeting, and of such teachers, ministers, or (private) members, who may be sent as delegates from the other churches. It is considered necessary that every church, or, where the distance is too great, several churches together, should send two, three, or more delegates to the annual meeting. The yearly meeting is to take place as heretofore on Pentecost or Whitsuntide, and the council-meeting to be held on Friday and Saturday before, to which end the delegates ought to arrive in the neighborhood on Thursday evening. The public meeting begins on Sunday, when a love-feast will be held, and the church is at liberty to invite thereto also neighboring churches as usual. The proceedings of the council-meeting should be immediately recorded in writing, and as much as possible communicated to all the churches.

Why was Pentecost the date for Yearly Meeting? In his encyclopedia of 1866 Kurtz quoted Quaker sources which said that Yearly Meeting met then because traveling was easier at that season. But the Church historian has not far to conjecture another reason. Though the "plain people" rebelled against liturgy it was still a part of them. In the liturgical Church year, Pentecost has a place with Easter and Christmas. Pentecost was a natural time for such a meaningful Brotherhood gathering. Not until 1902 was exception allowed to the Pentecost date, and not until 1917 was there a permanent departure.

It was about 1830 that Henry Kurtz made contact with the Yearly Meeting, of which he wrote some twenty years later.[4]

---

[4] *Gospel Visitor*, Volume 3, Number 1 (1853). Page 11.

His description gives us vivid impressions of the meetings.

When, many years ago, it was our privilege to attend yearly meeting for the first time, we saw, as it were, at a glance, that this was quite a different affair from those things, which are likewise held now-a-days yearly, under different names, such as conferences, associations, conventions, synods or general assemblies. . . . This (our yearly) meeting was altogether a new thing to us, if we except our common council meetings, with which we had some acquaintance previously.

These, our common council meetings I had learned to consider as practical schools of Christian wisdom and Christian morality, where the general principles of the gospel were applied to individual cases; where every Christian virtue, such as love, humility, patience, forbearance, etc., was called into exercise and where every moral evil was to be set in its true light, in order to remove it. And such a school, I now found was also the yearly meeting, only on a much larger and higher scale.

Such were our thoughts some twenty years ago at the first yearly meeting we ever attended, and being willing and desirous to learn, we formed then a resolution, that as long as the Lord should spare our life and strength, we would endeavor to avail ourselves of those blessed opportunities for our own improvement.

He proceeds to express regret at his slowness to learn and his hesitancy about going to Yearly Meetings for fear that love would not prevail and that he somehow might be to blame. But he is glad he kept going and love was manifested.

He who understands the real intent and working of the Yearly Meeting understands the Church. Henry Kurtz gained such an understanding, and, as long-time clerk of the meeting and as editor, he shared liberally his insights.

The character of Standing Committee is well indicated in the minutes of 1846:

On the 29th day of May, A. D. 1846, the brethren convened in Annual Meeting at the house of Bro. John Royer, on Trout Creek, in Lancaster County, Pennsylvania, and the meeting being opened with singing, exhortation, and prayer, it was concluded that all the ordained elders present should retire, as a committee to receive all those matters which were to be laid before the Yearly Meeting.

One of our clearest views of early Annual Meeting comes out of the minutes of that same year, 1846:

Art. 1. As regards the way and manner of holding Annual Meetings, so as to enjoy more order, convenience, and satisfaction.

Considered, in the fear of the Lord, that the counsel of the Yearly Meeting in the year 1837, in this respect, was proper and expedient, if observed, and that the best plan will not mend the matter if it is not carried out. Different plans were proposed, and after a long discussion and mature reflection, it was resolved to make no material change but this: That our western brethren shall have the privilege of taking the Yearly Meeting every other year, if they request it, and that our eastern brethren should not fail to attend the same; that it should be explicitly understood and given out, that Friday and Saturday there will only be private council-meeting—all the ordained elders to form the committee to take in and bring before the meeting those matters to be considered. The public meeting should be on Sunday and, if possible, not in the same place where the council-meeting is held.

But there was pressure for a delegated meeting; and so in 1847 Conference procedure was up again. The atmosphere was charged with emotion, as the account of the writing clerk, Henry Kurtz, well indicates:

It was on the 21st day of May, A. D. 1847, that the brethren from the East, West, North, and South assembled in Annual Meeting at the house of Bro. Isaac Deardorff, in Franklin County, Pennsylvania, and on the day following entered upon the business of the church, which seemed to be somewhat involved in clouds, and these appeared to lower themselves and become darker. This produced an anxious concern for the future peace and welfare of the church, and at length the Lord in mercy was pleased once more to smile upon his troubled children, and to grant them a joyful expectation of his helping his servants in the arduous task before them. Thus, then, the points and queries were considered and discussed, with rather unusual unanimity, in the fear of the Lord, as follows:

Article 1. Whether we could not amend our plan in holding our Yearly Meetings, that the business might be conducted more quietly and orderly?

Concluded, in regard to our Yearly Meetings, that the brethren meet on Saturday, before Pentecost, and have public meeting till Sunday evening. Love-feast to be held either on Saturday or Sunday evening, at the option of the church where the Yearly Meeting is held. On Monday the council-meeting to begin, and continue until all the business is transacted or disposed of. The council to consist of delegates, not more than two, to be sent from each church, with a written certificate, containing, also, the queries to be presented (by the church whom they represent) to the Yearly Meeting. The delegates to constitute a committee of the whole, to receive and examine all matters communicated to the Yearly Meeting, and to arrange all the queries and questions for public discussion; and after they are publicly discussed, and the general sentiments heard, then the delegates are to decide; and if two-thirds or more of the delegates agree, let the decision thus made be final; but if the nature of the case be such that two-thirds do not give their consent, let it be delayed, until it receives the voice of at least two-thirds of the legal representatives. The Yearly Meetings to be attended by as many teachers and members as may think proper to do so, and the privilege in discussion to be free and open to all who may desire to participate in the same, as heretofore.

It is with some anticipation that we reach the minutes of 1846.

On Monday morning, June 12th, after Saturday and Sunday having been occupied with public worship, the council-meeting was begun at 8 o'clock A. M., solemnly, fasting and prayer having been recommended to all the members present, at early morning worship, and after singing, exhortation and prayer, and also reading the fifteenth chapter of the Acts, business was entered upon by Brethren George Hoke, Jos. Gerber, John Hart, Peter Nead, John Kline, Philip Boyle, and Henry Kurtz, being appointed as a committee to receive the messages from the churches.

Whole number of delegates was 95, and among them were—ordained elders, 24; elders, 31; teachers, 14; deacons, 15; and private members, 11. Churches represented 59; and though as fully represented as ever before, it is believed that only about one-third of the churches had sent messengers. The number of papers handed in, amounted to 63. Considering that the reading of all the papers, by one committee, would take up too much time, it was concluded to distribute them among ten committees, which were to examine them, and report thereon to the meeting. These committees were selected from the delegates. . . .

Art. 29. The committee to whom the letters concerning our Yearly Meetings had been referred, reported as follows: No less than twelve letters, from all parts of the church, had been presented in regard to this important matter, and after reading and weighing them all, and taking also in view the general state of feeling and experience of the present meeting, we propose the following in the fear of the Lord:

Considered, that this Yearly Meeting is as anxious and unanimous in the desire of following in the track of the apostles (Acts 15) as our beloved brethren were eleven years ago, at the Yearly Meeting in 1837. We find, however, by experience, that the change of the time of holding the council after public meeting doth work well—removing from us the great crowd of strangers. We are also satisfied that the sending of delegates or messengers from all the churches is necessary and proper, as also that all the elders, who come to us, ought to be members of the meeting, whether sent or not. A general committee of five or seven elders is to be appointed, as heretofore, and as many special committees as may be deemed proper or necessary in order to dispatch business. But as to voting, we hold that it will be best to aim always at unanimity, and dispose of business as hitherto. Should the meeting not be able to agree on any one point, let it be postponed to a future meeting. In addition it was proposed that all the churches should be admonished to use every diligence in sending, every year, two delegates, or at all events one to the Yearly Meeting. The above was unanimously adopted, without a dissenting voice.

This became the procedure until 1866. We are at the mid-point of the nineteenth century.

## Chapter 20

# ANNUAL MEETING AND CHURCH POLITY
# AFTER 1848

It is ninety-nine years from the adoption of the plan of 1848 to the report of the Committee of Fifteen to the Orlando Conference of 1947. The present system of working through the General Brotherhood Board and the regional setup has come by gradual evolution.

The first change after 1848 came in 1856 with the "proposal for forming districts of five, six, or more adjoining churches for the purpose of meeting jointly at least once a year, settling difficulties, etc., and thus lessening the business of our general Yearly Meeting."

This was the beginning of districts and may well have been the decisive point in the development of Brethren government in the nineteenth century. If the districts had been made strong with responsibility we could have taken the direction of the Quakers, who now have fifty Yearly Meetings that are practically autonomous and have little connection; their setup requires the direct face-to-face type of fellowship that is possible only in relatively small groups. But the delegation of authority to our districts was weak and they were slow in becoming administrative agencies of consequence.

In 1866 a plan for holding Annual Meeting was adopted. The meeting assembled on Monday morning after Whitsunday with two hundred delegates representing one hundred sixty-five churches. They were divided into fifteen subcommittees to prepare the business for the General Conference. The general session began on Tuesday morning, taking up deferred business and then the report of the committee that had been appointed to devise a plan for holding Annual Meetings.

The introductory section of the report dealt with the authority in Acts 15 for holding such meetings. It was pointed out that the questions submitted were to be those that could not be settled locally, that the bishops and also certain others should assemble to settle the questions upon which the brethren differ, that the local church is responsible for bringing them on their way, and that the council meeting should be for conference only.

It was recommended

that the Annual Council be formed by delegates sent by the district meetings, and by all the ordained elders present; that the meeting be held at the place designated by the council the preceding year, to commence on the first Tuesday after Whit Sunday, the previous Lord's-day (Whit Sunday) to be spent as it has hitherto been by the brethren in worship; . . . that the meeting still be held alternately, in the east and in the west.

The next section of the report deals with district meetings. These meetings were to be formed by one or two representatives from each organized church. The meetings were to be kept simple, on the order of common council meetings. A record of their proceedings was to be kept but not published. They were to endeavor to settle all questions of a local character, but to refer to Annual Meeting any that could not be thus settled, together with all matters of general concern. Queries sent to Annual Meeting were to have suggested answers attached; otherwise they were to come first to Standing Committee. Scripture authority was to be attached to all answers, whether by district meeting or Annual Meeting.

Business for district meeting was to be passed by the local church in which it originated. Any member falling under the counsel of the church could appeal to Annual Meeting through Standing Committee by presenting a petition signed by a number of members. The way was open for any member to present himself before Standing Committee. The church entertaining the district meeting was not to provide a boarding tent for a mixed multitude but entertain the brethren and the sisters privately. All churches were to have the privilege to call on General Council Meetings for committees to investigate grievances.

Another section of the report dealt with the organization of Annual Meeting. The bishop and the elders of the church entertaining the Annual Meeting were to select the Standing Committee from among the bishops present. Virginia, Maryland, Pennsylvania, Ohio, Indiana, and Illinois were each entitled to three, if that many were present. The remaining states were entitled to two or three in case a state had ten bishops. The Standing Committee was to choose its own moderator, two clerks, and a doorkeeper. The duties of each of these offices were prescribed, as was the manner of procedure of Standing Committee. The Standing Committee as a whole was to channel all queries, subcommittees being dispensed with.

Proceedings of Annual Meetings were to be published and were to be carried to all the churches for reading and observance. If any overseers of churches failed to see this through, Standing Committee was to appoint a committee to set things in order.

The committee's report was adopted "for at least a sufficient length of time to give it a fair trial."

In 1868 an advance step had been taken in representative government by providing that Standing Committee members be elected in the district meetings to represent their respective districts. Standing Committee was also allowed to elect its officers, other than moderator, from the members attending the meeting, not necessarily from its own number.

Upon being given the responsibility of electing Standing Committee members, the districts became more stable. Their dignity as governmental units was enhanced.

In 1877 a significant provision was made about passage
of queries at Annual Meeting. It was freely charged that the
crowds that thronged the meeting, including many non-
members, unduly influenced the deliberations and affected the
vote. So the provision was added that if a decision cannot be
obtained by general consent, "it shall be decided by vote of the
Standing Committee and delegates present."

In 1882 it was decided that no elder should serve on
Standing Committee more than two years in four; also that
each congregation having a membership of two hundred or
fewer might send one delegate. Congregations of over two
hundred members might send two. "The delegates thus sent
with the Standing Committee shall compose the voting power
of Annual Meeting." All members were given the right to
participate in discussion. A two-thirds majority vote of delegates and Standing Committee was required for passage. Thus
was established a definite representative government. The
"town meeting" type of democracy was at an end.

This decision coincided with the schism in the Church.
Before taking up the developments from that point, it is fitting
that we turn aside to see the directions taken by the "Old
Orders" and the "Progressives" in regard to Annual Meeting.

The Old Order Brethren in 1882 returned to the pure
Yearly Meeting type of familistic fraternalism expressed in
1848. The congregation then is simply those individual parts of
the brotherhood who live in a district or area and meet for
worship as they conveniently can. They are under the care of
an elder, who is at one with all other elders of the Yearly
Meeting. Christian conduct is guided by the advice and
decrees of Yearly Meeting. The Yearly Meeting interprets
what the imitation of Christ is for the Brethren in our time.

The constituting of the Progressive Brethren was a direct
repudiation of this view. They declared repeatedly that all
authority resides in the congregation. The congregationalism
was so strong that at first Annual Conference was repudiated

and omitted. After a preliminary self-appointed committee had convened and issued a call for a meeting, a "convention" met at Ashland, Ohio, June 29 and 30, 1882. The next year, on June 6, a meeting convened in Dayton, Ohio. This was properly the first General Conference. The next Conference met at Ashland, Ohio, September 21-23, 1887. Attendance was voluntary response to a published invitation. The Pentecost tradition was ignored in this and future meetings. There was an uneasy feeling over the avowed congregationalism, and this Conference of 1887 "defined that the apostolic idea of congregational church government relates alone to the incidental affairs of the congregation, and not to doctrinal practices, which must be universal."[1]

At the third Progressive Conference, that of 1892, a short Brethren creed was propounded and congregational government was declared but also "that . . . faith, character, and practice of each and all are under the same divine law of government, under Christ and the Holy Spirit, to each other, as the Word of God teaches."[2] The name *Brethren General Conference* was adopted. The fourth week of August was set as the time for regular meetings. But the Brethren General Conference never attained the proportions of the great family reunion which the old Yearly Meeting held. It became an inspirational gathering in which delegates of theoretically independent congregations listened to reports and plans and made appointments to voluntary agencies, which offered themselves as the channels of service of these independent congregations.

Soon the Progressive Brethren (Brethren Church) had learned how to exercise control over autonomous units. A Pastors' Association was formed, and by scrutinizing its members and requiring subscription to its statements, it controlled the ministry and hence the Church.

---

[1] Holsinger, *History of the Tunkers and the Brethren Church.* Page 545.
[2] *Op. cit.* Page 546.

We return to the Conservative body of the Church. After 1882 Annual Meeting adopted the device of appointing responsible boards or permanent committees to carry out the will of Conference. This had been forecast in 1880 with the Domestic and Foreign Missions Board. The Danish mission was put under the care of this board. This mission was the result of the interest and devotion of a remarkable immigrant brother, Christian Hope. Tracts and letters to his old friends and countrymen had led to inquiries, and the District of Northern Illinois had held a special district meeting in 1875 and sent a delegation of two elders and Brother Hope as interpreter. Northern Illinois carried this on until the formation of the Domestic and Foreign Missions Board in 1880.

After the strain of 1882 was over, a more careful plan was adopted, and the board was replaced by the General Church Erection and Missionary Committee. The plan contemplated the formation of missionary committees in the districts. It proposed that each district organization be a miniature of the general organization. Theoretically the general committee approached the congregation through the district committee. The district mission board had to sanction all requests for aid. This board was the most important district agency until the 1930's. Its status was due to the evangelistic zeal of the people as well as to its priority in time. The plan of 1884 provided for congregational solicitors and offerings to support the evangelizing work.

Another development took place about this time. Brethren long have had enthusiasm for writing and circulating tracts. The Brethren's Book and Tract Committee was established by Conference in 1885 and continued until 1895, when the two committees were combined into the General Mission Board and Tract Committee of the German Baptist Brethren Church. In 1908, when the denominational name was changed, the Mission Board became the General Mission Board of the Church of the Brethren.

While these events were transpiring another development occurred, little appreciated but profound in its implications. The Conference became a legal corporation. From 1884 the possibility of the Church's holding property was discussed. In 1887 the project of collecting endowment by the Book and Tract Committee precipitated the matter. Galen B. Royer has preserved the story in detail.[3] A leaflet, put out in 1886, presented the desirability of a permanent fund for the tract work. The fund was to be held as an endowment, the interest on which was to be used for the book and tract work. It was proposed that twenty dollars constitute one life membership, entitling the giver to one dollar's worth of books and tracts annually.

The Mission Board followed suit, and began to gather endowment. When the actual incorporation resolution passed Annual Meeting in 1889[4] there had already been collected over $30,000.00 endowment by the two subsidiary corporations of the Conference.

What a revolution! On the Conference floor there was no question as to the wisdom of incorporating with a view to holding investment property and collecting interest. The Church was a corporate partner in finance capitalism! Yet the minutes still abounded in advice on such subjects as interest and insurance. Since then the Church has gathered endowment extensively. In 1950 the various corporations of the Church had permanent funds of approximately $5,000,000.00. However, there always have been some Brethren who have doubted the wisdom of endowments. It was the incorporation of the Church under Roman law by Constantine in 321 A.D. that started it on its ignoble career of land ownership and political sovereignty.

The corporate pattern, fully established, now found

---

[3] *Thirty-Three Years of Missions in the Church of the Brethren.* Pages 131 and 132.

[4] The Church was incorporated as the German Baptist or Brethren Church under the laws of Wisconsin. Later the title had to be changed to German Baptist Brethren.

many new expressions. In 1893 the Annual Meeting expressed the view that it would be a good thing for the Church to own its own publishing interests. It was thought that a Church-owned press would contribute to unity. Through the efforts of Elder Daniel Vaniman and others and the generosity of the stockholders, a $50,000.00 corporate enterprise was deeded to the Church on March 31, 1897. The Mission Board was made the board of trustees of the Brethren Publishing House.[5]

The business had been located at Mt. Morris, Illinois, but was moved to Elgin, Illinois, in quest of better mail and freight connections. A new brick building was erected in 1899. Writing in 1919, Otho Winger said:

The growth of the business at Elgin has been rapid. Additional building was done at different times, until 1906 saw the present large four-story building. One hundred and fifty thousand dollars has been invested in the House, including a large amount put in up-to-date machinery.[6]

The Publishing House was a department of the Mission Board's work until 1916, when it was incorporated as a "separate corporate entity," its directors being members of the Mission Board. At the Conference in 1949 the House reported assets of a half million dollars. The sale of the book bindery at a profit of $25,209.07 was also reported. Thus was demonstrated the fact that the Church may divest itself of corporate structure as well as acquire it.

In 1896 a Sunday School Advisory Committee of three members was appointed. In 1911 this became the General Sunday School Board, which had five members and had power to employ a field secretary and carry forward a promotional program. This led logically to district Sunday-school boards and to district secretaries, some of whom were very effective workers. In the recasting of machinery in 1928 the General Sunday School Board became the Board of Religious Educa-

---

[5] In 1947 the legal name became House of the Church of the Brethren, but the old trade name continues.
[6] *History and Doctrines of the Church of the Brethren.* Page 153.

tion[7] and absorbed the General Welfare Board, which had originated in 1924,[8] and the Music Committee, which also had originated in 1924.[9]

In 1908 the General Educational Board was created to supervise the Brethren schools. From 1890 until 1908 there had been visiting committees of three elders "to watch over the moral and religious influence of the schools, and see that the principles of the Gospel and church government be carried out as defined by Annual Meeting." The change to a permanent board of seven members was made in 1908 to carry through the difficult task. In 1916 the board membership was reduced to five, two of whom were not to be connected with the schools. In 1927 it was reconstituted to consist of three chosen by Standing Committee plus the heads of all Brethren "recognized educational institutions."

The ministry being at the very heart of the life of the Church, it is strange that we did not get a General Ministerial Board until 1921. And in this case the usual process from general Brotherhood to district and local church was reversed. Recommended in 1912, the very fundamental study entitled *Election and Support of Pastors* was finally accepted by Conference in 1917. This study recommended that each district establish a board of three, two of whom must be elders. At the Annual Meeting of 1921 a plan was passed calling for the completed series of boards—local and district and the General Ministerial Board. The General Board was to have five members to supervise, guide, and develop the ministry of the Church. Through the employment of fieldworkers this became a very important part of the Church's machinery.

At the special Goshen Conference, called in January 1918,

---

[7] In 1932 the Annual Conference changed the name to Board of Christian Education.

[8] The General Welfare Board was itself the merger of three boards, the Dress Reform Committee (1914), the Temperance and Purity Committee (1907), and the Peace Committee (1911).

[9] The term *General Music Committee* had been used for several years and was then shortened without explanation.

the Committee on Relief and Reconstruction was appointed; in July 1921 it closed its work and its books. The 1932 Conference charged the Board of Christian Education with the task of dispensing funds in times of suffering, and instructed that board to work with the Mennonites and the Friends. When World War II loomed in 1939, the Board of Christian Education and the General Mission Board each appointed two members, and a fifth was chosen from neither board. This sub-board was now called the Brethren Service Committee.

At the special called meeting of the Standing Committee (the equivalent of a special session of Conference) held in Chicago, December 18 and 19, 1940, the Brethren Service Committee became a board. It was to consist of five members. Each general board was authorized to appoint one ex-officio member, and other Brethren denominations were granted associate representation if they desired it.

We have traced the main committees or boards through the period 1882-1947, which might well be called the committee period of the Brethren. We have not named all the committees. As one reads the annals of these years he is impressed with the patience and good temper of the rank and file of the Church membership. Changes in the denominational organization often required changes in district and local organization. The frequency of change inevitably brought confusion. With the adoption in 1947 of the plan proposed by the Conference-appointed Committee of Fifteen, it is to be hoped that the multiplicity of changes will end and the Church will have a chance to make its machinery function.

We pause to note several brief items before considering the General Brotherhood Board.

The districts have achieved strength and a family feeling through the years. In some districts there have developed assemblies, ministeriums, camps, district missions, old people's homes, and college ownership. The relative stability of the district has been a blessing to the Brethren.

One district institution is of uncertain record—the district elders' meeting. It grew out of a twofold source. One is the old institution of "adjoining elders." Before the pastoral era, if a church needed help it called in the adjoining elders. In important elections, discipline of officials, or irregularity of doctrine or practice, the adjoining elders either were called in or intervened. No usage could have been more characteristic of the fraternalism which the Brethren understood was the very nature of the Church. The second factor that may have entered into the institution of the district elders' meeting was the early custom of assembling the elders at Annual Conference. Prior to 1868 all elders present constituted Standing Committee.

It was a tremendous wrench of fraternal relations and a direct concession to commercialism when free entertainment of the Yearly Meeting was discontinued. The first charge for meals was at Lanark, Illinois, in 1880. It occasioned much discussion and disgust, and resulted in the following resolution:

Whereas, the present ticket arrangement does not give general satisfaction; therefore

Resolved, First, That sisters and their special female friends shall pay fifty cents for their tickets.

Resolved, Second, That in addition to regular tickets, meal tickets at fifteen cents each shall be kept for sale.

The matter of feeding the Conference attendants had been dealt with in 1879. It was complicated by the attendance of a mixed multitude as well as by the increasing cost of entertaining the increasing crowd.

The Old Order fraternity preserves the original hospitality. The country is divided by them into four areas, and the area assists the local church in the entertaining. Lodging in homes and barns is free, and a large tent is used for meals. One of the most impressive religious spectacles on the North American continent is this religious denomination gathered in conference eating together. In 1950, near Lima, Ohio, the dining tent had seven hundred eighty seats at one table sitting.

Within the present generation more changes have been made than ever before in the conduct of our Annual Meeting. In 1924 it was decreed that the moderator should be chosen a year in advance. In 1933 it was indicated that the moderator-elect should begin his term of service with presiding over Standing Committee the year following his election. He now has responsibility for the welfare of the Church and for representing the Church in certain outside contacts during the year preceding his presiding over Conference.

In 1924 the annual election of writing clerk was superseded by electing a secretary (the older term is still used) for a term of three years.

The schedule of Conference has been adjusted repeatedly until now the Standing Committee convenes on Sunday or Monday, the Conference opens on Tuesday evening, Wednesday is given to sectional meetings, the Conference business begins on Thursday morning and concludes on Saturday afternoon or evening, and the interspersed inspirational meetings come to a climax in the missionary convocation on Sunday evening.

Since 1946 the region has been a definite part of the governmental structure of the Church of the Brethren. There are five regions: Southeastern, Eastern, Central, Western, and Pacific Coast. The regional organization was a matter of growth, with Conference encouragement, from 1931.

The correlation of boards and their several programs was long a problem. In 1923 a Council of Promotion was formed of one representative from each Conference board and Standing Committee representation. In 1928 a Council of Boards, including all board members, was sanctioned. But the Committee of Fifteen recommended a single board of twenty-five members to be known as the General Brotherhood Board. This plan came to reality in 1947. The General Brotherhood Board formed five commissions, as follows: Foreign Mission Commission, Ministry and Home Mission Commission, Christian

Education Commission, Brethren Service Commission, and Finance Commission. The board employs a general secretary and each commission has its staff, employed by the board through its executive committee.

The report of the Committee of Fifteen was virtually a constitution for the Church, though it was not so named. Its chief organizational factors were the establishment of one General Brotherhood Board and the recognition of regions. In the judgment of the present writer the foreign element in the report was the ambiguity it introduced regarding the eldership. In the New Testament the elder is a bishop. All Christendom except the Calvinistic Churches recognizes this. The Brethren have not repudiated the New Testament concept of an elder; they have just put a new commercial patch on the old Biblical garment that will probably be corrected in time. The report also has the weakness that it deals lightly with the ministry, which is no negligible factor in the Church's life.

In summary, up to about 1880 in Dunker history the governmental principle was face-to-face democracy of the fraternal council. This was modified by a certain patriarchalism which we had in common with people of Bible times. About 1880 the practice of representative democracy or republicanism took the place of the earlier procedure. Delegated authority became the method of acting. Its favorite form was the corporation—the board or committee. The Church's polity since 1947 may be called conciliarism. It acts through a series of councils and assemblies—the councils exercising delegated powers and deriving from and reporting to the larger assemblies. The council is a concession to ecclesiasticism. In government the period 1880-1947 may be viewed in the future as one of awkward, adolescent growth in an awkward, fumbling society.

With confidence in the rank and file and with clear purpose among people, ministry, and council members and the councils' fieldworkers, we face the latter half of the twentieth century.

## Chapter 21

## THE GOSPEL VISITOR AND ITS EDITOR

The *Gospel Visitor* and its direct descendant, the *Gospel Messenger,* constitute a bridge across the century from 1851 to the present. "Every denomination almost publishes a paper of their own," wrote Henry Kurtz in 1851. But few indeed of the papers then published are still in existence. The officially owned publication of the Church of the Brethren is the third oldest religious periodical now being issued in the United States.

Elder Henry Kurtz was born in Germany on July 22, 1796, and given a classical education there looking toward the ministry. At twenty-one he migrated to the New World and became a teacher. On June 10, 1819, he was admitted to the Lutheran Synod and given his first charge in Northampton County, Pennsylvania. Four years later he moved to a pastorate in Pittsburgh. In 1820 he had married a worthy young woman, Anna Catherine Loehr. To them were born four sons, who became worthy men.

While he was at Pittsburgh his mind was stirred over the subject of baptism. Study and observation convinced him that faith was essential to proper baptism, and therefore he could no longer baptize infants. After some debate and hesitation the Synod deposed and excommunicated him. He moved to Ohio and within a few years was located on a farm near Poland, where he came in touch with the Brethren. He was baptized on April 6, 1828, by Elder George Hoke. Two years later he was elected to the ministry. He at once became very active. In 1842 he moved into the Mahoning congregation, and was ordained as an elder in 1844. He held the oversight of that congregation until his death in 1874.

In 1837 he was chosen writing clerk of Yearly Meeting, and with the exception of the years 1839 and 1850, he held this position for twenty years. He had superior educational qualifications for this work.

While he was a Lutheran pastor in Pittsburgh he had published a small parish paper. In 1833 and again in 1836 he launched short-lived publications. These later ventures were intended to serve the Brethren but failed for lack of patronage. No known copy of either of them exists. A great upheaval was then stirring intellectual activity everywhere in America. The Brethren themselves were changing from the use of German to English. The old records mention that the Yearly Meeting of 1850 was conducted bilingually. One of the reasons Kurtz was clerk for so long was that he was at home in both languages.

It was during this period that Peter Nead was composing and publishing his books: *Primitive Christianity* (1833), *Nead's Theology* (1850), and *Wisdom and Power of God* (1866). And so it was not strange that Kurtz, bitten by the printer's "bug," could not forget his plan for a church periodical. He continued to talk of it, and in 1850 intended to test the sentiment of Yearly Meeting on it. Illness prevented him from attending, but he felt it was the providential time to venture on his project.

At the meeting of 1850, in Kurtz's absence, a query was presented and answered as follows:

Art. 21. Whether there is any danger to be apprehended from publishing a paper among us?

This subject to lay over till next Annual Meeting.

The introduction to the first issue of the *Gospel Visitor* sets forth the purpose and plan.

Peace be unto you! Luke 24: 36. Dearest Brothers and Sisters, Friends and Fellow Travelers to Eternity!

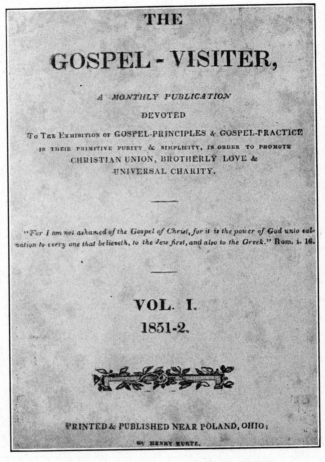

THE

GOSPEL - VISITER,

*A MONTHLY PUBLICATION*

DEVOTED

To The Exhibition of GOSPEL-PRINCIPLES & GOSPEL-PRACTICE
IN THEIR PRIMITIVE PURITY & SIMPLICITY, IN ORDER TO PROMOTE
CHRISTIAN UNION, BROTHERLY LOVE &
UNIVERSAL CHARITY.

*"For I am not ashamed of the Gospel of Christ, for it is the power of God unto salvation to every one that believeth, to the Jew first, and also to the Greek."* Rom. i. 16.

VOL. I.
1851-2.

PRINTED & PUBLISHED NEAR POLAND, OHIO,
BY HENRY KURTZ.

Cover Page, Volume I of the Gospel Visitor

Peace be unto you! Not the peace which the world may give but that peace which cometh from on high.

With this salutation we send the Visiter in the midst of you. Will you bid him welcome? . . . But you will ask, How may we know, that he is not an imposter? We answer,—By carefully examining and scrutinizing him in a spirit of candor according to the Gospel; by watching him closely, and by trying his spirit, whether he is of God, because many false prophets are gone out into the world." 1 John 4: 1.

A long time has elapsed, since we sent out the queries, proposed in July 1849. . . . But we cannot defer it any longer. We have prayerfully considered every objection; we have already felt the difficulties; we shrink from the responsibility. Yet there is one word of God staring us in the face, which will deprive us of our peace unless we obey it. It is this. James 4: 17 "Therefore to him that knoweth to do good, and doeth it not, to him it is sin." Consider with us the following facts.

Thousands of presses are daily working in this our country, and are issuing a multitude of publications, some good, some indifferent, some, alas! too many absolutely bad and hurtful. . . . Should we not use every means in our power to counteract the evil tendencies of our time, and to labor in every possible way for the good of our fellowmen, and for the glory of God and his truth as it is in Christ Jesus?

. . . . .

But we are asked: What do you want to print, and what is your object? We will try to answer in a few words. We are as a people devoted to the truth, as it is in Christ Jesus. We believe the church as a whole, possesses understandingly that truth, and every item of it. But individually we are all learners, and are progressing with more or less speed in the knowledge of the truth. For this purpose we need each other's assistance. But we live too far apart. If one in his seeking after a more perfect knowledge becomes involved in difficulty, which he is unable to overcome, this paper opens unto him a channel, of stating his difficulty, and we have not the least doubt, but among the many readers there will be some one, who has past the same difficult place, and can give such advice, as will satisfy the other.

Again—a brother is solemnly impressed with a view of the Gospel-truth or Gospel-practice, which appears to him to throw additional light on some particular point. . . . This paper will open a channel, to have wrong views corrected, and right views promulgated.

While we would thus invite and crave the cooperation of our beloved brethren in this our undertaking, we would candidly state here, that in making our selections, we shall be guided by a sincere love of truth, and publish only what may appear to us most generally useful.

Finally our humble prayer is, that the Lord in his infinite mercy may grant his blessing to us and to you all, and to this little work, so that none of us shall be ashamed in His coming, when He shall require of us an account of our stewardship.[1]

---

[1] *Gospel Visitor,* Volume I. Pages 1 and 2.

The reactions of the Brethren after they had seen the early numbers of the *Visitor* are reflected in the minutes of 1851:

Art. 8. What is the opinion of the Yearly Meeting, with regard to having a paper published under the title, "The Monthly Gospel Visitor"?

Considered, at this council, that we will not forbid Bro. Henry Kurtz to go on with the paper for one year, and that all the brethren or churches will impartially examine the "Gospel Visitor," and if found wrong, or injurious, let them send in their objection at the next Annual Meeting.

Kurtz carried through the first volume of the paper, but not without difficulty. The issues show great sincerity of spirit and contents, excellent literary style, and marked humility and good sense on the part of the editor. In appearance the paper was fully abreast of the best of its age. It looks very much like the *Niles Register,* which was the leading literary-news weekly journal of the United States of that period. This is the more remarkable when one remembers that the paper was printed on a handpress on the second floor of a small farm spring-house in a comparatively new region of Ohio. The copies were printed, addressed by hand, and hauled three miles to the post office at Poland, Ohio.

Some quotations from the closing pages of Volume I will indicate the situation in the editor's own words:

This present No. will conclude the first volume of the "Gospel-Visiter," for which purpose a title page and table of contents will accompany the same. Having added two full Numbers extra, we hope, our subscribers will see, that we have tried to do as much as we could in this point of view. Being compelled by unforeseen circumstances, such as being left alone by our young partner, before one half of the volume was out, to do most all the work, till lately, by ourselves, and within our own family, we have been enabled to get along without sustaining any pecuniary loss, chiefly owing to the slow, but constant increase of our subscription-list, for which we make here once more our grateful acknowledgements. . . .

As to the continuation of the Visiter we will decide nothing, before the pending yearly meeting is over. We have already intimated, that we are apprised of a strong opposition to be urged against the Visiter there. We are preparing to meet it. Though the publication is carried on as our own private business, on our own private responsibility, we are willing to learn, if it is contrary either to the spirit or to the letter of the Gospel, or detrimental to the well-being of society, and if we are convinced of this, or even, if self-interest should blind us, so that we could not be convinced, if the assembled brethren should unanimously consider it so, we will try to submit, whatever it may cost us, as we never intended to revolt against the counsel of the church. ...

We will then simply announce the fact, that the question about the continuation of the Visiter was brought up at the last yearly meeting, and decided as follows, (see Art. IV. of the Minutes;)

"In regard to the continuation of the Gospel-Visiter it was concluded, that in as much as there is a diversity of opinion upon the subject, some in favor, and others opposed, we cannot forbid its publication at this time, and hope, those brethren, opposed to it, will exercise forbearance, and let it stand or fall on its own merits."

And in justice to ourselves we must merely add, that though we had to perform the duties of clerk in the meeting, we scarcely occupied 5 minutes in the defence of our case, and had no hand at all in the formation of the above conclusion.

Relieved in a measure by this declaration of the Yearly Meeting, which was all we could reasonably expect under existing circumstances, and encouraged by renewed subscriptions of those, who had been readers of the first volume, and by a goodly number of new subscribers, we now venture to say, that with the permission and help of God, on whom we only rely, we will try to commence the second volume with the June-No. as soon as possible. The title, aim and object shall be the same, as heretofore, and it shall be our constant endeavour not to lose sight of it, either in our own compositions, or in making selections from the communications sent in. We beg our correspondents to bear this also in mind, and to help us in our endeavours or excuse us from inserting their articles. We will also studiously try to avoid all personal or sectional references, which may be calculated to give offence, contrary to our intentions. And in order to put at rest every brother, that is afraid of a division, that might be caused by the Visiter, we would humbly yet solemnly assure him, that so far from harboring any thought like that of causing a division in the body of Christ, we would rather pull out our right eye or cut off our right hand, than that through our instrumentality such a calamity should come over our brotherhood.

As to the TERMS of the Visiter we do not see that we can alter them yet, but we shall do as in the first volume, that is, give as many extra No's as we can possibly afford.

But to our dear *ministering* brethren, who are sacrificing often their time and their energies to the cause of Christ, while others can be at home, taking care of their own concerns and families, we feel to offer more liberal terms. If they will send us their address, we shall send one copy for examination, and continue to send altogether on their own terms. If they feel willing and able to pay, well and good; if they would like to read it, and do not feel able to pay for it, it shall be sent gratis; and *any poor* brother, that sends us 5 subscribers and pay, shall have a free copy.[2]

Subscriptions did not increase as the editor hoped. Some members still opposed this new thing. Some still feared it would bring division in the Church. Some felt they could not afford the paper. Some thought the price was too high. Some feared the starting of rival papers, resulting in controversy. Some objected that Kurtz was making merchandise of the gospel. The editor had answers for all, and was encouraged by the interest and enthusiasm of some, the assurance that some were getting the gospel and the teaching of the Brethren who would not otherwise have had these privileges, and the belief that great good could come through the project. So he labored on with meager finances, under pressure of farm duties, with handicaps of uncertain help and occasional illness. Sometimes the issues were late, but he always gave good measure and more. The regular issues were in English, but he added German editions as he could.

In January 1852 he proposed:

1. If within two months one hundred new subscribers are sent, we shall send two more No's extra for this first volume to all subscribers. [They at that time numbered four hundred twenty-eight.]

2. If within three months two hundred new subscribers come in, we will add four No's to the Volume.

3. If five hundred new subscribers are furnished within five months, we will enlarge each number to 24 pages, and continue the first volume till next December, furnishing new subscribers with back copies from the beginning, until exhausted, so that the first volume shall at least contain 320 pages, all at the price of One Dollar paid in advance.[3]

---

[2] Volume I. Pages 250-252.
[3] Volume I. Pages 166-168.

Toward the end of the second volume, he said:

We feel encouraged and willing by the permission of the Lord and with His assistance to continue our labors for another year, and to commence our third volume, as soon as the present one is completed. By that time we will have given seven numbers in German extra, as a proof of our desire, to do rather a little more than our conditions would require.

Wishing to improve the outward appearance of the Visitor, we contemplate to procure new type for the third volume, if the support will warrant the expense, and with regard to its contents, we will only say, that we hope with the assistance of our correspondents, old and new, to make our columns more and more interesting and useful.[4]

There was a major crisis in the *Visitor's* life in the spring of 1854. The editor writes:

By the grace and tender mercy of our God and heavenly Father we have been enabled thus to come to the conclusion of the third volume of this humble publication. For three years we have been constantly engaged in the difficult, laborious and responsible task of editing a paper devoted to the exhibition and defence of Gospel Principles and Gospel-Practice in their primitive purity and simplicity, in order to promote Christian Union, Brotherly Love and Universal Charity.

True, this cause was worthy of a better and more able advocate, than we in our individual capacity could presume to be.

He goes on to speak of his personal handicap in being a German by birth and education without English schooling, his dependence on a younger helper with English training, and his gratitude for the Lord's help even in spite of human failures. He expresses his desire for a rest for his health's sake, possibly a trip to Europe, and his expectation of postponing the fourth volume.[5]

However, the following month (June 1854) brings another issue with its preface to Volume IV. The troubled times in Europe made it inadvisable for him to take the much-desired trip to visit his aged mother and beloved sister. Many had expressed their desire to have the publication continued and

---

[4] Volume II. Page 268.

[5] See the May number, 1854, pages 282-284.

he had no one else in whose hands to place it; so he determined to carry on.[6]

In 1856 Kurtz found an assistant editor in the person of a young elder, James Quinter. In the autumn of that same year a young novice, Henry R. Holsinger, came to live in the Kurtz household for a few months and work on the *Visitor*. 1856 was Kurtz's last year as writing clerk of Yearly Meeting, except that he served in 1863. The publication office of the *Visitor* was moved to Columbiana, Ohio, in May 1857. James Quinter was the sole editor from 1864. Kurtz devoted his leisure to the *Brethren Encyclopedia,* which appeared in 1867. In 1873 he sold his interest in the *Visitor* to Quinter.

H. R. Holsinger felt that there should be a weekly religious paper among the Brethren, but the proprietors of the *Visitor* did not see fit to make the change. He taught school for several years after working in the *Visitor* office and edited a secular newspaper. Then in 1864 he started a new paper, the *Christian Family Companion*. It was a weekly paper with a broad policy, and much trouble arose over the freedom with which individual members were allowed to express themselves in its columns. It solicited church news and thus became popular with many. It continued until June 1, 1874, when it was consolidated with the *Gospel Visitor,* becoming the *Christian Family Companion and Gospel Visitor*.

The editors of the consolidated paper were James Quinter and J. W. Beer. The title page claimed permission of the "Church of the Brethren." It was issued from Dale City (later Meyersdale), Pennsylvania. On January 1, 1876, the name was shortened to *Primitive Christian*.

Another weekly paper, the *Pilgrim,* was edited by H. B. and J. B. Brumbaugh and published at James Creek, Pennsylvania, from 1870. With a milder policy than that of the *Christian Family Companion* it gained a good circulation, but since its purpose was not greatly different from that of the *Primitive*

---

[6] June number, 1854. Pages 1 and 4.

*Christian* the two papers were united on October 24, 1876. Quinter and the Brumbaugh brothers published the combined paper at Huntingdon, Pennsylvania.

In January 1876, at Germantown, Pennsylvania, J. T. Myers and L. A. Plate started the *Brethren's Messenger*. In August of that year it was moved to Lanark, Illinois, and its name was changed to *Brethren at Work*. J. H. Moore, J. T. Myers, and M. M. Eshelman were the editors. It held the same conservative course in the West that the *Primitive Christian* held in the East. The two papers were combined in June 1883 under the now-familiar name, *Gospel Messenger*.

The *Gospel Messenger* has been making its weekly visits since June 1883. For years the paper was published in Mt. Morris, Ill., and Huntingdon, Pa. At first, Elder James Quinter was editor-in-chief, H. B. Brumbaugh, Eastern editor, J. H. Moore, office editor, and Joseph Amick, business manager. D. L. Miller soon took up the work as office editor and he continued in this position until he succeeded as editor Elder James Quinter, who died in 1888. Elder Miller continues as editor-in-chief to the present [1919]. In 1891 Elder J. H. Moore became office editor and continued as such until October 1, 1915, when he was succeeded by Elder Edward Frantz.[7]

Elder Frantz remained as editor until January 1944, ably assisted by H. A. Brandt. Desmond Bittinger followed Elder Frantz, and was succeeded in July 1950 by Kenneth I. Morse.

Henry Kurtz started all this. The era of inventions had arrived. The real significance of Henry Kurtz is in connection therewith. He was an earnest champion of the Brethren faith and practice. We read his doctrinal expositions and defenses today with profit. Certainly a main purpose of launching the *Gospel Visitor* was to maintain and further develop the unity of the Brotherhood. He feared the effect of geographical dispersion. He fearlessly plunged into the use of the new industrial-social techniques of the age of invention to maintain the unity and the message of the church.

---

[7] Otho Winger, *History and Doctrines of the Church of the Brethren.* Page 150. Many of the preceding facts have been drawn from Winger's book.

Cover Pages of Ten Brethren Periodicals

It is not alone that he demonstrated that a church paper could be successfully maintained among the Dunkers; it is that he used the columns of that paper to advocate some new and far-reaching policies. We shall see some of these in succeeding chapters. A thorough conservative, the little elder was a fearless spirit. He would certainly not approve today those who rest in comfortable adjustment and stop on past achievements. Kurtz wished to use the devices of society about him and not be used by them.

As the surge of new conditions threatened to disrupt the unity of the Brotherhood he published his *Brethren Encyclopedia*. It appeared in the troubled days of the period following the Civil War. It is the most scholarly and ambitious work that he undertook, and he must have died believing that it was his greatest work. Behind and throughout the *Encyclopedia* is the proposition that the devices of the new age must be utilized in the service of the old faith.

Kurtz died in 1874. Although spared the pain of 1881-1883, he was the true ancestor of the conservative or center party.

# Chapter 22

# THE STRUGGLE FOR BRETHREN SCHOOLS

One of the ideas that Elder Kurtz advocated in the columns of his paper was the establishment of Church-affiliated schools. In a more active program of education, definitely under the auspices of Brethren, Elder Kurtz saw the future of the Church. Yet he was clearly aware that in this he was adjusting to the contemporary society of his day.

When Henry Kurtz first conceived the idea of a Church-affiliated school is uncertain. The desire for advanced academic training was in the air in his day. The school that he and his assistant editor, James Quinter, launched at New Vienna, Ohio, on September 14, 1861, was the first school by Brethren for Brethren. It therefore has valid claim to being counted the first Brethren school, though Kishacoquilas Academy was begun and operated by Brother S. Z. Sharp six months earlier.

Kishacoquilas Academy was a purely private affair. It was a defunct academy with Presbyterian antecedents when Solomon Zook Sharp got hold of it. Sharp began to operate it on April 1, 1861. He was a member, not a minister, of the Church. Some of his pupils were from Brethren homes. He prepared his pupils for teaching. He had been baptized only six months before and it is not likely that he thought of his venture as a Brethren school until he reflected upon the matter in later years.

It was Kurtz and Quinter who brought forward the idea of a Brethren school. The New Vienna Academy was the fruit of their planning. Kishacoquilas was incidentally Brethren; New Vienna was designedly so. In spirit the two schools were so much alike that the question of priority seems rather incidental. But to Kurtz and Quinter belongs the credit for naturalizing education in the Church.

The columns of the *Gospel Visitor* carried the proposal for a school and became the medium for give and take on the matter of education in the Church. The proposition was first set forth in unique fashion. Quinter went traveling and wrote a letter to Kurtz, and Kurtz printed the letter with a parenthetical comment. The paragraphs about the proposed school must be quoted!

Upon serious reflection upon our contemplated school, some ideas have been presented to my mind, which I offer to you for your consideration. One important desideratum is, well qualified teachers—teachers possessing both literary and moral qualifications. It has occurred to my mind, that if there are brethren among us, possessing qualifications sufficient to enable them to discharge the duties of teachers in such an institution, perhaps they would not feel free to abandon other callings in which they are now engaged. I have therefore thought, it would be proper to send one or two of our young brethren to school, to qualify them for teachers. Two perhaps would be better than one. I would prefer poor young men, young men who look for success in life, to their own exertions, and the blessing of heaven. I have a person now before my mind, who might answer for one.

Two ways of meeting the tuition expenses, have occurred to my mind. The first is, to present the matter to such of the brethren as we think would be likely to favor the project, and solicit subscriptions of such, to defray the expenses of educating brethren for teachers; this I think could be done without difficulty. The other plan is this! Some of the brethren might become security for these young brethren to be educated, to the institution in which they might receive their education, for their tuition fees. This money to be payed by those brethren who become teachers, out of their salary, after they become teachers.

I merely submit these thoughts to you for consideration, thinking that something of this kind might further an object we both think important and desirable, as an auxiliary for the advancement of Gospel truth.

(The last mentioned object requires a few words of explanation from us. Years ago we could find many brethren, who had received only a common-school education, engaged in teaching school, where the Bible and the New Testament was read, and probably both English and German was taught. But now so much is required of school-teachers, that many of those old teachers cannot pass examination any more, and others have taken their places, who need the Bible no longer, and our children are deprived of a vital element of education, namely the moral and religious.

This want is supplied by some or most religious denominations by Sunday or Sabbath-schools; but even this is denied in a great measure to our children for want of teachers. Hence the idea, which struck us both, though unknown to each other at first, to establish a school to educate young brethren for school-teachers.)[1]

There had indeed been a school in the remote past taught by Sister Susan Douglass in the "parsonage" at Germantown, but it was a neighborhood school like a host of others in the colonial and early national period. Only an unwarranted glorifying of the remote past could give standing to that as a Brethren school. The letter of Quinter and Kurtz is the first known proposal for a Brethren school.

That was in March 1856. Kurtz kept the subject alive. In June he set forth his educational philosophy in a rather extended article under the heading, "German English Schools on Gospel Principles." He indicated appreciation for the public school system that made education possible for rich and poor, native and foreign alike, but expressed the view that it was not meeting the needs of those who spoke no English before going to school. Such pupils learned to spell words and imitate writing without knowing the meaning of what they were doing. German and French children ought to learn English with the help of their native languages, understandingly. Teachers are needed who know the native languages of the pupils as well as English. He goes on to say:

But we need something more than mere teachers of spelling, reading, etc. for our children; we need Christian teachers, Godfearing men, who love the Bible, and will inspire our children with love for the same; who will not exclude the Bible from the school, and thus withhold

---

[1] *Gospel Visitor*, March 1856. Pages 75 and 76.

from our children the divine lessons of religion and morality which are calculated more than anything else to enlighten their understandings, to ennoble their minds, and to prepare them for all the vicissitudes of their after-life, to make them good citizens, good neighbors, and better still, if the influence of the Bible takes once by grace full possession of their hearts, good Christians and happy heirs of immortality.

Such teachers we need for our children.[2]

The September issue in the same year carried a long communication from one called Rufus who had serious doubts about the school matter. The assistant editor replied with care. The similarity in style of article and reply indicates that Quinter may have reworked the article. The heading is "The Contemplated School." "Rufus" was a long-time reader and appreciated what the editor was doing, but he feared that the contemplated school would do more harm than good. He thought high schools to be dangerous. He argued that if God needed a Moses he could prepare him without having the Church start a school. He greatly feared an educated ministry. He felt that only God knows what the consequences might be.

The reply pointed to the general interest and awakening in liberal education. Many young people are not satisfied with a common-school education. Some parents keep their sons from going away to school, but as soon as the sons are free from parental authority they satisfy their inclination for learning and do it under adverse conditions. Some go to institutions without Christian influence and their spiritual welfare is endangered. Many go to schools of other denominations and lose their respect for ours. So, he argues, it is not only the right but the duty of the Church to encourage institutions in which our youth may acquire useful knowledge. We quote his description of the kind of school he had in mind:

We would then expect such an institution to be under the influence of spiritually minded brethren. We would want religious teachers— teachers who would have a regard to the religious as well as to the intellectual improvement of students,—consequently the students would

---

[2] *Gospel Visitor*, 1856. Page 159.

have religious counsel administered to them. We would have the Bible daily used in the institution. We would have the students to board in a religious family—and have them led daily to a throne of grace and heaven's blessings invoked upon them. In short, we would have the school to resemble a pious family, under such rules as would discountenance whatever is evil, and encourage whatever is good.

Now would it be dangerous for youth, to have them placed under such circumstances? It may be said, to bring a school under such regulations, could not easily be done. But do we think it would be impossible? If we do, then we doubt the practicability of the principles of Christianity. It is true, it requires energy and perseverance. But these are required in our family devotions, and in all our relations in life, in which we reduce Christianity to practice.

.    .    .    .    .

We should always try to distinguish between the abuse of a thing, and its proper use. How has it been with our common schools? How immoral have many teachers been! And what bad conduct have many youth learned at the common schools! But will we repudiate the common schools altogether? By no means. They have been much improved. And so have high schools and colleges since Luther's time. Brother Rufus thinks that learned men are sometimes needed, and when they are, God will raise them up. He mentions the circumstance related by old Brother Mack—it was this, the brethren needed some information, and a brother came among them, who understood Greek—this was regarded as a providential occurrence. It certainly was an interesting circumstance. But where did the brother learn his Greek? It is not likely that he was taught it miraculously. He acquired it by study. We shall not pursue the subject further at present. We have not been trying to prove the necessity or utility of education. We are happy to find that Brother Rufus does not deny this. Our object has been to show, that as our youth desire to acquire knowledge, we should afford them suitable opportunities.

J. Q.[3]

In December 1856 the *Gospel Visitor* carried an article by James Quinter under the heading, "The Sons of the Prophets." This was a discussion of education, an indirect appeal for schools, and a sincere lamentation over the current educational practice.

The next spring Kurtz and Quinter moved to Columbiana,

---

[3] *Gospel Visitor,* September 1856. Pages 246-250.

Ohio. The May issue of the 1857 *Gospel Visitor* reports the move and promises an explanation as soon as there is time to write it. The June issue fulfilled the promise. We quote the explanation in part:

. . . It was not only to increase our facilities to send out our Publication, that we desired a more favorable location, but the idea of establishing a school, a subject heretofore introduced, to meet the wants of such of the brethren who desire better opportunities than are now enjoyed among us for obtaining an intellectual and christian education for their youth, to prepare them for the useful occupations of life, has not been abandoned by us. The propriety of an institution of the kind contemplated, becomes more apparent as our observations extend, and our reflections upon the subject multiply.

Knowing that some of our beloved brethren do not favor the idea of a school, such as we wish to have established, we have refrained from urging it forward too fast, hoping that if it should meet the approbation of the Lord, the plan would in time be matured, and the various means for its execution obtained. We desire the brethren to give this subject a place in their prayers, and to favor us with any suggestions or encouragements that they may have to offer.

We think our location here would in many respects be a favorable one for a school of the kind contemplated. . . .[4]

Annual Meeting had dealt with the school proposition in 1852 and 1853 in a vein of caution and warning. In 1857 it considered it again.

Art. 19. What are the views of the present Annual Council in regard to the contemplated school, that was alluded to sometime since, in the Gospel Visitor? Ans.—It is conforming to the world. The Apostle Paul says, "Knowledge puffeth up but charity edifieth."

But the school matter was not dropped. In October 1857 an article, "The Contemplated School," appeared in the *Visitor;* it was by a Virginian who supported the idea with well-seasoned reasoning. A negative communication by one "J. S." in May 1858 under the same head drew forth from James Quinter a lengthy reply which reveals the nature of the struggle so well that we quote it in full:

[4] *Gospel Visitor*, June 1857. Pages 189 and 190.

As the above communication from br. J. S., contains the principal objections we meet with from different places against the propriety of institutions similar to the contemplated School, we shall examine some of the objections brought forward. We are by no means fond of controversy. And we are particularly sorry that we are compelled to differ with any of our dear brethren. And although we may differ in our opinions upon some matters, we hope that God will help us to observe the apostolic injunction contained in the following words: "Love as brethren, be pitiful, be courteous." We fully agree with br. J. S., that the subject under consideration is one "requiring much serious consideration." We think we have given it much serious consideration, and we candidly confess that the more we consider the subject, the more are we impressed with, not only the propriety, but with the necessity of such facilities among us as a good school affords for meeting the wants of our rising generation.

In relation to the propriety of acquiring useful knowledge, we are glad to find, so far as we have become acquainted with the views of the brethren, that there is a general agreement among us. Br. J. S. after stating the many bad effects which he is fearful "high school knowledge" will lead to says: "Yet all this ought not to discourage the pursuit of acquiring useful knowledge, which is laudable in all, if the motive be good." And concerning the facilities enjoyed for obtaining education, he further says: "Now inasmuch as almost all the states in this country have made provision for all necessary learning, (and I rejoice that such ample provision is made, and placed within the reach) I see no necessity for the church to be particularly concerned about that matter, as all the branches are taught in the schools now in operation, and about being put into operation" &c. Now as br. J. S. says that it is laudable in all to acquire useful knowledge when the motive is good, and as he rejoices that the states have established school systems, we confess it appears remarkably strange to us, that he should be so much opposed to institutions for learning such as we have in contemplations.

As it seems exceedingly difficult to prevent such a matter from being misapprehended when it is proposed, it would appear that the design of the school we would like to see established, has been very much, if not entirely, misunderstood. It seems to be thought by many that the design of the school under consideration, is to educate young men for the ministry. From the general drift of the remarks in the communication of br. J. S., we judge this is the conception he has formed of the institution. We are sorry that such an idea should be entertained by any. Such by no means is the design of the school. The design is no more to qualify young men for the ministry, than it is to qualify them for farmers, or mechanics, or school teachers, or any of the avocations of life. The design is to offer to our youth the facilities for acquiring the various branches of useful knowledge which they may wish to acquire, in order that they may be qualified for whatever calling in life their inclinations may prefer, or that Providence may lead them to, apart from those influences which have a tendency to lead them from that pure Christianity, which we as guardians and parents must be exceedingly anxious for them to embrace, if our attachment to, and preference for, the doctrines of our church be sincere.

But it is assumed by those who differ with us upon the propriety of a school among us such as we plead for, that all the facilities for acquiring all the knowledge that is desirable are afforded by the school systems established by the different States, and especially in those States in which the union or graded schools have been introduced, as in the higher grades of these schools the higher branches are taught, consequently, there is no necessity for the Brethren concerning themselves about the establishment of a seminary for the advantages of their youth. Bro. J. S., after enumerating a great many branches of knowledge taught in the schools now in operation, adds: "Now if these things, or this knowledge is all taught and placed within the reach of the Brethren's children without the ministers of the church leaving the word of God to serve tables, where exists the necessity, or propriety, of their so doing?" What does the beloved brother mean when he says all this knowledge, meaning the branches he has enumerated, such as the Hebrew, Greek, German, and French languages, is all placed within reach of the Brethren's children? Does he mean that our sons and daughters can board with their parents and be under their watchful care, and attend school where all the branches of knowledge noticed can be acquired? We presume he can not mean this, since even where the union schools are in operation, it is only those who live in close proximity to them that can enjoy their advantages. Or does he mean that there are enough institutions of learning throughout the country to which Brethren can send their sons and daughters without concerning themselves to establish one of their own? If the latter is his meaning, we admit there are many schools, and many of them good of their kind, but they are by no means all *we* could wish them to be in every respect, in relation to the pure Christian influence which they exert. We believe br. J. S. to be an affectionate father, and warmly attached to the church of his adoption, and we put the question home to him, whether he would not much prefer, if he had children to educate, and if they insisted on going from home to obtain education, and if he should concede to their wishes, to place them in a school under the control of the brethren, where they could associate with brethren, and where they could attend the holy sanctuary of God with the brethren? We cannot but think that the brother would much prefer to have his children among the Brethren.

Now, notwithstanding we are often told that we need no such school as we have under consideration, since the excellent systems of education established by law are sufficient, yet if theories and assertions are not confirmed by facts, such theories and assertions should be abandoned. And what are some of the facts relating to the case? Why, there are many brethren in *New Jersey, Pennsylvania, Ohio, Indiana, Illinois* and perhaps in other States too, who find the schools established by the laws of those States inadequate to answer the demands of their sons and daughters for obtaining education, and they are sent from home to school. There are now scores and perhaps hundreds of the children of brethren from home attending school. And according to the common course of things, this number will be annually increased. We entreat br. J. S., and the class of brethren which he represents, to consider seriously and prayerfully these facts.

Being fully aware of these facts, the question, what shall be done? with no ordinary amount of responsibility, comes home to the hearts of many. And the propriety, and indeed the necessity, of providing an asylum, where our youth shall, while they are acquiring education, be preserved from those influences which are likely to lead them into other denominations and be placed under circumstances favorable to a conversion to what we regard a pure Christianity, becomes very apparent. We do not wish to insinuate that those who have the control of the institutions of learning which abound in our age, make the proselyting of the students to their respective denominations, a prominent object. We do not think that this is generally done; but there is a very strong influence exerted, notwithstanding, by the teachers over the pupils. We recently heard with sorrow, a brother relate the consequences of sending his children to a school where the influence was not such in every respect, as he could have wished. His children wished to go to school, and there was none of our own to send them to, and he was compelled to send them, if he sent them at all, to an institution under the influence of another denomination. And much to the grief, apparently, of the parents, some of them joined the denomination having the control of the school they attended. We confess we feel a deep interest in the welfare of the rising generation. From this class the official stations in the church are . . . to be filled, and the responsible places in society supplied.

An anxious solicitude for the spiritual welfare of their children characterized the early Christians. "Their great desire and constant endeavor was to train up their children in the fear of God, to conduct their education at home, to withdraw them as much as possible from temptation, and to make them so happy in their own quiet homes that they should neither desire the noisy amusements of the world nor subject themselves to its temptations. The children found their happiness in their parents, and the parents in their children. Such families were the nurseries of pure, consistent, efficient churches; such Christians were the lights of the world, which could not be hid; the salt of the earth, which never lost its savour." *Coleman's Ancient Christianity*. Now to imitate the early Christians in withdrawing our youth as much as possible from temptation, does it not become our duty to provide them with the means of education among ourselves? Can we consistently with our principles, which we as a church hold, send our children away to schools under the influence of other denominations, and strictly carry out the apostolic injunction which requires us to "bring them up in the nurture and admonition of the Lord?" This is a grave question, and deserving of the serious consideration of the brethren. Now as the custom of sending our sons and daughters away to school is growing among us, what better can we do than to afford them the means for obtaining the education they may desire? We wish it understood, that a knowledge of this custom, has produced the strong conviction which exists in the minds of many, of the propriety of such a school among us as we are advocating. Had common schools been found sufficient to answer the wants of our brethren, the propriety of any other kind might then have been more justly denied. But since, as we have seen, common schools are not sufficient, the propriety of affording something more for our youth, should, we think, be apparent to all.

But br. J. S., is fearful that evils will grow out of a school, and especially the evil of making merchandise of the Gospel. It is very true that

"Each pleasure has its poison too,
And ev'ry sweet a snare."

And we cannot be too watchful in guarding against evil. But whatever evils the brother fears from a school of our own, we fear our young men will be exposed to greater evils in obtaining education, should we afford them no school such as they may desire. Our preachers of the present time are men of more education than our preachers were thirty years ago. In saying this, we do not say that our preachers of the present day are more efficient preachers, or better men, than those were who lived thirty years ago. Upon these points we offer no opinion. Now thirty years from this time our preachers will be better educated than those of us at the present time are. Now as the brethren will send their children away to schools, (and there is no manner of use whatever to oppose them,) under the influence of other denominations if there is none of our own to send them to, and as some of these will be likely to become members of the church, a number of those who will fill the office of preachers in our church thirty years hence, will have been educated in the schools of other denominations, and consequently will be much more likely to be "gospel sellers," (an evil the brother fears,) than if they are educated in institutions of our own. Now keeping in view the strong probability that education will be sought after and pursued, we should, by all means, both out of regard to the welfare of our children and the welfare of the church, supply our members with the means for educating their sons and daughters.—And whatever evils may attend the establishing of such a school as we wish to see among us, we give the conviction of our mind, resulting from observation and reflection, that, ultimately, greater evils will follow the want of such a school.

Br. J. S. speaks about the ministers leaving the word of God to serve tables. Taking these words in the connection in which they occur, we suppose the br. thinks it improper for ministers to leave preaching and teach school. In relation to his views upon this subject, we remark, first, that we do not by any means think that none but ministers can conduct the school. And, secondly, as the br. does not think it right to sell the gospel, ministers as well as other men, must follow some business for a livelihood, or how are they to live? Now many of our preachers follow farming to procure a maintenance for themselves and their families; and does the brother think they are leaving the word of God to serve tables? We presume he does not. Because a preacher attends to some profession or calling in life besides that of preaching the gospel, it does not follow that he must leave preaching the gospel.

The brother says that "High school knowledge will never be able to make a person wise unto salvation." Does he believe that any of the advocates of the school contend that it will, or that we want to substitute knowledge for the converting power and truth of the gospel? We think the beloved brother cannot entertain such an opinion of our views and purposes. We hold no such erroneous views. We believe that the Church of Christ alone and the mighty truth it wields, can reform the world. His remarks here, seem to be foreign to the question under consideration; viz., the propriety of a school. And so do his allusions to the circumstance of the Savior having never learned letters in the ordinary way of learning, and to that of his having chosen unlearned and ignorant men for the first preachers of the gospel. Now does the brother think that because the Savior did not go to school, we should not send our children to school? We know he does not think so from what he has said. And does he think that because the Savior chose unlearned and ignorant men to preach the gospel, that we must when we call men to the ministry choose the unlearned and ignorant? We presume he does not. Then we cannot see that the argument drawn from these circumstances, is at all relevant to the question. It is true the kingdom of Christ is represented by a *stone cut out of the mountain without hands,* to show us that it is not to be established by human power. And Christianity was established not by human, but by divine power; its great Founder as well as his apostles being miraculously qualified for their work,—they were miraculously taught the knowledge of languages &c. But are we now to be miraculously taught? We think not. But by a proper exercise of the faculties with which God had indued us, and by a proper improvement of the opportunities with which he has surrounded us, and with his blessing upon our efforts, which will be given if humbly sought, we shall be qualified for the work allotted to us.

It is true, as the brother remarks, that the apostles have not intimated any thing about establishing schools. And as nothing is said either for or against such a school as we feel is needed among us— a school to answer the wants of a considerable number of the members of our church—a school in which our youth may acquire useful knowledge and at the same time have the opportunity of enjoying the means of grace as afforded by a church of the Brethren—a school in which none of the real wants of the students shall be overlooked,—the utility and propriety of such an institution, is to be settled as some other matters having an important bearing upon the welfare of our race and the prosperity of the church, by the exercise of our reasons and the decisions of our judgments as philanthropists and christians. And that we may decide correctly upon this and upon every other subject upon which we may be called upon to decide, our prayer is that we may all have the wisdom "that is from above, which is first pure, then peaceable, gentle, and easy to be entreated, full of mercy and good fruits, without partiality, and without hypocrisy."

The beloved brother claims to be sincere in the views he entertains. We do not doubt ours. And his expressions of love to us are, we assure him, kindly reciprocated.[5]

---

[5] *Gospel Visitor,* May 1858. Pages 110-114.

Several things are apparent from this extensive statement. First, the State public schools have become increasingly prevalent and are assumed to be a blessing by all parties involved in the discussion. Second, the possibility that a school might lead to professionalism was being dimly discerned. The editor's view that the school could not lead to a professional ministry is interesting in view of the fact that the plea for half a century now has been: "We must have schools to educate our own ministers and missionaries." Third, there is a most touching and naive faith in education as an abstract something that is good in itself. This seems to have been common to all writers. Fourth, the reasons given for establishing Church-affiliated schools appear clearly. The school promoters wanted to keep the young people among wholesome associates, to make it possible for them to attend their own Church services while getting their schooling, and to keep youth from being subtly proselyted by other denominations or even by non-Christian forces.

The Brethren were caught in the wholesale stampede for education which characterized America. As one looks back across ninety years, he must be struck with the fulfillment of the anticipations of both the foes and the friends of the proposed schools. Our schools have carried forward the urbanization and industrialization of the Brethren, but they have conserved the young people of Brethren homes for the Church.

The Annual Meeting minutes of 1858 carry the following decision:

Art. 51. We desire to know whether the Lord has commanded us to have a school besides our common schools such as the one contemplated in the Gospel Visitor? If we are, ought we not to have it soon? And if it is not commanded of the Lord, ought we to have one? And is it right to contend for or against such an institution publicly through the press, since our different views may become a stumbling block before the world? And if it is once decided, ought we not to keep forever silent about it? Ans.—Concerning the school proposed in the

Gospel Visitor, we think we have no right to interfere with an individual enterprise so long as there is no departure from Gospel principles.

There were no further queries until 1871.

Columbiana did not after all become the place for the school when it was undertaken. At New Vienna, Clinton County, Ohio, a very nice building was for sale. Members of the Fall Creek congregation offered to purchase it if the Brethren would occupy it with a school. Quinter moved to New Vienna. Business was then so bad that Kurtz could not move the paper. Quinter was to continue to serve on the paper from the new location. The school opened on October 14, 1861.

The events of the times were against the school. It was closed June 27, 1864, on account of the disturbed condition of the country during the Civil War. In this enterprise James Quinter was assisted by Bro. O. W. Miller, A. M., Sister Clara A. Haas and her daughter Hattie, Sister Mary Craig, and Lettie and Rachel Day.[6]

The school at Kishacoquilas fared better. Sharp says of it that the strain of three years bore heavily upon his wife's health and so he sold the school to Professor Martin Mohler, brother of our evangelist, J. M. Mohler. Brethren continued to patronize this school until one was started at Huntingdon, Pennsylvania. Among the earlier students under Sharp's ownership of the school was J. B. Brumbaugh, in whose mind originated the idea of starting the school which developed into Juniata College.

It is noteworthy that the aversion to a professional ministry was so strong among the Brethren that when they started schools no Biblical or formal religious instruction was offered. They depended upon atmosphere for religious influence. Retrospect over three generations of Brethren schools indicates that religious atmosphere has had the greatest molding effect upon the multitude of youth who have attended.

---

[6] S. Z. Sharp, *Educational History, Church of the Brethren.* Page 26.

# Chapter 23

# AN APPRAISAL OF BRETHREN SCHOOLS

From the first efforts in the 1860's until 1950 the operation of Church-sponsored schools may be said to have been a major interest of the Brethren.

In the ninety years since the outbreak of the Civil War there have been three major phases of Christian effort through which the Church has striven to bear a positive Christian witness. These are education, missions, and relief and rehabilitation work, which in all its multiform phases has become designated as service. Counting personnel engaged, years spent in active endeavor, money expended, and duration of time, education has the precedence among the three phases of effort.

The establishment of Church schools of advanced rank represents the thorough acceptance of Henry Kurtz's viewpoint of getting inside the institutions and techniques of contemporary society and working them for the Church and for God.

Since the establishment of the first schools of 1861, there can be designated twenty Brethren schools that have been in operation for a longer or a shorter time. In addition, a twenty-first endeavor at Berlin, Pennsylvania, might well be included because of the education it carried for the support of Church schools, though it never actually opened as a school. A number of smaller school efforts by Brethren did not attain enough permanence to get into the records. We are not counting the rather extensive school work, mostly of elementary rank, on the various mission fields. The schools established have done work of excellent quality related to our American national development, often in spite of meager resources. Data regarding particular schools will be found in the appendix.

The schools began largely as normal or teacher-training institutions. They have been mainly such until the past two decades. This is true not only of Brethren schools but pretty largely of liberal arts colleges in general. There were some pupils who turned to farming, because their families possessed land; a few who had capital or business connections that turned them to industry; a still smaller number who sought to enter the professions of medicine and law. After 1900, Brethren youth could add to the learned professions also the ministry. Now with the great increase of professionalization, corollary to our urbanized industrial society, there has been opened a multitude of choices to young college graduates.

The craft of yesterday is today a profession with standards of training. When the writer entered college a perennial debate topic was *Is Teaching a Profession?* The debate has ceased. Teaching is a profession. The writer's great-grandfather in pioneer Ohio was a blacksmith and served his countryside also as a dentist. He had tools and a strong arm. Neighbors tortured by dental troubles resorted to him. In his good-natured desire to relieve suffering he cured their toothache with a white-hot wire from the forge or with blacksmith pinchers. His benevolent efforts would now put him in jeopardy of prison. In the interests of health, safety, and justice in our interdependent society the State necessarily imposes its standards upon those who would exercise a calling.

In the bitter years of the depression in the 1930's the Brethren schools came under criticism for taking people from the soil and exposing them to the hazards of industrial life. The late President Otho Winger in his *Memories of Manchester* (1940) deals with this question:

> Some have wondered why more of our alumni have not gone back
> to the farm. It may be remembered that the depression of 1930 caught

many of our alumni in their younger years when the farm could not pay at all. Many had already started in that vocation but had to turn to other work because the farm did not pay. Many found that their only salvation for themselves and their families was that they were able to turn to another line of work because of their training in college.

One thing has been overlooked by those who have gone through the alumni bulletin to see how many are helping in their rural communities, for many who are listed as high school teachers, business men and housewives are working in rural communities, where they are making splendid contributions to the church and its work.[1]

At this date it is almost impossible to picture the expansion of education in the ranks of the Church of the Brethren. The writer of these lines has etched into his childhood memories the entertaining stories of his grandparents about the unusual Dunker preacher—a college graduate—who used to come to Mansfield, Ohio (Richland County church). And the perfectly marvelous thing about it was that you could understand what he said. And he was just as "common" and "sociable" as if he had never seen a college! He was the only such preacher they had ever seen, but they had forgotten his name. Years afterward, from the files of the Church periodicals I was able to identify this heroic, semimythical figure as S. Z. Sharp, during his period as president of Ashland College. For a long time it was considered that S. Z. Sharp was the first man in the Church to receive a liberal arts degree. He received the degree of Master of Arts from Washington and Jefferson College in 1875.

Now it is established that Lewis Kimmel was graduated from Allegheny College, Pennsylvania, with the Bachelor of Arts degree in 1859 and the Master of Arts in 1863. Kimmel was a dairyman and farmer from 1859 to 1906 near Elderton, Pennsylvania, retiring to Shelocta, Pennsylvania, where he died on August 7, 1907. D. C. Reber, one-time president of Elizabethtown College, is authority for the statement that up to 1900 not more than a dozen members of the Church had bona

---

[1] Otho Winger, *Memories of Manchester.* Page 89.

fide liberal arts degrees. In contrast, study by Forrest Weller in 1947 indicated that there were then between fifty and one hundred members of the Church teaching in colleges and universities not under the denomination's control.

Juniata, our oldest extant Brethren college, granted the first Bachelor of Arts degree in 1897. The situation at Manchester reported by Winger is typical of our colleges:

When I became president in 1911, there was no alumni association to turn to for any support. In the fifteen years that the college has been under the direction of the Brethren, there had been but nine graduates of the college department. There had been some other graduates, but not very many. I was a student here in 1900 when Troy Smith and George Tanreuther completed the A. B. degree. Two years later, in 1902, my last year as a student, S. P. Early and George Layman completed their college work. In 1903 D. O. Cottrell was the only graduate. In 1906 O. D. Foster, in 1908 Jesse Boone Studebaker, in 1909 David L. Stoner, and in 1910 M. E. Studebaker were the only graduates. In 1911 there were none. So it was a great advance when in 1912 there were three graduates, and likewise in 1913; but in 1914 we had made great progress, for eight people completed the work for the A. B. degree. In 1915 twenty-one people received degrees, and so we were off toward building up an alumni group.

The number of A. B. graduates continued to increase for about ten years, when we reached the peak of our college enrollment. From 125 to 150 each year completed the college course. These were the years when many students were completing the two-year course required of teachers in Indiana and Ohio. This added many graduates from other departments.

The following analysis is largely of the college department. Including the graduates of 1940, there have been 1193 men and 1012 women who have completed the college course. . . .[2]

Only in the magic land of America in the heyday of industrialization could such a phenomenal development occur.

It has to be chronicled soberly that the Brethren, both leaders and people, did not have clear perception of what was happening to them in the first three decades of the twentieth century. They exultantly counted the increased number of

---

[2] Winger, *op. cit.* Page 87.

college students. The college department was now larger than the academy! The college had decided to discontinue the academy! (A shout of triumph was raised.) Campaigns to build new buildings were enthusiastically staged. Endowment campaigns were begun as religious crusades. Each new step of State or college association recognition was proudly advertised. This authority or that student of affairs had declared the Brethren educational development unprecedented. The Brethren blazoned these facts abroad, oblivious of the dubious implications and innocent of the cause in American social development.

President Winger proudly stated:

The Alumni bulletins show that more than a thousand of our graduates have gone into educational work of some kind, most of them into high school teaching. Records show that about a hundred are principals of high schools or grade schools. More than fifty have become college or university professors. Thirty-two have become school superintendents. Six have become deans of colleges, and two have become college presidents.

Manchester has often been criticized for turning out so many teachers; but compared with other colleges, the record is not so bad. Even so, the college friends may feel proud of the record that the public school teachers of Manchester have made. For the most part, they are not merely so many teachers to fill the vacancies that occur year after year, but they have gone out from Manchester with high ideals and with a determination to give to their students something more than mere academic knowledge. Throughout northern Indiana and in many sections of other states, you will find these graduates doing splendid work, and in many places whole communities have been influenced by their splendid service.

Contrary to what many people would believe, the next largest group have entered some form of business work. These include almost every kind of business, from being employees in concerns small or large to being business executives, bank officials, and managers.

As might be and should be expected, Manchester has contributed many graduates to the work of the church. More than sixty are now active pastors. About forty others are serving the church as ministers while supporting themselves for the most part as schoolteachers, farmers, business representatives, and in other activities. Thirty-five of these graduates have become foreign missionaries and have gone to India, China and Africa, where they have been ambassadors of good will for the cause of the church of Jesus Christ. When we think of these, scattered throughout the world, we can begin to realize how largely the influence of the college has been felt.[3]

Kurtz's original idea of training teachers has succeeded beyond his greatest expectations. Brethren colleges have been normal schools. And it may be said that the overwhelming majority of teachers from Brethren colleges have gone "with high ideals and with a determination to give their students something more than mere academic knowledge." In the life of America it would be difficult to exaggerate the importance of this Christian witness in the public schools.

It will be recalled that Horace Mann, the father of the American public school, was born the same year as Henry Kurtz (1796). The development of elementary and high schools was getting under way in Kurtz's time. Mann was dedicated to the philosophy of the improvability of the human race through education. He had the first normal schools in America established in Massachusetts. He proposed the reduction of religious instruction in the schools to the reading of the Bible without comment. Education was counted to be training for living in the environing society. The times were ripe for such schools. A complex structure of society required a trained people. Schooling was a short cut over apprenticeship.

In 1852 Mann left his work in New England and accepted the presidency of Antioch College at Yellow Springs, Ohio. Until his death in 1859 he sought to make Antioch a center of teacher training and of his educational philosophy. Elder Kurtz had around him the new type of schools. Mann was traveling up and down the state with the flaming zeal of a prophet when Kurtz began to write on education in the *Gospel Visitor*.

The trend is now toward State control of education. We in

---

[3] Winger, *op. cit.* Pages 87 and 88.

1950 are undergoing a political revolution, analogous to and corollary of the Industrial Revolution. All this has implications for our educational procedures.

It is probably because Brethren schools began with a major aim of training teachers that education in the Church has come to mean higher education. In the late twenties and the early thirties the academies were closed. The Church has practically limited its enterprises to education at the liberal arts college level. Was this wise?

In our sending thousands of Christian teachers into the public schools, uncounted thousands of boys and girls at the earlier ages have been touched indirectly by the Church. But there are those who think we turned the wrong direction when we closed the academies. Studies show that the age of determining one's fundamental life direction is much younger than was once thought. Most children choose their direction by twelve or at most fourteen years of age. Should we not, then, have direct educational contact with the younger age group? Could not higher education better have been left to the State if one level must be chosen?

In the late thirties skepticism arose as to the place of the Christian college. Demands were increasingly difficult to meet and the role of the college was less clear. Then came World War II. The struggle was hard. But after the war, college halls were crowded with students receiving G. I. assistance. Discussion about the place of the college receded, but the problems are not settled.

We close this chapter with a few self-evident propositions.

It may be said that the schools have greatly hastened the industrialization and urbanization of Brethren people, although they did not cause or create the process. Pastors and school promoters have glamorized and idealized "going away to school." The loftiest idealism has combined with a very matter-of-fact materialism to urge young people to "train for leadership," which in most cases has been unconsciously accepted as implying more money and easier working conditions—the rewards of a materialistic society.

It may be said that the schools have furnished educational guidance to hundreds, perhaps thousands, of boys and girls with a degree of effectiveness which could never have been exercised by any other institution or agency. Personal confusion was reduced.

The schools have trained the great majority of the missionaries and pastors of the Church.

The schools have trained large numbers of boys and girls from non-Brethren homes. Our neighbors often have been eager to place their children in Brethren schools. This, in the long perspective, may be our most significant missionary effort and social contribution. Few young people have passed through our schools without imbibing some of the emphasis on peace, kindliness, moral earnestness, religious respect, and humanitarianism which have been typical of the schools.

Today the existent schools remain as centers of wholesome moral life and Christian fraternal care in which young people may receive an education for contemporary society. There has been little of the pioneer exhibited in Brethren educational work. The inventor and innovator has been absent. But the work of the schools has been quietly honest and of thorough excellence. Moral character has always been held up as indispensable, without which intellectual training would be of no avail.

## Chapter 24

## OTHER VENTURES IN EDUCATION

Another idea that was advocated in the columns of the *Gospel Visitor* in the early years was the establishment of Sunday schools.

The Sunday school has been for over a century the chief educational agency of that part of the Protestant world which has accepted the State-controlled public school. Some religious societies operate parochial schools at either the elementary or the secondary level, but this is not general.

The Sunday school originated in England. A publisher named Robert Raikes (1735-1811) saw the factory towns teeming with untutored, idle children loafing on the streets on Sundays. He conceived the idea of gathering them into schools and teaching them to read, and employed a woman for this purpose. She taught them reading and writing as means for reading the Bible. He publicized the experiment in his *Gloucester Journal* and was swamped with inquiries. Begun in July 1780, at Ashbury, Berkshire, the movement spread until in 1800 it was claimed that one hundred fifty-six thousand four hundred English children were being taught in Sunday schools. The general procedure was to use a volunteer staff.

The first sure reference to an American Sunday school is to one held in 1794 in Passaic County, New Jersey, where the children from a cotton factory were given gratuitous instruction.

The Sunday school came as a device of the industrial age.

It was developed by earnest Christians to meet the needs in an industrialized society. The remarkable thing is that it was transferred to the countryside in many different nations. Its scope has been enlarged, in most areas, to cover all age groups, and a Bible study curriculum for all ages has been developed.

By 1825 the American Sunday School Union reported its membership as one thousand one hundred fifty Sunday schools with eleven thousand two hundred ninety-five teachers and eighty-two thousand six hundred ninety-seven scholars, and estimated that there were sixty-one thousand pupils enrolled in other Sunday schools in North America.

About that time the Brethren first met the Sunday school. As early as 1823 a union Sunday school was conducted at the old colonial Oley church, in Berks County, Pennsylvania. No preaching service was being held there at the time, and the school was popular. In 1845 a Sunday school was organized in the White Oak district of Eastern Pennsylvania by Brother and Sister Jonas Gibble. It lived until they moved away several years later. The third school known to us was started in Philadelphia in 1856. The same year, schools were started by Brethren in Mifflin County and Union County, Pennsylvania. At the latter place J. G. Royer began his service as a Sunday-school teacher.

As early as 1789 the Yearly Meeting had laid upon parents the responsibility of teaching their children the Word of God. In 1838, the Meeting advised against Sunday schools. The establishment of three schools in 1856 brought a reconsideration and, in 1857, the decision was: "We know of no Scripture that condemns Sabbath schools, if conducted in gospel order, and if they are made a means of teaching scholars a knowledge of the Scriptures."

This was quite a concession. The speed of organization thereupon and the lack of supervision of the early schools brought some disorder. But those early Sunday schools were a testimony to the sincerity of multitudes who participated in them and sat down in groups to read the Bible and memorize sections of it. The decision of 1857 was reaffirmed in 1862, but the Sunday schools were a factor in the division of 1881-1882. There was some ground for the opposition in that the Sunday schools grew out of the industrial order, not out of the familistic order of which the Brethren have been sturdy exemplars.

This was well stated in 1908 by Elizabeth Meyer in her address at the Bi-centennial Conference, from which we quote:

> Though the good results of the Sunday School are manifest everywhere, today, notwithstanding the opposition which Sunday-school workers were obliged to face, yet we believe that some of our old brethren were sincere in their opposition, because of a righteous fear concerning the effects of this work. Bro. J. G. Royer thinks they were not opposed to Sunday school because the Scriptures were taught there, but they feared that it would prove a means of releasing parents from a sense of their responsibility for the religious instruction and care of their own children; and that as a result of this tendency, the work and influence of the Sunday school would be liable to bear adversely on the family, which was meant to be God's primal training agency for the human race. The divine injunction to parents is—Deut. 6: 6, 7; 32: 46, 47: . . .

> The home thus ordained by God must not be hindered in its mission, nor can it safely be rivalled or slighted. The Sunday school must prove its cooperation with the family, or yield its claim to divine authority (1 Cor. 4: 15; Rom. 8: 28). It would not be right to ignore this fear of our early Brethren, for it is only too well founded. Is it not true that there are in the Brethren's Church today, members who are enthusiastic Sunday-school workers, yet neglect the teaching of the Scriptures in their homes? What a pity that in some localities, Brethren's children come to Sunday school without having even studied the lesson! . . .[1]

In 1876 our first Brethren Sunday-school helps were published. The first Sunday-school papers were pioneers in the field of children's magazines and newspapers. They were novel and thrilling to children and young people. The chil-

---

[1] *Two Centuries of the Church of the Brethren.* Pages 251-252.

dren's newspapers that are now sold through the public schools, the comic books, radio skits, television, and moving pictures have to a considerable extent encroached upon the interest in the Sunday-school papers.

Lesson helps have been furnished as aids, not substitutes, for direct Bible study. Our church has participated in the co-operative undertaking of building lesson outlines, and it provides graded lesson materials for children and uniform lesson materials and electives for older age groups through our own Sunday-school editorial department.

In 1886 the Annual Meeting decided that a minority in a church should not hinder the majority from organizing and conducting Sunday schools in harmony with the principles of the Brotherhood. In 1896 the Sunday School Advisory Board was appointed by the Conference. This is the ancestor of our Christian Education Commission of the General Brotherhood Board.

The Sunday school has not quite held its own in recent decades. The top enrollment reported—one hundred thirty-nine thousand nine hundred fifteen—was in 1921. In 1950, the schools sending in report blanks had a total enrollment of one hundred twenty-nine thousand three hundred three.

Certain other educational agencies have developed in the last three decades. The first one to note is the daily vacation Bible school. The origin of this movement is credited to Robert G. Boville in a Baptist mission society in New York City. He had several schools in 1901 to utilize the vacation time of children for Bible instruction. An association was organized in 1906. The movement swept the country over-night. The record for the Brethren is as follows:

| | | | |
|---|---|---|---|
| 1919 | 8 | 1923 | 357 |
| 1920 | 88 | 1924 | 287 |
| 1921 | 292 | 1925 | 254 |
| 1922 | 329 | | |

Then the novelty wore off. Also, many of our churches joined in union schools. But there has survived a sturdy vacation school movement among us.

The weekday religious education movement also came to the Brethren. It has had ups and downs, but now seems to have a new surge of interest. This movement on the local level is largely a union, community affair. For two years the compiling of statistics was undertaken by the Board of Christian Education. The number of pupils that Brethren congregations reported under instruction was:

|  | 1930 | 1931 |
|---|---|---|
| In daily vacation Bible school | 14,841 | 16,424 |
| In weekday religious education | 1,781 | 1,187 |

The camping movement illustrates the reaction of our industrialized urban population to its artificial environment of town street, shop, store, factory, and laboratory. The Church has shown remarkable wisdom in availing itself of the natural instinctive longing of man for the out of doors and in linking its teaching program to the environment of natural beauty which a well-chosen camp affords.

It is not always possible to distinguish a meeting, a conference, and a camp. The religious camping movement proper may not go back farther than the 1880's. At Lake Geneva in Wisconsin in 1914 the first permanent religious camp in America was established. It was established under the International Council of Religious Education and is still operated under the direction of the council. It is interdenominational and functions widely in training leaders.

The first Brethren camp was organized at Beatrice, Nebraska, in 1916 by Edgar Rothrock and Virgil C. Finnell. This was not permanent. In 1920 C. H. Shamberger, employed by the Christian Workers' Board as youth secretary, made a study of camping procedures, and in 1921 held the first camp-conference for Brethren young people at Winona Lake,

Indiana. The attendance was nearly one hundred, with the following leaders: E. B. Hoff, J. Hugh Heckman, L. W. Shultz, J. J. Yoder, Perry Rohrer, Charles D. Bonsack, M. R. Zigler, Eva Lichty, and A. F. Brightbill. As such camp-conferences multiplied in succeeding years, they moved in the direction of camps more than conferences.

It cannot be definitely stated which camp among those growing up as permanent Church camp sites was the first to be put into operation. Camp Harmony, near Johnstown, Pennsylvania, and Camp La Verne, in Southern California, undertook camping schedules in 1924. In 1925, Camp Mack, near Milford, Indiana, was available to campers. This became the largest of the Brethren camps. Camp Sugar Grove in Southern Ohio came in 1926; Camp Bethel, near Roanoke, Virginia, in 1927.

The two "pattern" camps through the years have been Harmony and Mack. The former centers around the personalities of W. J. Hamilton and H. B. Speicher, the latter around the personalities of Professor L. W. Shultz and his wife.

The first intermediate boys' camp was probably that carried on near Plymouth, Indiana, for the boys of the Douglas Park and Hastings Street missions in Chicago. Galen Sargent, Perry Huffaker, and the writer were leaders.

Other camps were organized within the Brotherhood. A quartet of leaders covered five to seven thousand miles in an old Studebaker sedan each of four summers, 1927-1930, to staff the camps. These were C. H. Shamberger, Dan West, Perry Rohrer, and Alvin Brightbill; occasionally also Joe Van Dyke. Besides camp leadership, there were other products of this touring, e.g. creation of recreational literature through the Recreational Fellowship, and the "hill-top" method of developing leaders.

By the end of 1939 the total number of Church-owned and Church-operated camps was twenty-nine, located in thirteen states and Canada. This had come down to twenty-two by

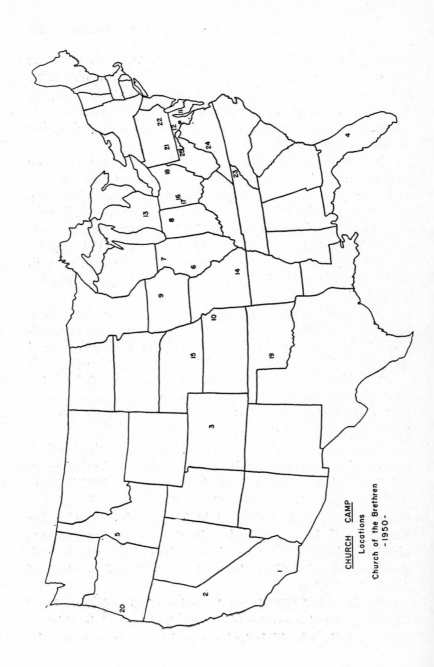

CHURCH CAMP

Locations

Church of the Brethren

-1950-

### Key to Map Showing Church Camp Locations

1. California: Camp LaVerne
2. California: Camp Peaceful Pines
3. Colorado: Camp Colorado
4. Florida: Camp Ithiel
5. Idaho: Camp Stover
6. Illinois: Camp Emmanuel
7. Illinois: Camp Emmaus
8. Indiana: Camp Alexander Mack
9. Iowa: Camp Pine Lake
10. Kansas: Mt. Hermon Camp
11. Maryland: Camp Mardela
12. Maryland: Camp Peniel
13. Michigan: Church of the Brethren Camp
14. Missouri: Camp of the Ozarks
15. Nebraska: Camp Schwarzenau
16. Ohio: Camp Mountain Lake
17. Ohio: Camp Sugar Grove
18. Ohio: Camp Zion
19. Oklahoma: Camp Spring Lake
20. Oregon: Camp Myrtlewood
21. Pennsylvania: Camp Harmony
22. Pennsylvania: Camp Swatara
23. Tennessee: Camp Placid
24. Virginia: Camp Bethel
25. West Virginia: Camp Galilee

1950. Camp planners' meetings have been held and some direction has been given to the movement by the Board of Christian Education, now the Christian Education Commission of the General Brotherhood Board.

A quotation from Harry K. Zeller, Jr., puts the camp contribution aptly:

The world is getting out of doors again. The young people of the Church of the Brethren are not only getting out of doors again but they are getting from the out of doors a new experience and a new relationship with God and with their fellow young people. The Christian camp is the youngest member of the Christian educational auxiliaries to religion and it is playing a most vital part in the Christian training of children, young people, and adults. One reason for this tremendous impact of camp upon life is that it brings people together for all twenty-four hours of the day instead of one or two. Our church feels sufficiently the value of this impact upon the lives of its members that it has institutionalized the camping to a high degree. The question of the moment concerns the direction and emphasis of the camping movement in the years immediately to come.

One newly developed phase of camping deserves separate mention—the work camp.

The work camp came into being in 1920 through the

experience of a Swiss named Pierre Ceresole.[2] He wanted to devise a plan to "kill enmity rather than enemies." His idea was to go and help where there was need. He gathered about him some "peace soldiers" and worked for six months at Verdun, helping the French peasants rebuild their homes and plant their crops. In 1934 the first work camp was brought to the United States under the American Friends Service Committee. In 1937 they invited Brethren and Mennonites to join in a project with them.

This experience greatly influenced the five Brethren who participated. In the 1938 Conference at Lawrence, Kansas, a peace program was adopted that gave consent to two things with respect to work camps: (1) co-operation with Friends and Mennonites and other Christian groups; (2) constructive local community and church projects.

Some figures make concrete the growth of our work camps:

|  | United States | Europe |
|---|---|---|
| 1939 Number of camps | 2 | none |
| Number of campers | 31 | none |
| 1949 Number of camps | 11 | 2 |
| Number of campers | 143 | 23 |

In 1949 we had as many camps in Europe as we had in the United States the first year of our work camp program, and almost as many campers.

The work camp is the steppingstone to "volunteer service."

We must here conclude our discussion of education. In recent years, Brethren experiments in education have tended toward informal types. One thing we may hazard: The various types of informal education must surely foster in the individual the sense of vocation as something entrusted to himself in the midst of an evil world. When the individual sees his life as

---

[2] See Allan Hunter's *White Corpuscles in Europe*, pages 33-35, for details of origin.

something infinitely precious which he must not waste, will he not then turn anew to THE LIFE—Jesus? When the individual feels the burden of life-investment as a major problem of his finite existence, maybe then he will see anew Him who is THE TRUTH. Our ways are subject to further development, but we have glimpsed THE WAY.

## Chapter 25

## THE FOREIGN MISSIONARY DEVELOPMENT

Foreign missions have long ranked with education as a major Christian interest and mode of testimony in the world. Foreign missions arrived later than the schools. They are as clear an example as we can cite of the development of a specialized branch of the growing professionalization of our modern world.

The modern missionary movement began with William Carey (1761-1834). He passed his youth in the environment of England's industrialization and expanding geographical knowledge. He himself was a rare combination of scientific, linguistic, and religious enthusiasm. He was fired by tales of early Moravian missionary devotion, but he dreamed out a plan different from theirs. They went out as colonists who became indigenous residents of the areas to which they went and expected to support themselves. He developed the idea of a society of "ropeholders" that became the pattern for all the mission societies and boards that have been organized since his time.

The first such organization was the Baptist Missionary Society, started October 2, 1792. It represented an adaptation of the joint stock company to the religious purposes of the Christian Church. The time was ripe for such a new device. The powerful evangelical revival had deeply moved men for the salvation of their fellows, and the world was being woven together in a new unity. The successful demonstration of the steamboat in 1807 led to a great expansion of trade. The arrival of steam navigation made it easy to believe that the modern missionary movement had arrived "for such a time as this."

Carey and John Thomas were sent to India under the newly formed missionary society in 1793, just one hundred one years before our Wilbur Stovers and Bertha Ryan were sent to the same land to initiate Brethren mission work in the non-Christian world. The going of Carey and Thomas marked the beginning of a new profession—that of the foreign missionary. Christians had been zealous for propagating their faith long before that time, but prior to 1792 Christian propagandists were either crown chaplains—pastors and neighbors who worked with their immediate neighbors—or colonists such as the Moravians.

Carey and Thomas moved into a remote society, non-Christian in thought and adherence, and gave themselves to full-time Christian propaganda. They were to be supported by members of the society on the home base, who were to pray and contribute financially. The directors of the society were the link between the home base and the field. The plan was simple, clear, and beautiful in Christian zeal.

The pattern at once commended itself to the contemporary Christian world. Although it did not work in Carey's case and he was soon supporting the society and its work by his earnings as linguist and superintendent of an indigo factory instead of their supporting him, soon other societies were organized—four before 1800 in England. In America the term *board* was used instead of *society*. The first American board was formed in 1812. Others followed.

The earliest inquiry relative to non-Christian areas came to the Brethren Yearly Meeting in 1852. It was answered by a statement of principle. Our people were hardly industrialized enough to understand the implications of the foreign mission movement.

The first Brethren preacher to be sent abroad was

Christian Hope, a Dane who, with his family, was sent to his homeland on January 1, 1876. This action was the answer to the call of a young man who had read our literature and had written to Brother Hope asking for baptism. At a special district meeting held at Cherry Grove in Northern Illinois, on November 12, 1875, it had been decided to send Brother Hope and Elders Enoch Eby and Paul Wetzel on this mission. Elder Daniel Fry ultimately replaced Elder Wetzel on the delegation. The elders went in 1877 and organized a church, remaining until February 1878. This project was but an extension of the old Brethren system of traveling or adjacent elders. The unique elements were the distance and the fact that first the district, then the entire fraternity, united in offerings to assist them.

The story of foreign missions from here on has been capably and voluminously told in Galen B. Royer's *Thirty Three Years of Missions in the Church of the Brethren*[1] and Elgin S. Moyer's *Missions in the Church of the Brethren*[2], supplemented by numerous theses, pamphlets, sermons, brochures, special histories, and annual reports.

The first mission board came into existence by Conference appointment in 1880—the Foreign and Domestic Mission Board. To it by official action was assigned the care of the Danish mission work. The period, 1880-1884, was one of transition. There was some evangelistic traveling in addition to the transmission of funds and the giving of advice to Denmark.

The new era began in 1884 with the appointment of the General Church Erection and Missionary Committee. One of the members was D. L. Miller, of venerable memory. Nearly three decades later he wrote in the preface of Royer's above-named history:

A backward look takes us to a grassy slope under the shade of an apple tree in the yard of Brother Moses Miller, near Dayton, Ohio,

---

[1] Brethren Publishing House, 1914.
[2] Brethren Publishing House, 1931.

within a stone's throw of the Tabernacle where the Conference of 1884 was held. It was a beautiful June day and here the newly-appointed General Mission Board met and organized for business. A few days later, June 13, 1884, the first business meeting was held at Mt. Morris, Illinois. Then the treasurer reported $8.69 on hand, not enough to even think of beginning work. Contrast this with the money and assets of the General Mission Board in this year of grace, 1913. We now have annual receipts, aggregating about $100,000 with assets, including endowment, the Gish Fund, and the Publishing Department, of nearly $1,000,000. Then we had but a single missionary in foreign lands,— Brother Hope in Scandinavia,—now, including the outgoing missionaries for 1913, we have in India thirty-eight missionaries, in China eighteen, and five in Scandinavia. Noting the contrast here drawn, surely one is led to rejoice with an exceeding great joy and to exclaim, in the fulness of the heart, "Behold what God hath wrought among his people."

From 1884 to the outbreak of World War II (1939) most Brethren would have held missions, or foreign missions, to be the primary work of the church. This idea was convincingly set forth by Wilbur Stover. On his furloughs and after his retirement he traveled the length and breadth of the Church, spreading everywhere his enthusiasm for missions. The Student Volunteer Movement aided until 1923 with its slogan, "The Evangelization of the World in This Generation."

Economic events after World War I profoundly affected the missionary course of the Christian Church, Brethren included. The agricultural deflation that hit America in the winter of 1921-1922 devastated whole areas of the Brotherhood. Hundreds of prosperous families were brought to the verge of bankruptcy. Seven years later came the crash of 1929 and a decade of the worst depression in Occidental history. The West rallied from it only by beginning the armament race which led on to September 1939. Something fundamental happened to us in the depression of the 1930's. Its problems we never solved; we left them to prepare for and fight another war.

The missionary effort has brought some remarkable results. The work in Denmark spread to Sweden and was carried on with varying zeal until 1947. The *Yearbook* for 1950 reported one church with fifteen members in Denmark, and twenty-nine members in Sweden. Since many families had moved to the United States and the rest could be shepherded by other Christian groups, the work was suspended. There have been missionary endeavors for short periods in Asia Minor, Switzerland, and France.

Our first adventure into the heathen world, undertaken in 1894, has proved the most successful. The *Yearbook* of 1950 reports a growing Church of eight thousand five hundred seventeen members, with twenty ministers and eight licentiates, in India.

Fourteen years after the mission party sailed to India, the pioneers left for China. They were the Frank Crumpackers, the George Hiltons, and Emma Horning. The work in Shansi Province has been through war, famine, and upheaval. The 1950 *Yearbook* reports a membership of two thousand twenty-four in North China, a thousand fewer than two years earlier. The social revolution has swept the Church in China into isolation; it is in the keeping of Providence.

Fourteen years after the beginning in China, A. D. Helser and H. Stover Kulp were off to Nigeria, British West Africa. Their wives and the Dr. Homer Burkes joined them some months later. Thus the Africa mission was launched. The Church there now numbers seven hundred thirty.

Ecuador, in South America, is the last major field. The work was formally opened there twenty-four years after that in Nigeria. The Benton Rhoadeses went in 1946, followed by the Claude Wolfes in 1948. It has an economic advantage over the other fields in that it lies within the dollar area. This may be a providential advantage in the infant days of the mission.

The growth in our mission work since 1885 has been gratifying. The first annual report in that year showed an expenditure of $3,552.09. For the fiscal year ending February 29, 1950, the expenditures of the Foreign Mission Commission

LOCATION OF MEMBERSHIP
the World
Church of the Brethren
- 1950 -

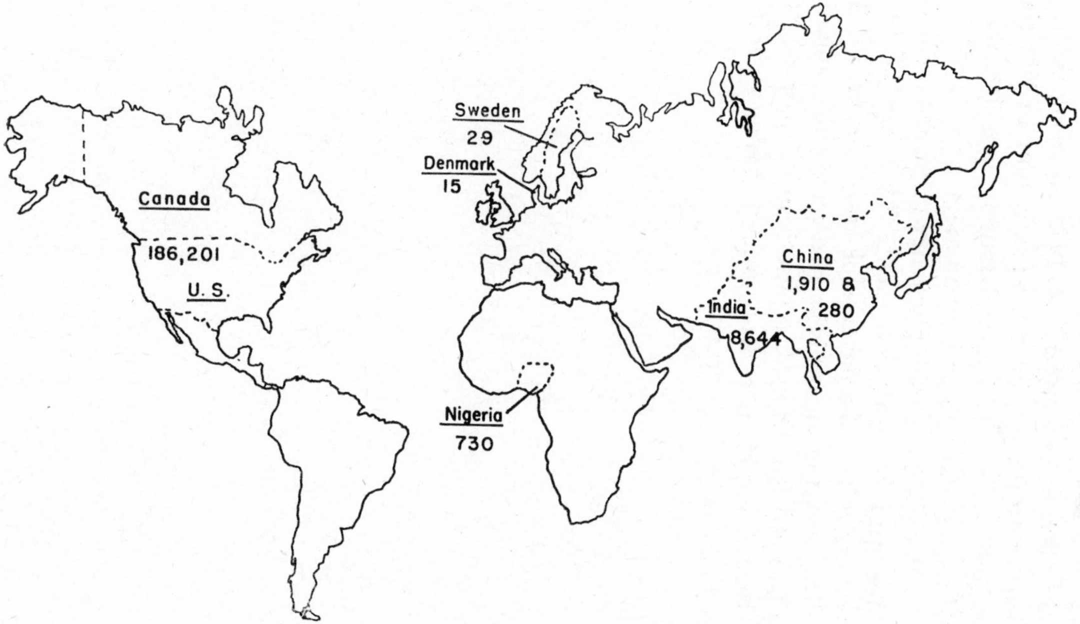

Canada
186,201
U.S.

Sweden
29
Denmark
15

Nigeria
730

China
1,910 &
India
8,64    280

had been $310,707.26. In 1885 there was one worker, with his faithful wife, in Europe. The 1950 *Yearbook* shows eighty-nine persons on the mission fields: forty-four in Nigeria, thirty-one in India, ten in China, and four in Ecuador, with numerous others on furlough or in retirement.

We neither philosophize nor guess about the future of the "modern missionary movement." There are those who look for a return of the colonial type of missionary effort. The modern missionary movement is carried on within capitalistic culture. The Lord has deigned to bless it in the past, and the future is His. It is not He nor His Church that is on trial. It is our social organizations and forms.

# Chapter 26

# BRETHREN SERVICE

The third major phase of the Church's attempt to present its message in the contemporary world has acquired the name *Brethren Service*.[1]

The real charter for Brethren Service was adopted at the La Verne Annual Conference of 1941, and its prominence in the life of the Church began then. But its roots go back to the very beginning of the Church. The Church at Schwarzenau began practicing a community of goods and continued for seven years. The early records of Germantown, with its poor box, indicate that the common good was not forgotten. The deacon has had a real office in the Church. The present-day office of "relief worker" is an extension of the deaconate. At many times in Brethren annals emergencies have brought forth the spontaneous outpouring of fraternal help.

The closing action of the Yearly Meeting of 1865 is as follows:

Contributions for the brethren in Virginia and Tennessee: Bro. Wrightsman from Tennessee, and Bro. Mumaw from Virginia stated to the meeting that the brethren in those states, need assistance, and that they must suffer unless they get assistance; whereupon the meeting appointed D. P. Saylor as a receiver to receive contributions for the relief of said brethren. The meeting likewise directed him to appropriate the funds now in his hands, collected for the Oregon Mission, to the same purpose.

---

[1] The present Brethren Service Commission (March 1, 1947) was preceded by the Brethren Service Committee, the name of which was obviously suggested by the widely known Friends Service Committee—an instance of the inter-relatedness of the "historic peace churches."

D. P. Sayler's itemized reports through the *Gospel Visitor* of 1865 and 1866 show that he received at least $8,238.93 for relief, besides a fund of $396.95 for an impoverished brother, an elder in Tennessee, whose plight had touched the Brethren.

In the minutes of the Meeting of 1866 we find this item:

> In response to a petition from the brethren in Virginia for pecuniary help for Bro. Peter Crumpacker, an elder in the church, who lost three thousand dollars in getting his brethren out of prison, and by being robbed by the rebels, this Annual Meeting recommends to all the churches in the North to assist liberally this worthy brother to bear his loss, which he, through love to the brethren, sustains. And we appoint Bro. Benjamin Moomaw his receiver.[2]

In that same year Article 21 recommended the freedmen of the South to the generosity of the churches, since reports of their starving had reached the North. Indiana had already sent some donations.

The famine years of 1874 and 1875 in the West afford another instance. The need was desperate in Kansas, Nebraska, Missouri, and Colorado, and the columns of our church papers of those years were largely occupied with the appeals for relief funds and the accounting for the same. Falls City, Nebraska, became a central receiving and distributing point. Relief was given not only to Brethren but to others; in fact, the greater portion of it went to others, "to Baptists, Methodists, Presbyterians, Campbellites, Catholics and others making no profession." Non-Brethren participated also in the giving. The wider reach of service was counted a Christian duty. The Bible was used to prove that Brethren should help their needy neighbors. But it was also counted an opportunity for a spiritual ministry. Missionary enthusiasm motivated physical helpfulness. The Brethren hoped that kindness in physical ministration might make receptive ears for a "pure gospel." Brother Jacob Bahr wrote:

> Who knows but what the present suffering in Nebraska, Kansas,

---

[2] *Minutes of Annual Conference, 1866*, Article 48.

and Missouri . . . is one of the Lord's ways or means of spreading the gospel which we preach and practice in our churches at home? For if the Brethren combine through to the last as they have begun everywhere and see those suffering people provided for until they can raise a crop "their light shall break forth as the morning."[3]

A sister pled for ministers. She said, "By affliction God seems to be preparing these people to accept the plain, humble faith of the meek and lowly Savior."[4]

All this is in line with the Pietistic heritage of the Brethren. The emphasis on goodness and kindness predisposes to practical relief activities. The reading of the New Testament does the same.

The Relief and Reconstruction Committee of 1918-1921 administered relief to the needs growing out of World War I. A summarizing statement from the Annual Conference minutes of 1940 traces the development from 1921 to 1940:

For a number of years following the World War of 1914-1918 the call for relief funds and the disbursing of the same were done by a Relief and Reconstruction Committee. At the conclusion of these special efforts the remaining funds were turned over to the General Mission Board.

In 1932 the Anderson Conference placed the responsibility of developing a relief program in connection with the Friends and Mennonites upon the Board of Christian Education. Much relief work was done in Spain. Our workers there were instrumental in dispensing large quantities of food and clothing to those in need. They won their way into the hearts and good will of both sides and the military came to see that we were there on a Christian errand. Dan West, Martha Rupel, David Blickenstaff, and Paul Bowman, Jr., did excellent service as our representatives. Mrs. Ross D. Murphy represented our church upon the Friends Committee on Spain that had this work in charge.

When the distress of the peoples of the Orient became known relief work was planned and done through the General Mission Board and our mission in Shansi. It became apparent that a close relationship should exist between the boards involved so the Council of Boards decided in Nov., 1939, that the General Mission Board and the Board of Christian Education should serve together as a Brethren Service

[3] *Christian Family Companion and Gospel Visitor*, Volume 10. Page 104.
[4] Susan Crumpacker. *Ibid*, Volume 10. Page 524.

Committee in the field of relief and reconstruction work. Through an executive committee of five—two from each board and a fifth from without the boards—the work has been organized to care for relief, refugees, rehabilitation, peace education and finance.

This executive committee has been authorized by the two boards to make this report to the Annual Conference through Standing Committee. . . .[5]

Two factors brought a great expansion in Brethren Service activity from 1940. These were the unprecedented magnitude of the suffering of mankind and the emergence of responsibility for conducting the Civilian Public Service program. A special session of Standing Committee was held in Chicago, December 18, 1940, to plan for Civilian Public Service. The experience gained in administration of the camps for several thousand conscientious objectors and the vast sums handled brought visions of very large plans for relief and reconstruction. A special committee brought to the Conference of 1941 a "charter" for the Brethren Service Committee. It read as follows:

I. Function of the Committee.

The Brethren Service Committee finds its charter in the words of the Master: "I was hungry and ye gave me to eat; . . . I was a stranger and ye took me in; I was naked and ye clothed me; I was sick and ye visited me; I was in prison and ye came unto me . . . inasmuch as ye did it unto one of these my brethren, even these least, ye did it unto me."

This committee represents the Church of the Brethren in the area of social action. Its primary function is that of personal rehabilitation and social reconstruction in the name and spirit of Christ. Its fields of service are as follows:

1. To arrest and eliminate, in so far as possible, those forces in human society which contribute to the disintegration of personality and character, and to social instability. The Brethren recognize war, intemperance, political corruption, and the breakdown of the family as important among these forces (1 Thess. 5: 14, 15).

2. To relieve human distress and suffering around the world without regard to barriers of race, creed or nationality. This includes the service of the church among refugees, exiles, prisoners, orphans, widows,

---

[5] *Minutes of Annual Conference, 1940.* Pages 41 and 42.

the aged and other conditions of human life in which there is need for physical and spiritual relief compatible with the ideals, traditions, and financial resources of the church (Gal. 6: 10).

3. To represent the church in the area of creative citizenship and Christian testimony on issues of national and international significance. This includes the program of Civilian Public Service and the relation of the church and its members to the government in regard to peace and war and situations where the principle of religious freedom is involved (I Peter 2: 12).

4. To develop, organize and apply the spiritual and financial resources of the church to the above areas of service as a concrete and practical expression of the spirit and teaching of Christ as the Brethren understand and interpret them. This shall include the expressional side of our peace program in an effort of world reconciliation and the preservation of goodwill and human understanding among all peoples and races. The work of the committee shall be carried on so far as possible on a voluntary basis (Rom. 12: 20, 21).

. . . . .

5. Since this committee represents in the church the function associated with the office of deacon in the New Testament church, it shall be understood that the adoption of the report by Annual Conference implies that that office shall be the medium through which the work of the Service Committee shall be implemented in the local congregation. The committee shall have the privilege where the office of deacon is inoperative of effecting the necessary organization within the local congregation to carry on its work.

6. The committee shall have the authority to incorporate and to hold property and funds associated with the service it represents.

7. The present Brethren Service Committee and the Committee on Counsel for Conscientious Objectors shall be dissolved with the passage of this report.[6]

There was never a decade in the life of the Church comparable to the 1940's. The idea in Civilian Public Service was to do some kind of constructive work, largely without compensation, as an alternative to war. The philosophy of service was basic in it. The particular form the service took was determined and for the most part very much limited by the times and conditions. The personnel—the Church administrators, draftees,

---

[6] *Minutes of Annual Conference, 1941.* Pages 52-53.

government officials, technical agency representatives, and others—also had much to do with the direction taken. Chief among those who carried administrative responsibilities for the Church were M. R. Zigler and W. Harold Row.

In this movement the nonresistance of a former day tended to become a hopeful pacifist philosophy. The Brethren tradition of humanitarian religion came under the influence, more or less unconsciously, of Protestant liberalism and brought forth the purpose to witness positively for peace. The Church was called upon to accept permanent responsibility for an alternative to war. "As long as there is war or compulsory military training the church will be called on to sacrifice. An alternative to war as a testimony of our belief and conviction that war is not the right way to adjust difficulties between nations and classes of people is an essential part of our future planning."[7]

It is too early to evaluate properly the shades of thinking in this area. The pacifist philosophy cannot be appraised when we stand so close to it. But one could hardly expect a minority group to have a wholly rational view while the world of which it is a part is going insane.

The relief and rehabilitation aspects of the service work came to assume enormous proportions. There is no exact record of all the places and families on the earth touched by Brethren Service in its global outreach. The report to the Annual Conference of 1948 speaks of work in progress in Austria, France, Germany, Poland, Holland, England, China, Japan, Ethiopia, Ecuador, and Texas. Brethren centers were being maintained at New Windsor, Maryland, and Nappanee, Indiana, with subsidiary ones at McPherson, Kansas, and Roanoke and Harrisonburg, Virginia. In that same year the heifer project shipped one thousand eight hundred seven animals to Italy, China, Poland, and Greece. Projects assisted

---

[7] From the Brethren Service Committee report to Annual Conference in 1943.

local neighborhoods; two units of volunteers were operated in mental hospitals; and there was a beginning of an interracial ministry, besides other activities.

Here are some financial statistics:

| Year (Church Fiscal) | Brethren Gifts | B. S. Income | B. S. Expenditures |
|---|---|---|---|
| 1940 a | $ 13,706.38 | $ 13,706.38 | $ 17,643.78 |
| 1941 | 67,541.56 | 67,541.56 | 33,747.23 |
| 1942 | 177,858.70 | 198,196.09 b | 155,938.64 |
| 1943 | 340,222.97 | 462,010.11 b | 446,786.67 |
| 1944 | 386,483.06 | 480,476.24 b | 523,878.66 |
| 1945 | 427,710.49 | 530,677.43 b | 528,524.57 |
| 1946 | 1,055,798.17 | 1,148,658.19 b | 1,037,324.83 |
| 1947 | 669,531.64 | 757,468.62 c | 793,500.34 |
| 1948 | 591,448.60 | 650,222.18 c | 688,577.38 |
| 1949 | 303,876.69 | 355,716.28 | 409,011.35 |
| 1950 | 244,703.26 | 249,871.86 d | 296,058.15 |

a. The year started with a balance of $25,359.36 on hand.

b. In these years the difference is largely accounted for by non-Brethren payments to maintain the C. P. S. camps.

c. In these years tardy C. P. S. income continued and the committee benefited by sundry subsidies from outside the Church.

d. In this year the funds of Brethren Service show a deficit of $46,186.29.

Throughout there is no accounting for real goods, which sometimes came near the value of the money shown.

The budget expenditures recorded above in no way indicate the full stream of relief in goods and money. This tabulation of goods administered in 1946 makes this plain:

| | |
|---|---|
| Value of all contributed materials handled by Brethren Service, except cattle | $3,153,000 |
| Livestock attendant program | 1,491,000 |
| Cash spent at Elgin, exclusive of administrative costs | 1,213,000 |
| Ocean freight paid by others on Brethren Service gifts | 757,000 |
| Value of cattle-heifer project committee | 470,000 |
| Administrative costs | 105,000 |
| Total program | $7,189,000[8] |

[8] *Gospel Messenger*, July 12, 1947.

The year 1949 marked the turning point in the service program. The symbol of this was the merging of the budget of the Service Commission with the other Brotherhood funds. Before that time the relief work of the Church could be regarded as the meeting of an emergency. Even Civilian Public Service was an improvisation. But the emergency was becoming permanent. The unusual efforts of the war years were to become the usual effort of the Church. If it had not been so, Brethren Service would have been liquidated and its residuum handed back to the Christian Education Commission. As it is, we have two commissions—the older (Christian Education) with an approved budget of $84,000 (including $12,000 for special college relief), and the newer (service) with an approved budget of $250,000.

It would be hazardous to predict whether relief and reconstruction, with social education and action, are to remain a normal part of the Church's program. Relief and rehabilitation are corrective. There is no such thing as political education without specifying evils and abuses, not incidentally but constantly and insistently. It is loosely said that the older nonresistance was a negative approach, but in reality the exact opposite is true. The term *pacifist* has been praised as positive, for the pacifist seeks to permeate all society with his principle of active goodwill. But in actual practice those pacifists who have tried it have either found themselves in the midst of the unholy strife of the world or have more or less consciously resumed nonresistant ground.

Emergencies do occur continually, and the abnormal is always present in the world. It is possible that, with the increasing militarization and debasement of society which some think they see coming in the twentieth century, the service emphasis might become a primary one in the Church —as it has been in the last decade. Then the Church would become, in effect, an "Order of Christian Humanitarian Service."

# Chapter 27

# NONCONFORMITY AND THE DRESS QUESTION

*WHEREAS, The principle of non-conformity in giving form to our costume, as well as in everything else, has been a peculiar characteristic of our fraternity, and is so stated in our written history, and has had its influence with our non-swearing, and non-combatant, and our general principles identifying our fraternity with the primitive and apostolic church in preserving us from the extravagant expenditures which both the religious and secular world have fallen into, and in obtaining for us as a body the characters of simple honesty, purity, and uprightness in the world; . . .*

*Resolved, First, that we will labor in the spirit of the gospel and in brotherly love to maintain the principle of non-conformity in giving form to our costume, and in every way that the recognized peculiarities of our fraternity require.*
*—From the Minutes of Annual Meeting of 1880, Article 23.*

We have sought to trace the results of Elder Henry Kurtz's belief that he could use the devices of the Industrial Revolution to overcome the effects of the revolutionary geographical upheaval. From that conviction there came, besides the Church press, a threefold development: Church schools, organized missions, and organized Brethren Service. Elder Kurtz never saw the last-named agency, but he would have approved it.

But Elder Kurtz would have been disappointed with what has been done. We have pushed none of these lines of endeavor vigorously enough to realize its possibilities. And in some cases these activities have become ends in themselves. This particularly would displease him, for to him the entry into these endeavors was never merely humanitarianism or citizenship improvement; it was a means of serving the Church. He was vividly aware that the Christian's citizenship is in heaven.

There is another whole series of effects that were not in the plans of Elder Kurtz. These were the effects that the industrial society exerted upon the Church itself. A threefold action is also here discernible: (1) the challenge to the Church's vivid sense of nonconformity, apparent in relation to the distinctive form of dress; (2) the challenge to the twin principles of nonresistance and nonparticipation in war; and (3) the demand for professionalization of the ministry.

The first two decades of the present century saw the intensification of these items. The ethical teachings of Jesus were then coming to the fore within Protestantism in liberalism and the social gospel. Many Brethren became profusely apologetic for the aloof attitude and policies of the Church. The current reaction to the liberal trend has not at this date had much effect upon Brethren thought. We could come nearer to discerning the future of the Church of the Brethren if we knew the outcome of these struggles.

We now take up the earliest of the challenges—the challenge to the Church's sense of nonconformity. The most obvious phase of Brethren nonconformity was dress, or costume. The principle, however, was rooted within; it covered the whole of life: furniture, buildings, amusements, expenditures of every kind—in fact, all the details of living.

The clothing a person wears is an inseparable part of himself in society. Before the day of machine production man spent a larger percentage of his income on clothing. There was not then a great variety of things to buy. Clothing was largely made at home by the family. Both materials and style were largely matters of the tradition of the family or the social class, sometimes of the region. With the coming of industrialism, materials of dress were produced in factories, with frequent changes, and soon clothing was being designed and made in the shops and mills. This changed the design of garments. These things help us understand why the nineteenth century saw the real beginnings of the discussion about dress.

Prior to the age of industrialism, Europe had been dominated by certain prevailing types of clothing. Religion was a factor in determining these. Other factors were climate and materials available. Many a tribal or regional garb was designed by the bishop or monastic association that evangelized the area. Christian ideas of dress came from the practices of the ancient Orient and express Biblical ideas and the practices of the earliest Christian Church.

That is why every tribal costume of western Europe makes provision for the primitive Christian teaching concerning women having their heads covered in worship (1 Corinthians 11:1-16). Among the Teutonic peoples of middle Europe, a white cap or hoodlike headpiece was the usual form. In other parts of Europe the color of the headdress was different (sometimes black) and among the Latin tribes instead of a cap-shaped headdress the flowing mantilla was the prevailing type. The mantilla is probably nearer the "veil" that Saint Paul wrote about in 1 Corinthians 11, as the sari of India today would testify. The Roman Catholic discipline came out of the Latin setting; so the nun today wears a mantillalike headdress. But the sister of the "plain people," who came out of middle and northern Europe, wears the white cap.

Commercial manufacturers of clothing knew little of Christian antiquities and cared less. Their designs were made to sell at the largest profit. They tickled the pride of the common people by copying court styles. The custom of women wearing hats goes back to the French court women of the late seventeenth and the eighteenth century. The hat was originally a masculine design. Certain influential women of the court chose to dress in masculine style. Shaving was originally a custom of the French court. The Bible was a book of bearded men. Shaving could not become general until industrialism developed good, cheap cutlery.

It has become commonplace among writers to say that Brethren adopted their early garb from the Quakers. This is true as far as it goes but it is only a part of the explanation. The Brethren and the eastern Mennonites did borrow certain specific features of their garb from the Quakers, but the early Friends themselves were from the same vein of thinking and historical background which naturally related dress to religion.

In the Orient a man's membership in any social group even today is shown by his dress. The commonest group criterion is religion. That sentiment was transplanted to western Europe and became indigenous. In medieval Europe there were norms of dress for the laity and for the clergy. Each religious order had its own uniform dress. The Reformation was largely a nationalistic movement and said little directly about dress. It eliminated classes, but it did not lift all to become priests, for moral laxity soon became so common that no man was a priest. This was the forecast of our contemporary secularism.

When zealous groups like the Quakers, Mennonites, and Brethren arose against the background of the Reformation emphasizing individual conversion and dedication, it was in effect a revival of the religious vocation. The primary business of each person was to witness to the truth of God, regardless of national or class consequences or family advantage. It would have been strange if these groups had overlooked costume.

Both Continental Anabaptists and English Friends began early to apply their witness against all forms of luxury, self-indulgence and worldliness to the subject of dress. The strict disciplinary party of Mennonites in the late seventeenth century decreed against the use of finery, including buttons. Buttons were then hand-carved, a species of jewelry worn by the extravagant. The substance used was bone—sometimes human bone. So the refusal to use buttons showed abhorrence of cruelty and bloodshed as well as aversion to luxury.

In 1668 George Fox expressed his concern about dress:

Away with your skimming-dish hats, and your unnecessary buttons on the top of your sleeves, shoulders, backs, and behind your coats and cloaks. . . . And away with your visors whereby you are not distinguished from bad women, and bare necks, and needless flying scarves like rollers on your back.[1]

Ten years previously Fox had written a "warning to all the merchants in London and such as buy and sell, with an advertisement to them to lay aside their superfluity and with it to nourish the poor."[2]

Very early the question of color entered Quaker discussions. The adoption of gray as the badge of Quaker plainness came only gradually.[3] In its inception it was a protest against expensive, luxuriously dyed and finished cloth. Later the motivation became uniformity.

By the early decades of the eighteenth century the plain coat and the broad-brimmed hat had become fixed for the male Friend. The woman wore the bonnet with a crown. The shawl was not distinctive until the wearing of coats by women became so general that the religious groups wearing the shawl found themselves different from others.

Among Brethren, color never assumed the importance that it did for Quakers and some Mennonites. There were protests, however, as for instance the strong stand against black as an expensive and fashionable cloth by David Murray in the *Vindicator* for March 15, 1871.[4] Gray or other "lindsey" colors were variegated and much more easily done. In Dunker tradition, while there was a leaning to somber colors, it was never enforced by discipline. The stronger feeling was against several colors at one time. This is now exemplified among the Old Order Brethren, among whom a sister has the liberty to pick the color of her costume, as long as it is the same color

[1] Sidney Lucas, *The Quaker Story.* Page 56.
[2] Braithwaite, *The Beginnings of Quakerism.* Page 523.
[3] See Braithwaite, *The Second Period of Quakerism,* pages 515 and 516. A detailed account of Quaker dress regulations for men and women may be found on pages 512-514.
[4] Volume 2, pages 46 and 47.

from neck line to skirt hem.There is something in the Pennsylvania Dutch temperament that loves bright colors, and the
Brethren Yearly Meeting never forbade them.

There is one unusual thing about the Quaker garb; the
Quakers never insisted on the wearing of the beard. George
Fox had a hairless face. The Quakers came from the upper
class and were accustomed to shaving. It was different with the
Brethren. Among the Pennsylvania Germans the frivolous
custom of shaving never was countenanced by religious people.
When Christopher Sauer was arrested on May 25, 1778, his
persecutors deprived him of his broad-brimmed hat, his beard,
and his hair—marks of his religious profession. They inflicted
upon him not only physical suffering but the anguish of shame.

There were numerous items in the Brethren's minutes
advising both sexes regarding the proper and decent care of the
hair. The plain brother  was to have his hair moderately long.
The "blocked" haircut still prevails in some quarters.[5] Home
haircuts needed to be simple in style, and a closely clipped skull
would hardly fit with a flowing beard. It is possible that the
custom of wearing the hair long goes back to the Quakers who
were long-haired Royalists.

There has always been a taboo among Brethren against
the wearing of a mustache without a beard. The mustache was
permitted when it was worn as a part of the beard. But the
preferred custom of both Dunker and Mennonite has been a
beard with a shaven upper lip. There is no evidence that the
fraternal kiss as a Church rite had anything to do with this.
The mustache was a symbol of the army officer caste, and to
peace people represented one of the most abhorred occupations.
The brother could wear a full beard; he could be of shaven
face: or he might be bearded with shaven upper lip.

It is now apparent that the Brethren's plain dress was not
a late innovation, as some superficially hold. The thing that is

---

[5] Reference to the "apple butter crock" haircut is a jest, and one that is
of questionable taste.

late (i. e., of the nineteenth century) is the challenge of the times to the practice of plainness and to the philosophy of separation from the world. This challenge produced an intensive discussion of the garb and the idea underlying it. Many have mistaken this as the beginning of the plain dress itself.

Testimonies from the eighteenth century are not lacking. Morgan Edwards, our recorder from the days of the American Revolution, says: "They use great plainness of language and dress, like the Quakers . . . . They commonly wear their beards."[6]

The first historian of Pennsylvania, Robert Proud, wrote between the years 1776 and 1780:

Those people in Pennsylvania, called Dunkards, Tunkers, or Dumplers, are another species of German Baptists. They are singular in some of their opinions and customs; and perhaps more so in their manner of living, and personal appearance, than any others of that nature in the province.[7]

Speaking of the Dunker view of the Christian life as a way of piety, good works, and obedience to the commandments of Christ, Gillin observes:

This position naturally includes the Dunker doctrine of simplicity of life, especially of dress. . . .

The insistence of the Dunkers on plain dress is, in part, attributable to their doctrine of the gospel as the law of the Christian life (I Tim. 2:9, I Pet. 3:3). In part it is to be explained by their imitation of the sects that had preceded them. But, more profoundly, it was due to their feeling of unlikeness to the people that formed the membership of the tolerated churches. On the part of the learned and great, it was a period of elegance and over refinement in dress. Ordinary people could not afford to dress in the prevailing expensive fashion. They naturally felt that when wrong views of religion and ethics and a taste for fine clothes were combined in the same persons, especially when those persons were their persecutors, the elegant apparel must be as wrong as the immorality and the persecuting spirit.[8]

---

[6] Quoted from Brumbaugh, *History of the German Baptist Brethren.* Page 526.

[7] Brumbaugh, *op. cit.* Pages 523 and 524.

[8] Gillin, *The Dunkers.* Pages 30, 42-45.

The earliest known discussion of dress with Brethren connections is that in the *Ephrata Chronicle*.[9] Describing events immediately following 1732, it is stated that although the superintendent lived like the Mennonites in simplicity and lowliness of life, some of his followers with Quaker background dressed him like a Quaker, and this became the special garb of the Solitary Brethren. It is implied that Mennonite clothing was fashioned on the poorest scale, while that of the (English) Quakers was more sophisticated. This, however, did not cause the superintendent to abandon his most rigorous disciplines. On pages 88-90 of the *Chronicle* the dress of both sexes is described in some detail.

The term, "conformity to the world," later much used in relation to dress, occurs in the Yearly Meeting minutes of 1791. But 1804 brings the first specific mention of garb in the minutes. Article 5 advises against ordaining as a bishop a brother who shaves his beard. Article 9 says:

Concerning the evil which grieves God and the angels in heaven, and also the faithful souls on earth, namely, the new fashions which are in vogue in the world, and also here and there are believers who gratify too much the lust of the eye (Num. 15: 39), and conforming therein themselves to the world; . . . therefore

It has been unanimously deemed good that the bishops and ministers, as also all fathers and mothers of families, should use all diligence to counteract such things that they might spread no further, but rather be put out of the way; especially when persons desire to be received [into the church] it should be laid before them, that such things are contrary to the wholesome doctrine, and that it is their duty to deny themselves; and when they are willing to lay them aside, then they may be baptized in hope, that they will permit themselves to be further instructed. . . .[10]

Dress was here viewed as a family as well as a personal problem. One wonders whether the instruction here mentioned in receiving members was practiced prior to this date, as it certainly was throughout the nineteenth century.

---

[9] *Ephrata Chronicle.* Pages 54 and 55.
[10] Brumbaugh, *op. cit.* Pages 243f.

# Chapter 28

# THE DRESS QUESTION AFTER 1804

Documentation on the story of garb among the Brethren is practically endless after 1804. There was no complete agreement; variations developed in various parts of the country. Some were liberal, some conservative. This difference brought extensive discussions and frequent rulings from Annual Conference.

The first period following 1804 extends to the chronological dividing point of 1851. This period of a little over a generation—practically a half century—may be designated as the period of axiomatic acceptance and gradual challenge. The writings of Henry Kurtz mirror the status of the fraternity's faith and practice in regard to nonconformity at the midpoint in the nineteenth century.

The period from the midcentury to the schism—1851 to 1881-1882—is the period of sharp challenge of the garb. Issues became pronounced and feeling tense.

In the division, the Progressive group threw off all allegiance to the distinctive garb, and despite their reversion to conservative theology they have never revived any interest in it. The Old Order Brethren, on the other hand, reasserted the garb irrevocably and today (1950) are its exemplars. They have been consistent in their position and have prospered therein.

We are following the largest group, the Moderates, or Conservatives (later called the Church of the Brethren), for whom the schism set no new direction.

Annual Conference condemned the extremes represented by the Progressives and the Old Orders and proceeded on its middle course. Approximately two generations have passed since that date; they may be designated the period of gradual abandonment of the garb. It divides rather evenly at the St. Joseph Conference of 1911.

### The Period of Axiomatic Acceptance and Gradual Challenge (1804-1851)

Thirteen years passed after 1804 until the dress question was again brought to the Yearly Meeting. In 1817 we find:

Art. 2. Concerning conformity to the world in wearing fashionable clothing and everything that is high, without exception,

It was considered, that when a member should therein be found guilty, he should be admonished; and if the admonition would not be heeded, we could not hold such in full fellowship, . . .

Five years later:

It was considered, for the third time in the great council, that when a member has been admonished in love once and again, we would not break bread with such. . . . Also such who permit those high fashions in their children who are yet under their control, and especially the bishops and ministers in the church should be examples of the flock.[1]

A query appeared again in 1834 and received a sharp answer. Others came in 1837 and 1840, again in 1845, 1847, 1848, and 1849. The impact of industrialism was beginning to be felt in relation to garb.

In the first issue of the *Gospel Visitor,* Elder Henry Kurtz began a series of extensive editorials on "The Fraternity of German Baptists." His first article dealt at length with nonconformity and represents well the attitude of the Church in his time. "The third principle, which the Brethren hold to be of primary importance, and requisite for every member to study and observe, is—Humility, and Non-conformity to the world."[2]

---

[1] Minutes, 1822, Article 8.
[2] *Gospel Visitor,* June 1851. Page 37. The discussion proceeds on succeeding pages and in the issues for July, August, and September.

The article proceeds at length to emphasize humility, deprecate pride, and contrast the world and the Church. On this point he observes:

No true church ever fell into lasting decay, while it maintained that contrast, which the scriptures inculcate, to be necessarily existing between the church and the world, and while it continued to observe the apostolic injunction, Be not conformed to this world.

He enlarges upon the matter of nonconformity and the objections thereto. Then he raises the question of how far nonconformity is to extend and brings up such scriptures as Philippians 4:8; Ephesians 5:12; and 1 Corinthians 11:1.

In like manner, our old brethren, that have gone before us, did not bind heavy burdens, and grievous to be borne, and lay them on men's shoulders, as the Pharisees of old did . . . neither did they make a law or rule for others, of what they deemed their own duty in the practice of the principle, we have had under consideration, leaving it altogether to the teachings of the Holy Spirit and to the power of the truth and to the free will and option of every individual member, how far they felt themselves called to follow in this practice, and never taking under dealings, as far as we could learn, any member for shortcomings in this practice, unless it was connected with a gross violation of the principle itself; only teaching and exhorting their fellow-members, to live and act consistent with their professed principles, to which all had given their free and full assent, when received into the communion of the church, and so far from exercising an illiberal spirit in this matter, the obvious difference of appearance in our members generally proves the very contrary to be the fact, and that the danger [lies] rather on the other side. To guard us from this danger, and in conformity with the apostolic doctrine, methinks, we hear the voice of our ancient, faithful brethren from their very graves, all with one accord, saying with the apostle, Those things, which ye have both learned, and received, and heard, and seen in us, as we tried to follow Christ, do, and the God of peace shall be with you. Amen.

The Brethren felt themselves a separated people, even to the details of their daily lives. And a fashion of dressing set by the Church group was not felt to be a burden, except to him who was weak in faith. There had been enforcement; with the dreaded penalty of excommunication, but it was felt that for the most part the very logic and reasonableness of nonconformity would persuade the sincere. Hence the action on a query of 1849:

Art. 25. Whether it would not be agreeable to the gospel, to advise those members, who have been in the church two or three years, and are still conformed to this world, not to come to communion until they deny themselves, and become transformed from the world, after being admonished thereto?

Considered, that conforming to the world presents itself in such varied ways, that we cannot erect a standard in regard to it, so as to authorize the church to prohibit such members from partaking of the communion; but such members should be admonished and reproved by the church, again and again.[3]

This confidence that nonconformity was an eminently rational thing represented the high spiritual ground of the leaders, but the rank and file of mankind does not always respond to the highest and clearest reasoning.

### The Period of Sharp Challenge (1851-1882)

This was a period in which industrialization was proceeding and wealth was increasing phenomenally. The challenge to simplicity and abstemiousness became extreme. Everywhere around the Brethren, self-indulgence and conspicuous consumption were increasing. Since the Brethren shared in the increasing wealth, it was indeed hard to restrain the "weaker" members from that which the majority felt was worldly.

Consequently there was a great increase of queries to Yearly Meeting. The queries produced hours of intense discussion. The entire fraternity was embroiled in it, including almost every congregation and preacher. The subject of dress became emotionalized. Ingenious arguments were developed for and against the distinctive costume. It was an age in which everything was in transition. The conservative temperament was filled with terror and tended to clutch familiar landmarks with a sevenfold tenacity lest the faith itself slip.

---

[3] Minutes, 1849, Article 25.

The agitation may be felt in H. R. Holsinger's account from the viewpoint of the Progressive faction, of which he became the leader. In his history[4] he satirizes the incompetence of the elders who held the authority of the Church in their grasp, and charges them with counting order in dress more important in the ordaining of elders than ability and piety. A man "with short hair or store-bought garments and a worldly education with a godly life and holy conversation" had no chance. Controversies became bitter, "until, sad to say, Christian affection and brotherly love were strangers in the camp of Israel."

In 1853 there was one query on dress, and one on the beard; in 1854, another beard query; in 1857, one on garb; in 1858, three on garb. Two Yearly Meetings were then free of queries on attire. Then from 1861 until 1881, there was only a single year (1865) when the dress question was not on the floor of the meeting. Altogether, those twenty years saw forty-six queries directly on dress, besides eleven others involving procedures of discipline, most of which arose out of dress problems.

One result of this prolonged discussion was that the Dunker garb became more defined and standardized. For example, Article 47, 1866 (which was re-enacted verbatim in 1893):

Resolved, by this Annual Meeting, that the churches throughout the brotherhood enforce plainness of dress, and a plain manner of wearing the hair and beard, upon the preachers and officers of the churches. By plainness of dress, we mean the common order of giving shape to dress, as practiced by the old brethren and sisters generally, and by plainness of hair we mean the hair parted on the top of the head, or all combed back in a plain manner, or combed straight down all around the head, and not having the hair and beard trimmed according to the custom of the world.

Considered, that this Annual Meeting unanimously adopt this reso-

---

[4] H. R. Holsinger, *History of the Tunkers and the Brethren Church.* Pages 473-478.

lution, according to Rom. 12: 2; 1 Peter 1: 14; 1 John 2: 15-16; and that all preachers and officers that follow the fashions of the world in the foregoing particulars, violate the order of the gospel by doing so, and render themselves liable to be brought under the counsel of the church.

That Annual Meeting refused to specify whether the coat should have a rolling or a standing collar,[5] but the next year another query came:

IX. We petition Annual Meeting to reconsider Art. 11, of 1876, and so amend its answer that it make the standing collar on the coat the old order recognized by the Brethren.

Answer: This Annual Meeting reconsiders the above article and grants the request.

From this time on the plain coat was of one preferred kind.

But sharpness of tone and tenseness of feeling increased with the years. Congregations began to defy the authority of committees sent by the Annual Meeting.[6] A charge of political manipulation and falsification of records was made against the Standing Committee of 1876. The Committee of 1877 vindicated its predecessor but had to admit the muddle-headedness of its clerk.

A group of fourteen elders from the Miami Valley presented a petition to the 1880 Annual Meeting through the district meeting of Southern Ohio. It specified the innovations that had crept into Church life after 1851, together with disregard of nonconformity:

The causes of the troubles . . . the high schools [7] among us, popular Sunday schools, with their conventions and celebrations, long protracted meetings and the way they are generally conducted by singing revival hymns and giving invitations to rise or come forward; a salaried ministry, and the single-mode of feet-washing.[8]

---

[5] There have been three types of "plain coat"; (a) one which buttons completely up the neck and then has a small lapel-collar turned over; (b) the so-called "college coat," which is entirely without collar but resembles a buttoned sweater; and (c) the one with a standing collar.

[6] Minutes of 1876, Article 26; 1877, Article 33; 1878, addendum; 1880, addendum.

[7] A protest against Church ownership of schools.

[8] Minutes, 1880, Article 23.

These elders had presented their dissatisfaction legally but were given a temporizing answer; so naturally they withdrew.

An Annual Meeting committee was sent to the Berlin, Pennsylvania, church, but, under the leadership of Elder H. R. Holsinger, the church refused to accept the procedure set up by the committee. The Meeting of 1882 disfellowshipped the elder and warned the church, but lacked the power of discipline.[9]

The "sharp challenge" thus issued in three groups of Brethren, each company going as it felt it must under the guidance of God's Word and Spirit.

## From the Schism to the St. Joseph Conference Dress Report (1882-1911)

This generation in theory held tenaciously to the distinctive garb as the best method of exemplifying the principle of nonconformity. There was a great deal of discussion in the period over principles and methods. Principles were held to be of divine authority and methods were recognized as subject to change. Yet methods were held to be no mere whims or nonessentials; they were counted important. The garb was held to be the best method of exemplifying plainness and simplicity.

The Church, especially its leadership, was strong for the garb. The schism had taken out those to whom it was distasteful. It had also taken those who would impose it under penalty of excommunication. The moderates who were left were conservative as to the garb but unwilling to make it a legal matter, subject to compulsion. They wanted to rely upon moral suasion as had been done earlier in the nineteenth century. But they had to reckon with an environment that was rapidly changing.

Cloth was no longer made at home. Sewing was rapidly being transferred to shops. Money was flowing with greater

---

[*] Minutes, 1880, Article 23.

**A Brethren Couple, Dressed According to the Mode of Their Time**

The attire and personal appearance of Elder and Sister
Daniel P. Sayler were typical of the accepted mode during
the nineteenth and early twentieth centuries.

ease, and the ready-made-clothing industry was making an ever-greater variety of articles for sale.

The influence of industrialism is well illustrated by the decision to allow brethren to wear caps. In 1887, upon request from the Elkhart church in Northern Indiana, the decision of 1849 was repealed, and brethren were permitted to wear caps in cases of necessity. The *Full Report of the Minutes of Annual Conference* gives a lengthy and confusing discussion

**Typical Brethren Attire, Late Nineteenth and Early Twentieth Centuries**

Pictured here, left to right, are Elder I. W. Taylor, Elder S. H. Hertzler, and Elder J. H. Longenecker.

of this issue.[10] The next year the discussion was continued.[11] The confusion seems to have had in its background the fact that wearing the broad-brimmed hat was a time-honored custom, but no one remembered the reason for it. Now the machine age had brought the cheap and serviceable (and ugly!) man's cap within reach of everyone. Utility took precedence over tradition and sentiment.

Some dress irregularities were recognized by the 1898 Conference. The Standing Committee of that year drew up a rather comprehensive statement:

The *brethren* likewise should dress themselves in plain attire, not wearing fashionable hats and neckties, gold for ornament or other superfluities.

Inconsistency exists to some slight extent, resulting from a violation of the decisions of Annual Meeting. Upon examination seventy-four decisions covering the various phases of non-conformity to the world in dress and in adorning the body are found on our Minutes. . . . The fault lies in our practice. . . . More decisions will not remove the inconsistency. . . . But a more intelligent understanding of the important gospel principles of non-conformity to the world, plain dressing and plain living is what is needed.[12]

The situation had not materially altered by 1909, when two papers came to Conference complaining of confusion on the dress question. In response to these papers it was decided to appoint "a committee of seven faithful, intelligent, conservative brethren." Instructions given to the committee were:

. . . to examine carefully and exhaustively the scriptural ground on the subject of Christian attire, that the practice of the primitive church be investigated and the position and teaching of our own church fathers and the Minutes of our Conference be examined, with a view of giving us a clear, concise restatement of our position on this vexed question, so that all may understand alike and be unified and dwell together as becometh children of the family of God—in love and peace and harmony.

Pending the report of this committee, the matter was not

---

[10] *Full Report,* 1887, Article 9.
[11] *Full Report,* 1889, page 100, Article 12.
[12] Minutes, 1898, Article 3.

to be discussed in the *Messenger,* but people were to communicate their concerns to the committee, and leaders in the churches were to teach earnestly the scriptural doctrine of plain dressing and plain living.

The committee appointed was: D. L. Miller, L. W. Teeter, Daniel Hays, A. C. Wieand, L. T. Holsinger, B. E. Kesler, G. W. Lentz.[13]

This was the beginning of the St. Joseph dress decision.

The next year, 1910, the committee submitted an excellent report which approved the substance of all that was in the minute book.[14] But Conference was not satisfied. It adopted the report and appointed a new committee of five "to take the whole matter under advisement and to make a restatement." The new committee was H. C. Early, John Heckman, Galen B. Royer, C. D. Bonsack, and J. W. Lear. This committee submitted its report to the St. Joseph, Missouri, Conference the next year. It is a classic in the whole literature of this phase of the "plain people's" thinking. Reason, Scripture, Brethren tradition, and early Christian tradition are all skillfully woven into the brief yet thorough treatises of 1910 and 1911 on the dress question. The 1911 paper differed from that of 1910 in prescribing the essentials of a uniform garb. It closed with the provision: "Upon the final adopting of this report it shall supersede all else in the Minutes on the subject of dress." What a reduction in the size of the minute book!

## Today (1911-1950)

Speaking for the generation since 1911, one cannot but ask, "What happened?" Some of the staunch elders who served on the committees of 1910 and 1911 have expressed great amazement and grief over the course of events. They intended their reports to be guides and educational directives, and never wanted to encourage abandonment of the distinctive costume.

---

[13] Minutes, 1909, Article 5.
[14] Minutes, 1910, Article 5.

The reports affected the trend not so much by what they said as by what they did *not* say. The real question in the minds of the restless minority of 1911 was "Is the garb necessary?" This question had been in the minds of some since 1882. The St. Joseph decision recommended the garb but failed to say simply and clearly that he who would not wear it was to be cut off from the fellowship. That had really been the official position of the Church, but the appeal to reason had evidently lost its power. About 1918-1921, it began to be apparent what was happening: the distinctive garb was fast disappearing. Dismay registered itself in a small schism, the Dunker Brethren Church, in 1926. Elder B. E. Kesler was its leader.

Today some who helped break down the garb in the twenties and thirties sincerely wonder what they did. It was eloquently argued in those days that the peculiarity of God's people was to be in manner of life and in zeal for missions, educational endeavor, and the like, and such things were independent of a form of dress.

Two things contributed to the direction. Many of our younger ministers and leaders took training in Yale, Crozer, the University of Chicago, and elsewhere, and got the optimistic outlook upon contemporary society. They became convinced that it was the business of the Church to transform society. They saw the tradition of nonconformity as a barrier, not against the evils of society, but against participation in society. They thus became indifferent and even hostile to the symbols of nonconformity. The spirit of H. R. Holsinger now expressed itself in the learned English of the classroom.

The second factor was the arrival of the automobile on the crest of the flood of wealth following World War I. It shifted peoples' consuming and spending habits. Someone wittily put it this way: "The Dunker elder bought an automobile and stepped on the gas; out of the window went his broadbrim, followed by his wife's bonnet, followed by his whiskers."

Conspicuous consumption transferred to automobiles. It had been said that the workingman's wife could not afford to keep up with the styles, which changed two to four times a year. But presently the workingman himself wanted a new car every two to four years because the styles of cars had changed! The argument against the expensive hat lost its relevance when the man spent twenty to thirty times the cost of the most expensive hat—for a pile of tin and iron on wheels.

Some of us have thought that with the greatly increased material prosperity of America there was more need than ever for a visible symbol and witness to the place of simplicity. The picture the world holds of a Dunker is a patriarchal-looking individual attired in plain garb with a beard and a serene, benevolent face. Beside him, the sister is attired in a bonnet and mayhap a shawl, with a sweet, kindly face of peace. We could wish that that image would never be erased.

Even in 1950 there walk among us individuals and surviving companies who are living witnesses of nonconformity to the world. Their presence is a blessing, for it is a reminder of dedication to God.

# Chapter 29

# WAR AND CHRISTIAN NONCONFORMITY

The Quakers became models for the "plain people" in regard to peace as well as dress.[1]

William Penn had planned to set up the Christian State. With boundless optimism he believed that such a State would be as a light to the world. But before he died (1718) difficulties had begun for him in administering the colony. He has not recorded what he thought as these difficulties mounted in his later years.

Penn thought that the pious Germans of the Rhine country were a population made to order to help him establish his ideal Christian commonwealth. And indeed they were. They helped him greatly.

The passage of the years saw two parties develop in colonial Pennsylvania—the religious and the nonreligious or secularist. The religious party (Quaker) represented those who carried on the "holy experiment." These held an ethical, religious interpretation of life. From Penn the leadership in his idealistic theocracy passed to the earnest section of the Society of Friends.

There were others—some Quakers among them—who were not in sympathy with this idealistic pattern. They wanted to operate Pennsylvania on the usual lines of worldly States.

. . . The Quaker government came under severe criticism by various governors of Pennsylvania and many other colonists because of its refusal to sponsor military measures to protect the inhabitants from

---

[1] The history of the Brethren in relation to peace is best told by Rufus D. Bowman in his book, *The Church of the Brethren and War, 1708-1941*.

the Indians. On January 10, 1740, Governor Thomas addressed the Assembly of Pennsylvania in the following way:

"I must lament the unhappy circumstances of a country, populous indeed, extensive in its trade, blessed with many natural advantages, and capable of defending itself; but from a religious principle of its Representatives against bearing of arms, subject to become the prey of the first invader, and more particularly of its powerful neighbors, who are known to be well armed, regular in their discipline, inured to fatigue, and from thence capable of making long marches, in alliance with many nations of Indians, and of a boundless ambition."

Governor Thomas made a stirring appeal for the defense of the province. From this time (1740) until the Quakers lost control of the government in 1756, there was trouble between the governors and the Quaker Assembly. Many people wanted a change of government. There were loud demands for severe measures against the Indians. Benjamin Franklin and many other outstanding citizens were critical of the Quaker Assembly. How did the Quakers, who represented a minority in the province, keep a majority in the legislature for so long? This was accomplished through the aid of the Germans. And the publications of Christopher Sower were the leading influence among them. It is probably true that the German publisher held the balance of power at least for a few years.

Dr. William Smith, who later became provost of the University of Pennsylvania, estimated the inhabitants of Pennsylvania at 220,000, of whom one half were Germans, and about 40,000 Quakers. Isaac Sharpless, Quaker historian, indicates that the Quakers stood in power through the influence of Christopher Sower and his publications. William Beidelman wrote: "Sower's German paper was the only German newspaper circulated among the Germans for many years, and it controlled their political action throughout." William Smith stated: "The Germans, who had hitherto been peaceful without meddling in elections, came down in shoals, and carried all before them. Near 1800 of them voted in the county of Philadelphia which threw the balance on the side of the Quakers; who having found out this secret, have ever since excluded all other persuasions from the Assembly, constantly calling in the Germans to their aid, by means of this printer." This was the election of 1744.

One can easily see how criticism developed against the Germans and especially against Christopher Sower. The people clamoring for a change of government saw that the Germans were standing in the way of that change. The people who wanted war with the Indians saw that the Germans were supporting the Quakers because they desired peace. . . .[2]

Benjamin Franklin proceeded to bypass the Assembly by organizing a voluntary association for military defense. He called in the aid of religion and proposed fasting and imploring the blessing of Heaven on the undertaking. He drew up a statement and had it translated into German for circulation throughout the province. He called attention to the ways in which the Quaker-controlled Assembly was breaking down under the embarrassments of civil administration.[3]

The election of 1756 was a crucial one. Christopher Sower printed a broadside addressed to the Germans. The Germans responded and came to the polls in great numbers. The Quakers won twenty-eight out of thirty-six Assembly seats. But in the spring of 1756, when the governor declared war against the French and the Indians, the Quakers resigned their seats. Thus ended the Quaker control.[4]

Here began a century of nonparticipation in government for both Quakers and Brethren. To most of the present generation of Brethren such aloofness seems remote and unrealistic. But it needs only to be realized that as voting has increased and emphasis upon the garb has lessened in recent times, the old aversion toward military service has softened and made way for tolerance of military participation. There is a direct relationship between participation in government and participation in military service.

In monarchical Europe the question of participation in government—and the attempt at directing society—did not occur. Only in the New World with its theory of democratic participation could the question be raised. The "godly" never had a better opportunity to try to mold society directly (in contrast to the indirect method of personal witness and peace-

---

[2] Rufus D. Bowman, *op. cit.* Pages 87-89.
[3] See *Autobiography of Benjamin Franklin*, pages 125-132.
[4] See Bowman, *op. cit.*, pages 90-91.

able teaching) than in eighteenth-century Pennsylvania. And that effort ended in nonparticipation.

At least by 1848—and perhaps for many years before that date—each applicant for Brethren membership was required to state his acceptance of nonresistance. The Brethren were united against bearing arms. This was tied in with nonparticipation in government. A quotation from the diary of John Kline in 1862 makes this clear:

FRIDAY, December 20. Write to John Hopkins, to John C. Woodson, and to Charles Lewis. I can but entreat these men to stand in defense of our Brethren, and try to devise some plan by which they can be exempted from the necessity of bearing arms. I feel sure that if we can be rightly understood as to our faith and life, there will be some way provided for their exemption. The Brotherhood is a unit, heart and hand against arms-bearing. These things I made known to these men; not, however, in any spirit of defiance, but in the spirit of meekness and obedience to what we in heart believe to be the will of the Lord. Many have already expressed to me their determination to flee from their homes rather than disobey God.[5]

So strong were the convictions on this matter that when Dr. Henry Geiger of Philadelphia decided to enter the medical division of the army, he felt that he had to resign both his ministry and his membership in the Church. Here is his letter to the First church of Philadelphia:

John Fox
Christian Custer        Elders of German Baptist Church

Being about to engage in the service of our country and thus violate the rules of our church, I respectfully beg leave to offer my resignation as a member. Be so kind as to receive in behalf of yourselves and the members generally my grateful thanks for the past kindness and allow me to remain

Very truly yours,
H. Geiger

Philadelphia, June 27, 1863[6]

The letter was accepted by the church after two separate readings and some serious discussion.

---

[5] Benjamin Funk, *Life and Labors of John Kline.* Page 446.
[6] Quoted by Bowman, *op. cit.* Page 117.

## A minute from the Annual Meeting of 1864 reads:

Art. 35. As our national troubles, consequent upon the rebellion now existing in our country, have caused considerable difficulty in our church, and have tried our non-resistant principles, and have caused several questions concerning the paying of bounty-money, voting, etc., to come before this council-meeting, what counsel will this Annual Meeting give upon these subjects?

Answer: We exhort the brethren to steadfastness in the faith, and believe that the times in which our lots are cast strongly demand of us a strict adherence to all our principles, and especially to our non-resistant principle, a principle dear to every subject of the Prince of Peace, and a prominent doctrine of our fraternity, and to endure whatever sufferings and to make whatever sacrifice the maintaining of the principle may require, and not to encourage in any way the practice of war. And we think it more in accordance with our principles, that instead of paying bounty-money, and especially in taking an active part in raising bounty-money, to await the demands of the government, whether general, state, or local, and pay the fines and taxes required of us, as the gospel permits, and, indeed, requires. Matt. 22: 21; Rom. 13: 7. And lest the position we have taken upon political matters in general, and war matters in particular, should seem to make us, as a body, appear to be indifferent to our government, or in opposition thereto, in its efforts to suppress the rebellion, we hereby declare that it has our sympathies and our prayers, and that it shall have our aid in any way which does not conflict with the principles of the gospel of Christ. But since, in our Christian profession, we regard these gospel principles as superior or paramount to all others, consistency requires that we so regard them in our practices.

The stand against the bearing of arms brought troubles. Individual Brethren met the strain in various ways. Some went to prison. Many paid financial penalties, in both the North and the South. Some suffered persecution, even loss of life. Many fled to the sparsely settled parts of the country in Ohio and Indiana.

## Stonewall Jackson testified:

There lives a people in the Valley of Virginia that are not hard to bring to the army. While there they are obedient to their officers. Nor is it difficult to have them take aim, but it is impossible to get them to take correct aim. I, therefore, think it better to leave them at their homes that they may produce supplies for the army.[7]

Some historians count the Spanish American War to be the point of decisive direction in American history. By some ironical twist of circumstances there is no mention of this war in the minutes of Annual Meeting.

Since then we have passed through two world wars. A voluminous amount of written material has emerged from this era. One is impressed by the constant complaint that the Church was not prepared for its trials. Take for instance the one discussed by Bowman on page 189 of his book:

The decisions of the Goshen Conference may have helped some Brethren boys to stand more firmly for their peace convictions, but the Conference actions came too late to change the tide toward service in the army. The official position of the Church of the Brethren was against non-combatant service but the functioning position was in favor of it. Some of the leaders of the church took it for granted that a member of the church would not fight, but they failed to realize that something had happened to their people. The young people had not been taught the peace principle. At least they had not been placed in an educational setting where through stimulating discussions they would think through the problem of war. Many of them were not prepared to withstand the pressure of the army officials.[8]

The complaint continues to this hour. But the complaint itself needs criticism. First, we should realize that there is no such thing as preparing completely beforehand for trials and emergencies. Only general preparation of mind and spirit is possible. A fraternity engaged in a transformation or cultural adaptation in relation to its environing society is necessarily unprepared to take a nonconformist position. That was our dilemma in World War I. Yet we emerged (but hardly triumphantly) as one of Christendom's "historic peace churches."

---

[7] Quoted by Bowman, *op. cit.* Page 118. Among the writer's childhood memories is the venerable "Uncle John" Trackler. His parents were Brethren, but he served three years in the Union army. Later in his old age he found consolation in the fact that he had always aimed his musket low and thus had never killed anyone in his soldier days.

[8] Bowman, *op. cit.* Page 189.

In the second place, specific and effective protests can hardly be made in advance of the demands. This was stated clearly in a *Gospel Messenger* article by H. C. Early, who was then moderator of Annual Conference:

> . . . the government shall first state what it demands of us, and then it is our duty to say whether or not we will accept it. It is hardly to be expected of the church to say what she will and will not do, previous to a statement of what the government defines as non-combatant duties. This is the reason, as I see it, why the church has not, up to this time, declared herself.[9]

The wearing of the uniform became an issue in World War I. W. J. Swigart, camp visitor, is reported as saying:

> "Those who stand firm from the start fare the best. Our brethren will simply have to choose between war and the church, . . . It is now plainly evident that the only safe thing to do is as the church urges, and that is, not to uniform. After they uniform, which is the symbol of war, it is hard to take a stand, and refuse what has been required of them."[10]

The Goshen special Conference in January 1918 made one of the most magnificent statements of the Brethren peace position ever penned. The anticlimax came in the panic of the Church leaders when the government threatened prosecution because of certain clauses in the statement. It is certain that, if such persecution had descended, our outlook now in 1950 would be vastly different. As it turned out, the government scored by tactful handling of the issue.

The Church adopted a "social viewpoint." Brethren came to believe that society as a whole could be uplifted and, if not actually redeemed, lifted to near redemption. All that was thought to be needed to bring about this utopian dream was greater faithfulness and devotion on the part of God's people. Society would be transformed; wars would cease. This is the social optimism of liberal Protestantism.

Through the 1930's when the American peace movement

---

[9] *Gospel Messenger*, November 10, 1917.
[10] Bowman, *op. cit.* Page 188.

was running strong and there seemed to be hope that international peace would be realized, the Annual Meeting passed resolution after resolution. Some of these sound strange now.

The calamity of World War II came upon us. The familiar cry, "Unprepared," was heard. And "unprepared" the Church indeed was!

The special session of Standing Committee, called at Chicago in December 1940, made a magnificent statement and voted support of alternative civilian public service. Its testimony rang true. But the Church was a long way from the resignation of Dr. Henry Geiger in 1863. Witness the facts in this paragraph from the Brethren Service Committee's report to Annual Conference in 1945:

The Ministry to Servicemen seeks to bring the goodwill, encouragement, comfort, and guidance of the church to all men and women under Selective Service. A recent study shows there are 25,243 members and friends of the church either in service or recently released for various causes; 17,685 of these are regular members. These figures include 1A's, 1AO's, those in Civilian Public Service and women in all types of work, as WACS, WAVES and nurses. There are 1,424 1AO's; 1,386 in Civilian Public Service; 14 in prison; 600 women in service; 301 reported as missing; 589 deceased; and 1,162 discharged.

Yet the Church of the Brethren remains one of the "historic peace churches." The 1948 Conference at Colorado Springs attempted to be true to the historic faith.

Our understanding of the life and teachings of Christ as revealed in the New Testament led our Annual Conference of 1934 to resolve: "All war is sin." . . . The church is therefore increasingly committing itself to the prevention of war in addition to its historical position of refusing to participate in war. . . . This statement embodies the stage of thought and action which the church has thus far achieved . . . and pledges itself to be receptive to new truth and better modes of expression as these are brought to its attention.[11]

These are brave words, indeed. We trust they are inspired by the Holy Spirit. May they be realized in deed and in truth! But the facts must not be hidden. The apathy of the pews is

[11] Minutes, 1948.

disconcerting. The record of the Brethren in the C. P. S. camps is not heartening. Of the three historic peace churches (as of March 1, 1947) the smallest (the Friends) had contributed eight per cent of the men; the largest (the Brethren), eleven per cent; the other (the Mennonites), thirty per cent. This totals only fifty-eight per cent from what would normally be considered to be the best pacifist background. Clement Bontrager, in a forceful article,[12] gives warning that in two of the peace churches pacifism is slipping. One of these is the Church of the Brethren. We are bowing the knee to Mars. He cites a weak leadership and an undue emphasis on freedom of conscience as over against the plain teachings of Jesus in the Sermon on the Mount. He warns that we dare not rest on shifting sand or be conditioned by circumstances. Peace believers are germ-bearers of a new order and must stand on changeless truth, conditioned by eternity and the will of God.

---

[12] *Gospel Messenger,* June 7, 1947.

## Chapter 30

# THE MINISTRY AND THE INDUSTRIALIZED SOCIETY

The third and final phase of the unintended effects of the industrialized society was the transformation brought about in the position of the ministry. It is one of the most important—but least discussed—aspects of our Brethren Church life. The future of the Church depends upon the surmounting of the problems that arise out of the change from the free to the professional ministry.

We are using the term *professional* here to indicate the service rendered where monetary compensation is made. A professional man in this sense is one whose calling is his principal occupation and hence furnishes his livelihood. The learned professions once were few, but have been multiplied under the specialization of modern times. It is in this social situation that our ministry has been professionalized.

There is no record before 1860 of any Dunker minister being paid anything like a stipend, wage, or salary for his services as a minister. The following quotations from the summary of a Yearly Meeting sermon by Henry Kurtz, as given on pages 184-186 of John Kline's diary, indicate well the attitude and fears of the Church in this regard:

SUNDAY, May 11, 1845. Meeting to-day. John 7 is read. Brother Henry Kurtz spoke from the eighteenth verse. . . . He said: "These are the words of Jesus Christ, who knew what was in man. It becomes every minister who preaches the Word, to examine himself prayerfully, in the light of Holy Truth, to know certainly what impels him to the work. If, by such examination, he becomes assured that the love of Christ and for Christ lures him on, and that the salvation of souls and the consequent glory of the Lord is the beginning and the end of his motives, he can go on with heart and tongue, under the Lord's banner, defying the very gates of hell. But if the love of self and the love of the world enter as the chief elements of his power and will in the work, it would be better for him, better for the cause, and less dishonorable to the Lord if he would stop off short. . . .

"There is one feature particularly in the order of our ministry that I have always advocated, and expect by the grace of God to advocate to the last, and that is an *unsalaried* ministry. The world will say to me right here: 'You are working against your own interest. . . .' In answer to this I have to say that God never meant for the Gospel to be used as a means for getting water to the preacher's mill, or grain into his garner. When the Gospel is converted into merchandise, the preacher becomes a merchant, and like all other merchants it becomes his interest to handle his goods in a way that will please his customers, and put them in such shape and procure for them such kinds, whether good, bad, or indifferent, as will suit their fancies and please their tastes. 'The love of money is a root of all evil,' no less in the ministry than anywhere else. . . ."

The earliest Brethren looked to the New Testament for patterns in government and organization as well as in ethics and ordinances. They found the ministry there. Mack seems to have been influenced in regard to the ministry by Anabaptist views, through the Mennonites. Neither Brethren nor many Mennonites availed themselves of the permission given in the Schleitheim Confession (1527) with respect to aiding ministers financially:

5. Ministers:—"The minister shall according to the teaching of Paul, be of good report of them that are without. He shall teach, exhort, and help all the members to advance in their spiritual life. When he has needs he shall be aided by the congregation which chose him to his work. If he should be driven away, or imprisoned, or killed, another minister shall at once be put into his place.[1]

There are two references to the ministry in Brethren writings prior to 1815. One is an allusion to the professional ministry in a poem by Alexander Mack, Jr., originally appearing in the *Geistliche Magazin,* Number 9:

---

[1] Quoted in Smith, *The Mennonites of America.* Page 43.

7. Many preachers among the body of the people
   By no means consent to be inconspicuous
   And as they offer the kingdom of heaven for sale
   They do not get there themselves.
   They shun the tribulation and the ignominy of Christ
   And go the way of them they have misled.[2]

The other is a startling statement by Samuel Sower, writing to his sister on November 10, 1813, regarding the situation at Baltimore, Maryland. He says:

It surprises me not a little that the few Dunker families have grown to such numbers. They seem to be in great earnest, for they have started prayer meetings in private houses. They are devising means for getting an English preacher of their own faith. I do not believe it would be a difficult matter for them to supply the means for his support.[3]

The Baltimore project lapsed, and the idea of paying the minister seems first to have emerged at Philadelphia. Roland L. Howe, author of *The History of a Church (Dunker)*, writes in a letter of March 1938:

As far back as the 60's, small sums at irregular intervals are shown to have been paid for the "support" of the minister. . . . I have good reasons for believing [that] one or more of the members undoubtedly passed money in a quiet way to the pastor by way of support that never reached the records."[4] [5]

There must have been a reason for the items in the Yearly Meeting minutes of that decade:

1861—Art. 13. Resolved, that we are opposed to a treasury for the exclusive benefit of the ministry, but that every church should encourage their ministers to be active in their calling, and also to support

---

[2] S. B. Heckman, *The Religious Poetry of Alexander Mack, Jr.* Page 169.

[3] Quoted by Brumbaugh, page 513. Samuel Sower was a grandson of Christopher Sauer, Sr., but seems not to have been regularly in touch with the Brethren.

[4] F. B. Hollingshead, *Development of the Ministerial Policy of the Church of the Brethren*, a Bethany Seminary thesis, 1938.

[5] Details of the situation in Philadelphia, the smaller recorded payment to one of the ministers other than the pastor, the proof that a larger amount was paid to the pastor, the Annual Meeting committee sent to settle the difficulties over the ministers, and the possible reason for the omission of salary statements from the local church records are presented by Rowland Howe in his book, *A History of a Church (Dunker)*, pages 64-66. See also Annual Meeting Minutes of 1876, Article 27.

them in all cases of necessity. Considered, that we fully concur in the sentiment above expressed.

1866—Art. 41. Is it according to the Gospel for members, or any body of members, to pay a stated salary to our ministering brethren, for the support of their families, that they may give themselves wholly to their ministerial labors? Answer: Not wrong to support the ministry, where it is needed. I Tim. v, 18; Luke x, 7. But we do not approve of paying a stated salary.

A letter from Brother S. W. Mohler, who as a child was present at this Meeting of 1866, says:

As near as I can remember, the salaried ministry was discussed and strongly advised against.

. . . That summer I heard Grandmother and some of my uncles discuss it. Grandmother said: "Well, boys, I won't live long enough to see it, but it is possible that some of you will live to see the time when all the Brethren preachers will have to be paid—the Philadelphia church pays their preacher $1,000." . . . For several years after that I used to hear the Brethren mention the $1,000 salary of the Philadelphia church.

The first full-time regularly salaried pastor was Tobias T. Myers, who began his service at Philadelphia in April 1891. A parsonage with a rental value of twenty-two dollars per month was purchased and made available to the pastor in 1897. The salary, sixty dollars per month, was provided by Sister Mary Geiger. Myers remained until 1901, the last two years on half time. The work prospered and an extension point was started; it became the Geiger Memorial church. J. W. Cline was pastor of this new church from 1896 to 1899, before going to California and becoming the first pastor there in the First church of Los Angeles in 1900 (at fifty dollars per month).

The employment of the traveling evangelist and the missionary under a board was familiarizing people with the idea of paying the minister. Elder John Heckman, of Polo, Illinois, reports an Illinois development:

"On July 29, 1891, Brother P. R. Keltner entered upon full-time pastoral service in the Sterling, Illinois, church. He did not receive a stipulated amount of salary but he made an accurate account of all his expenses and they were paid by the Mission Board of Northern Illinois and Wisconsin. He continued at Sterling as full-time pastor for fourteen years."[6]

Note that the payment here was not a stipulated amount, as in the case of T. T. Myers. Another instance is that of W. R. Miller in Chicago:

"Again on June 23, 1889, the Chicago church was organized with an enrollment of twenty charter members. At this same meeting W. R. Miller was elected to the ministry and immediately entered into active service as pastor of the Chicago church. He continued as pastor for over fifteen years.

"Before this time, W. R. Miller had been in the grocery business in Chicago, but he failed in business. When he was elected to the ministry he received only a very small part of his support from the members in the Chicago church. But he did receive some. What they lacked in making up for his support, his brother, D. L. Miller supplied. This I have from D. L. Miller himself. Brother W. R. Miller gave his full time to the pastorate beginning June 23, 1889."[7]

Still another instance comes from Illinois:

John W. Lear, who began pastoral service at Cerro Gordo, Illinois, in 1902 was the first pastor in his District, the third in the State and probably the fifth or sixth in the entire brotherhood. At first he gave part time services on an annual salary of three hundred dollars. After two years he was hired as full-time pastor and served there ten years. He said the problem of holding the young people forced the church to act in this direction.[8]

It is interesting to note that J. W. Lear, through this pioneering and his later service to ministerial education in Bethany Seminary, probably exercised as much influence as any single individual toward the professionalization of the ministry.

Our next step will be to summarize the most important minutes of Annual Conference on the ministry across the years.

---

[6] Quoted by Hollingshead, *op. cit.* Pages 45-46.

[7] Quoted by Hollingshead, *op. cit.*

[8] Quoted by Hollingshead, *op. cit.* Page 47. A wealthy member, George Fulk, sponsored J. W. Lear as Mary Geiger had sponsored T. T. Myers.

On the *election* of ministers:

1853, Article 44:   Choice by ballot and without the presence of neighboring elders, an innovation, is frowned upon.

1862, Article 33:   If both a minister and a deacon are to be chosen, the minister's election is to be held first.

1865, Article 17:   Electioneering, even by officials, is forbidden.

1865, Article 44:   In an election, the ministers are to cast their votes first.

1866, Article 35:   Unmarried men may become bishops.

1868, Article 9:   Ministers from other denominations who unite with our Church must be received in the regular order of the Church.

1871, Article 23:   A minister may marry a woman who is not a member.

1880, Article XX:   If in an election a majority of members say they have no choice, it is deemed best to consider no one elected.

1899, Query 2:   A more scriptural way of electing ministers "by allowing the official part of the church to set forth two or three Brethren and ask the church which one of these shall be the minister," is requested. A committee is appointed to report the following year.

On ministers in the *first degree*:

It is not clear just when the degrees of the ministry became three, as it is fairly evident that there were only two in colonial times. The first query recognizing three ranks is:

1856, Article 20:   "Is it the rule and order among the Brethren to forward a brother to baptize at the same time he is put in the ministry?

"Answer: No."

1858, Article 53:   Ministers in the first degree are advised to be cautious and consult the Church in making appointments or filling them.

1860, Article 7: Newly elected ministers who lack confidence should be patiently borne with by the Church and encouraged.

1864, Article 32: Scriptural authority for three grades in the ministry is requested. This indicates that the three grades are not firmly established. The answer is deferred until the following year.

1865, Article 52: In answer to a similar if not the same query, the reply is: "We have plain scripture to teach a grade of officers in the church. (See Eph. 4:11); 'He gave some, apostles; some, prophets; some, evangelists; and some pastors and teachers.'"

On ministers in the *second degree*:

1853, Article 4: The Church is always to be consulted in advancing ministers.

1858, Article 19: The ceremony of advancement to the second degree is reception by hand and kiss.

1859, Article 22: A second degree minister should not appoint prayer meetings without the consent of the bishop.

1871, Article 1: When a second degree minister is needed but the oldest man in office eligible does not enjoy the confidence of the Church, an attempt should be made to remove the cause of this brother's unpopularity, and if that is impossible, the next eligible man may be advanced instead. This indicates that advancements ordinarily went by turns.

On *elders*:

1851, Article 6: The ordination of an elder should have the consent of his congregation and of the other elders present.

1852, Article 9: Where an elder has the oversight of an adjoining congregation, he should see that they have necessary help in the way of bishops or ministers.

1854, Article 13; 1867, Article 26: Where a leading brother, ordained or not, commits a gross public fault, or where a housekeeper does not conform to the usages of the

Church, the adjoining elders have a right to step in and deal with the situation.

1855, Article 17: Where two men were simultaneously chosen to the first-degree ministry, and likewise simultaneously to the second degree, they may also if other things are equal be ordained at the same time.

1858, Article 56: It is inadvisable to ordain a brother whose children, even while under age, are worldly.

1865, Article 41: The procedure in ordaining an elder is prescribed. A request for an ordination is to be made by the church and approved by the elders present. Then the sense of each member is to be taken individually to find if they favor the ordination of the brother oldest in office. If there is no serious objection, he is to be ordained.

1867, Article 28: While in general no change is recommended, Annual Meeting thinks it permissible in certain cases to let the church vote on which man is to be ordained.

1881, Article XII: A query asks that the provision about ordaining the oldest in office be repealed since it has no scriptural support. Annual Meeting replies rather tartly that Paul's qualifications for elders are not being overlooked, but that it is the Church's rule to ordain the oldest in office if other qualifications are about the same. Where this is not true, a vote of the congregation may be taken.

1885, Article XVI: A query asks that ordinations shall first be approved by a majority of elders in the districts, but Annual Meeting rests on former rulings.

1890, Article 16: The decision just mentioned is reconsidered and more favorable action taken. The authority to ordain elders is now vested in the elders' body of the district; the initiative in an ordination may be taken either by that body or by the local church. (This is the practice in 1950.)

1896, Query 6: Upon the death or removal of an acting elder, another must not take charge without the choice of the church or appointment by some other authorized body.

On *a salaried ministry* (in addition to minutes already cited):

1882, Article XIX: "Whereas there is a tendency in places in our brotherhood toward a salaried ministry, will this District Meeting ask Annual Meeting that there be no specified sum per day, week, month or year, paid to ministers on missions or any other work; but the Mission Board or Committee having control of funds may donate to ministers such sums as in their judgment their circumstances require.

"Answer:  Passed by Annual Meeting as requested by the District Meeting."

1890, Article 17: Stipulated salaries are again condemned, but an exception is made for mission work. The query indicates that preaching for stated sums is going on.

On *women preaching*:

1859, Article 7: Annual Meeting cautiously says:

"As Paul recognizes a distinction, in Rom. 12:6, 7, between teaching, ministering, and prophesying, and as he evidently approves of females prophesying (1 Cor. 11:5), we then think that a female cannot teach or preach according to 1 Cor. 14:34; 1 Tim. 2:12, in the ordinary acceptation of those terms, yet we cannot, under all, forbid them to prophesy."

Since 1900 it has become more and more the custom of Annual Meeting to make comprehensive decisions after a year or more of committee study, instead of dealing with a multitude of little specific questions. Decisions usually are long and detailed, seeking to cover the whole general field in which the problem lies.

1905, Query 7:  A plan for the effective distribution of the ministerial force of the Church is asked for. A committee is appointed.

1906, Unfinished Business, Section 4:  The committee's report is passed. It recommends frequent elections, the choice of young men and those who are willing to go where needed, their encouragement by the congregation, their soundness in the faith, and the appointment of district ministerial committees to assist and supervise the churches in their ministerial problems.

1906, Query 4: A plan to elect ministers and deacons by a majority of the votes cast is requested. A committee is appointed.

1907, Unfinished Business, Section 6: The committee recommends that when in an election no brother receives a majority vote, the election is to be repeated, this time narrowing the number of candidates to those who represent a majority of the votes cast, and thus to continue until some candidate receives a majority. If a majority of voters, however, finally vote "no choice," the election should be called off. If two candidates tie eventually, they shall both be called. The report is spread on the minutes for a year.

1906, Query 6: A plan by which pastors and evangelists shall receive gospel support so that they may give themselves wholly to the work is requested. A committee is appointed.

1907, Unfinished Business, Section 8: The committee reports progress.

1908, Unfinished Business, Section 2: The committee brings in an inconclusive report which recommends caution and deals in various generalities.

1907, Query 7: Two requests that presiding elders serve in terms not more than three years in length, and that they be elected by majority vote from among all the elders in the congregation, are spread on the minutes for a year.

1911: Definite permission from Annual Meeting is requested for the engaging of pastors. A committee is appointed.

1912: The committee's report, not very favorable to the employment of pastors, is recommitted to a new committee along with two new queries.

1913: The new committee reports progress.

1914: Further progress is reported.

1915: The committee reports, recommending that young men be allowed to volunteer for the ministry, that certain definite educational standards be set up for the ministry, and that there be two degrees—that of minister and that of elder. Ministers able to do so are encouraged to give their service gratis, but permission is given to employ pastors. The report is spread on the minutes.

1916: The whole report is recommitted.

1917: A new report is adopted. It differs from the one of 1915 chiefly in that no definite educational standards are named although ministers are urged to prepare themselves to the best of their ability.

1919: New formulas for the installation of ministers and elders are given.

1919, Query 7: Permission to elect ministers by ballot under proper circumstances is granted.

1920, Query 3: A plan for effective placement of pastors is requested. A committee is appointed.

1921: The committee reports, recommending a system of local, district, and general ministerial boards. The report is adopted.

1921, Query 7: A probation period or "Exhorter's Degree" is requested for young ministers. A committee is appointed.

1922: The committee reports, recommending that beginning ministers be first licensed for a year to preach but not to perform the other functions of the ministry. After the first year the license may be renewed or discontinued, or the minister may be permanently installed. Sisters may also be licensed to preach and may eventually be permanently licensed. The report is adopted.

1924: A form for licensing ministers is presented by the General Ministerial Board and is adopted.

1924, Queries 10, 11, and 12: A more definite plan for the selection and support of pastors is requested. The General Ministerial Board is asked to report the following year.

1925: The board reports progress and makes some general recommendations.

1926: The board brings a detailed report outlining very fully the duties of the General Board, the district boards, and the local ministerial committees. The General Board is to keep accurate statistics and information on the whole ministerial situation, and the United States and Canada are to be divided into five regions, each region to be supervised by one member of the General Board. The report is spread on the minutes for a year.

1927: The report is adopted.

1928: An installation service for pastors is adopted.

1931: A new pronouncement is made on ministers who commit gross sins and are deposed. They may be restored to the ministry one degree at a time, beginning with the licentiate, providing they exhibit exemplary conduct.

The very volume of these decisions is indicative of restlessness, uncertainty, and transition. Out of the whole period we select two significant aspects for comment.

The year 1908 was the bicentennial year. It was also the year in which the committee appointed to consider the matter of supporting pastors and evangelists reported. This report was in answer to a query which came from the Berthold church, North Dakota. The report of the committee is in four short paragraphs. The third paragraph urges the churches to give generously. The fourth urges prayer and activity upon the mission boards. The first and second paragraphs follow:

> We recognize that, under the present unequal distribution of our ministry, too often needed help is not given, the work of the ministry is much hindered and the cause is made to suffer, because the ministry has these financial hindrances. But we also recognize that our ministry, as it stands in relation to the church today, is gradually undergoing material changes, and that any legislation or radical change, in advance of *this movement we seem to be undergoing,* would be injurious to the church and the sacred calling of our ministry.
>
> We therefore recommend that our Brotherhood exercise the utmost

care and patience, *while this conscious change is taking place.* We need to be exceedingly careful in attempting to effect improvements along this line, *when there seems to be an entire transformation coming over us,* that our ministry does not fall from the high standard it has always held among our people, and degenerate into a class of hirelings, and thereby lose our power.[9]

Italics in the above are not in the committee's report. We believe there is sufficient comment in the italicizing. It is not especially cheering to see that intellectual understanding is joined with a kind of pathetic helplessness in the face of impending social change! Such cannot be a permanent policy of a witnessing, teaching Church.

The other is the emergence of ministerial training courses and schools. From the beginning of the school movement, the movement toward an "educated" and hence a salaried ministry was feared. The columns of the periodicals abound in these discussions. But save for the instance of Philadelphia and its hypothetical "thousand dollar preacher," up until 1880 there was no regularly supported minister in the Church. The traveling evangelist was being paid, sometimes with excessive generosity. In 1876 Christian Hope had gone to Denmark and had been (ir)regularly supported. But the plan of 1880 did contemplate the employment of religious workers on some systematized financial basis. They who were definitely opposed withdrew. Those who agreed with H. R. Holsinger in his somewhat vociferous arguments for a salaried ministry withdrew, and slowly adopted a salaried ministry, each congregation for itself. The "center" party declared:

1882, Art. X. We also declare distinctly that our loyal and faithful Brotherhood should neither fellowship, countenance nor tolerate those who would undertake to establish, under any pretence or color whatever, theological schools, or theological departments of schools or colleges, having in contemplation or purpose the training or graduation of any youth specially for the ministry of the Brotherhood or elsewhere, but we should faithfully adhere to our long-established practice in calling brethren to the ministry.

[9] *Minutes*, 1908, Section 2.

And with a now-visible inconsistency the Church proceeded to reconstitute a mission board, which of course called for professional religious workers. And professional workers called for training.

In the late nineties the colleges began Bible courses of various sorts, and with the dawn of the twentieth century came Bible schools. All the latter were short-lived except Bethany Bible School. Bethany was founded in 1905 in Chicago and ultimately became Bethany Biblical Seminary.

The Church has been blessed in having this school. It was launched through the devoted labors and sacrifice of two elders, Albert C. Wieand and Emanuel B. Hoff. Wieand excelled as an administrator; Hoff was primarily a Bible student and teacher. Both were idealistic. But both poured their lives into the school and gained respect for their vision even from those who differed with them. The founders loved the Church and they gave the school an impetus and an emphasis which it still perpetuates. Their project was one of the few genuinely positive innovations since the generation of Henry Kurtz. It contrasts strikingly with the wistful yearning that characterized the committee report of 1908.

Writing in 1934, Lorell Weiss gave a fair and penetrating analysis:

We have already remarked that the early pastors quickly realized their need of special training. Furthermore, a number of young men deliberately took work at other seminaries to prepare themselves for the ministry. The time was ripe, therefore, for such a step when A. C. Wieand and E. B. Hoff founded Bethany Bible School in 1905. Wieand had been dreaming about such a project for years. He and Hoff both took work at the University of Chicago, but were not particularly interested in securing degrees. The discovery that some of our people were taking work at the Moody school spurred him on. In the Biblical Seminary of New York he found many of his educational ideals in operation. After travel in Palestine and some study of religious pedagogy in Germany, he and Hoff took the initiative in establishing a Biblical training school for the Brethren.

Its beginnings were modest. Interestingly enough, the other

educators in the church did not regard it very favorably because they feared competition with their own enterprises. On the other hand, the more conservative Brethren in the church welcomed the new school because it promised to safeguard the traditional faith of the church. The curriculum of Bethany in its early years had the following objectives: (a) training in spiritual power, which was considered most vital, (b) a thoroughgoing practical knowledge of the Bible, (c) a training in methods conforming to the best pedagogical and psychological principles, (4) training in oral expression, and (e) clinical experience. Wieand disapproved of the radical and critical tendencies . . . in the larger seminaries and aimed to make Bethany's courses bibliocentric. His hope was not for a theological school, which the Brethren traditionally abhorred, but a Bible school. The student was to begin with exegetical study of the Bible, and inductive reasoning toward a Biblical rather than a systematic theology. In recent years there has been a tendency to modify this principle in the curriculum, especially since the change in administration in 1932.

The school filled a real need. Its training school was very popular, especially during the World War. The seminary department has been rather small, though there has been a little growth in recent years. In 1925 Annual Conference approved the taking over of the school by the church as its official seminary.

The present situation in theological training is not too satisfactory, however. The enrollment at the seminary is far too small, and there are only a few young men securing training elsewhere. Quite a number of men are still going out into pastoral work with only a college education. As a rule they do not do as well as seminary graduates. . . .[10]

Since Weiss penned these lines, the D. W. Kurtz administration has been followed by that of Rufus D. Bowman (1937-1952). The classrooms have become crowded with young men, and some young women, studying the Bible and theological lore, many of them hopefully anticipating religious work as a profession.

The following statistical picture of the pastoral situation in the Church during the last three decades has been gathered from the *Yearbook*:

---

[10] Lorell Weiss, in a Bethany Seminary thesis. Pages 137-139.

|  | Full-Time Pastors | Part-Time Pastors | Totals |
|---|---|---|---|
| 1923 | 193 | 182 | 375 |
| 1924 | 203 | 178 | 381 |
| 1925 | 241 | 234 | 475 |
| 1926 | — | — | — |
| 1927 | 261 | 213 | 474 |
| 1928 | 267 | 177 | 444 |
| 1929 | 282 | 219 | 501 |
| 1930 | 277 | 222 | 499 |
| 1931 | 259 | 308 | 567 |
| 1932 | 255 | 338 | 593 |
| 1933 | 207 | 298 | 505 |
| 1934 | 218 | 272 | 490 |
| 1935 | 241 | 339 | 480 |
| 1936 | 247 | 241 | 488 |
| 1937 | 200 | 303 | 503 |
| 1938 | 240 | 355 | 595 |
| 1939 | 264 | 429 | 693 |
| 1940 | 232 | 465 | 697 |
| 1941 | 237 | 462 | 699 |
| 1942 | 255 | 459 | 714 |
| 1943 | 262 | 466 | 728 |
| 1944 | 264 | 475 | 739 |
| 1945 | 271 | 478 | 749 |
| 1946 | 302 | 467 | 769 |
| 1947 | 303 | 472 | 775 |
| 1948 | 389 | 383 | 772 |
| 1949 | 392 | 394 | 786 |
| 1950 | 405 | 366 | 771 |

There is no extensive comment to make on this table. To characterize it in a single sentence which may seem banal, it shows that we have reached the midpoint in the twentieth century! There is no longer prevalent the controversy which marked the early decades of this century—whether to have a salaried ministry or not. We have it. Or do we?

A large proportion of the ministers, especially the older ones, still work in the spirit and in the memory of the free ministry. In many quarters the Brethren have taken on a salaried ministry without appreciating some of the implications of a professional ministry. The rank and file think of the minister as the local church's hired man, rather than as a professional servant. The "hiring and firing" of industry has been carried into the Church all too literally. Most Brethren are Americans and are thoroughly indoctrinated in buying and selling, hiring and firing. They have passed from the familistic society into the capitalistic society, and the church-pastor relationship is readily understood in this category.

Now the thing that remains to do is to make it work. Will it? That is the question for the future.

There appear to be several possibilities. One is that here is the wedge that will break the wall of Dunker orthodoxy and lead to assimilation into the prevalent conventional Protestant model of Church life. Some congregations have adopted the associate membership. And recently there have developed efforts to build community-church organizations. What is the community church but the germ of a State Church on the local level?

Another possibility is to continue indefinitely as a small conventional denomination without any special emphasis. This cannot easily be done, for most people require a reason or a faith as the ground of personal sacrifice.

There is a possibility that, unless wisdom is used in administration, there may be a reaction against the whole idea of an official, supported ministry, such as that experienced in the Society of Friends.

Still another possibility—which deserves serious consideration—is that of establishing a central sustenance fund and eliminating all financial competition within the ministry. This plan transcends the commercial practices of contemporary society. Several denominations have adopted it with its regimen of uniform basic salary. Our own District of Oregon has been experimenting with it for more than a decade, with very good results.

The congregation is frequently too small a numerical and financial unit to pay an adequate salary. Yet such a congregation may be the most fruitful area for work.

The Church seems to be far from comprehending the import of attempting to carry forward religious work in an economic society. In order to solve the problems of the industrial age, we must first seek an understanding of them.

# Chapter 31

## LOOKING UNTO CHRIST

*But the boat was now in the midst of the sea, distressed by the waves; for the wind was contrary. And in the fourth watch of the night he came unto them, walking upon the sea. And when the disciples saw him walking on the sea, they were troubled, saying, It is a ghost; and they cried out for fear. But straightway Jesus spake unto them, saying, Be of good cheer; it is I; be not afraid. And Peter answered him and said, Lord, if it be thou, bid me come unto thee upon the waters. . . . And they that were in the boat worshipped him saying, Of a truth thou art the Son of God (Matthew 14: 24-28, 33).*

This scripture is a parable of the Christian life and a graphic vindication of the Church of the Brethren today.

The disciples were on the Sea of Galilee. The night wind arose. The shallow waters were extremely dangerous in a high wind. From an adjacent mountain Jesus looked out and saw the disciples toiling to no advantage.

That company of tossing, rowing, sweating, and disturbed disciples may stand as an image of the institutional Church. In recent times the winds of social change and environmental upheaval have risen stronger and grown more boisterous. The Christian Church everywhere has felt the impact. There are many today who are "fainting for fear and for expectation of the things which are coming on the world" (Luke 21:26).

In this book we have observed the waves of environment beating upon that company of Christian believers whom we call the Brethren. The Brethren have not taken refuge in the ivory tower of metaphysical creedalism. They have insisted ever that religion be applied to the affairs of daily living.

But that presupposes a standard. The standard is Jesus. As Peter could walk across the waves while he had his eyes on Jesus and then began to sink when he looked downward, so the Church. The Brethren have no message for the world except to tell men to keep their eyes on Jesus. They have insisted on this for themselves.

The center of the Brethren culture has been the New Testament ordinances, or symbols. In the observance of these we have escaped magical sacramentalism on the one hand and vague sentimentality on the other. The New Testament ordinances are the very expression of Jesus' own mind and character as He strove to impart them to His friends. These ritual acts focus attention upon relationships, the true relationships that exist between man and God, and man and man. They preserve enough of the legal to give definiteness to religious tradition, and withal, a genuine evangelical liberty for the individual.

The call of the Brethren to look at Jesus only has commonly taken the form of emphasizing certain ethical teachings of Jesus which tend to be overlooked in the Christian world. In a former day, Brethren felt that nonswearing and simplicity or "plainness" were principles which they needed to emphasize before their fellow Christians. In recent years the great burden of the Brethren testimony has been peace and effort looking toward a peaceful world. We have sought to direct the eyes of Christians to Jesus, the Prince of Peace.

Again, the Brethren testimony to the non-Christian world has been the message and spirit of Jesus. Our mission work has been heavily buttressed by hospitals, dispensaries, schools, and various forms of co-operative effort. We have endeavored to make out of non-Christians the highest type of practicing, ethical Christians.

A thread of continuity has run through this history. The purpose to live according to the New Testament, set forth at Schwarzenau, has been the vital core of this fraternity's life.

Brethren have been struggling continuously with their environment. The central body of Brethren—the Church of the
Brethren—have taken a very mild and accommodating attitude
toward the society about them. This is due to the pietistic
emphasis upon goodness and kindliness. The desire has been
to bring the blessing of Jesus to multitudes of men.

To appraise the degree of ultimate success is impossible
and unnecessary. Life is not a finished product. The Church
has never been assimilated in the purposes of the unregenerate
world-society, even though it has at times seemed to accommodate its forms to contemporary social life. The Church is
not *of* the world, but the Church militant is always *in* the
world. It is in the world for a purpose—to serve the Lord
Jesus and to carry His Word.

Beyond this world of time stretches the illimitable world.

"I do not pin my faith for the future to my country or
even to my race. I do not think it improbable that man, like
the grub that prepares a change for the winged thing that it
has never seen, but is to be, may have cosmic destinies that he
does not understand; and so beyond the vision of battling
races, and an impoverished earth, I catch a dreaming glimpse
of peace."[1]

It is the faith of the Church of the Brethren that the
guide to those dimly perceived cosmic destinies is Jesus, our
Savior.

---

[1] Author unknown.

# APPENDIX

## A Letter Written by Alexander Mack, Sr.

The following letter of Alexander Mack, Sr., the first elected minister of the Church of the Brethren, has been recovered through the studies of M. R. Zigler, Geneva, Switzerland, the Church's representative to the World Council of Churches.

Employing Dr. H. Renkewitz to work with him, he discovered this letter in the archives of the castle of the counts of Ysenburg-Buedingen. The official records of the Kreis-Stadt of Buedingen are combined with the ancient records of the count. Ysenburg is the county in which is Marienborn, the location of the second group of Brethren to be gathered. It was from the Marienborn district that Peter Becker had come, and his baptism had been the signal for a violent storm. Of the below-mentioned Eva Liss, it is deduced from the letter that she had already received apostolic baptism. She is of the large number who have followed truth without thought of personal sacrifice.

On June 14, 1951, this letter was carefully copied, and, as a further guarantee of authenticity, was photographed. This was possible by the kindly co-operation of Herr Scheidt, the archivist of the Ysenburgian records, who from his grandfather inherited a genuine interest in Anabaptist history.

Gracious Lord and Count

Since an order has been issued from the chancellery of the count, in the first place that Eva Liss, a poor widow, together with her daughters shall leave the country, and that I too shall leave the land of my gracious lord, and whoever shall give me a night lodging shall pay a fine of 5 fl., I feel myself urged to write to the lord count these few lines, and to have him reconsider before God, the judge of the living and the dead, whether these proceedings are taken according to the will of God, who has established government to punish the bad and to protect the good. In respect to the first, Eva Liss indeed has been at the chancellery and has been questioned, but not found guilty of any misdemeanor which would give the authorities the right to persecute her; on the other hand, I have not even been examined or questioned about the nature of my faith, much less been convicted of any misdeed. Such procedure, firstly, is counter to the Jewish law, John 7: 51, where Nicodemus says: "Does our law judge a man without first giving him a hearing and learning what he does?" Yes, it is counter to heathen rights, Acts 25: 16, where Festus says that it is not the custom of the Romans to kill anyone before the accused meet the accusers face to face and have opportunity

Gnädiger Herr Und graff

Weilen Von herrn graffen seiner Cantzley ein befehl ergangen, erstlich dass
die +Va lis, eine arme wittib sambt ihren töchtern, auss dem lande weichen soll.
Und ich solle auch auss dess gnädigen herrn seinem lande, wo mich aber in seinem
lande über nacht betreten solle, straff erfolgen, so finde ich mich gezwungen, dises we-
nige, dem herrn graffen zu überschreiben, Und ihme wohl zu bedencken geben, vor gott
dem richter der lebendigen Und der todten, ob dises Verfahren, gehet nach dem willen gottes
Welcher die obrigkeit gesetzet dass böse zu straffen Und dass gute zu beschützen.
Noch erstlich ist zwar die +Va lis auff der Cantzley gewesen, Und verhört worden
aber doch keiner übel that können überwiesen werden, worüber eine obrigkeit
und recht macht hätte, sie zu verfolgen, Noch ander bin ich nicht ein mahl verhört
worden, oder nur gefragt wass mein glaube sey, viel weniger überwiesen, einer
übel that, solches Verfahren streitet erstlich wider dass Jüdische gesetz, Johan 7 Cap
V. 51, da sagte nicodemus, richtet Unser gesetz auch einen menschen, ehe man ihn verhört
Und erkennet wass er thut, ia es streitet auch wider die heydnische rechte, actorum
Cap. V. 16, da sagte festus. es wäre nicht der römer weise einen menschen Um zu bringen
ehe der Verklagte habe seine kläger gegenwärtig. Und raum empfangen sich der an-
klage zu Verantworten, ia vom christenthum will ich nichtes melden, dass ein christ durch
den geist christi solches thun könnte, was aber nun mein verbrechen ist will ichs bekennen
frey Und öffentlich. dass ich Jesum christum der König aller Könige, Und herr aller herren.
dass einige wass wir thun achte haben will, dass der sünder solle busse thun, Und an
den herrn Jesum glauben, Und solle auff seinen glauben, sich tauffen lassen im wasser.
Und solle dann alles suchen zu halten, wass er Jesus befohlen, Und in seinem testament
öffentlich hinderlassen, thun wir nun hierinnen Unrecht, wider dass grossen befehle wort
heiliger schrifft, es sey in lehr leben Und wandel, so wollen wir Uns ia gerne weisen
lassen, kan Uns aber niemand dises erweisen, mit gründt der heiligen schrifft, Und
man Uns doch verfolget, so wollen wir zwar gerne alles leyden, Und dulten, um der
lehr iesu christi willen, so wollen wir es befehlen allein, an den oberrichter iesu christ; welcher
am tage der offenbahrung recht richten wird. Und einem ieglichen nach seinen wercken
Vergelten, ohne ansehung der person, wan nun iesus sagen wird, Matt. 25 Cap zu
denen zur lincken. gehet hin ihr verfluchten, weilen sie seine glieder nicht gespeiset
Und wie es ferner lautet, ey wass wird er sagen, zu denen die sie ohne recht Und ohne
Verhörung verfolget haben, die werden sagen müssen o ihr berge fallet über Uns, Und ihr
hügel bedecket Uns, denn wir können nicht bestehen, vor dem der auff dem stuhl sitzt

Geschrieben den 5. Herbstmonat 1711.

Alexander Mack ein
glied in Christo

to make his defense concerning the charge laid against him. Yes, I shall not claim for Christendom that a Christian through the spirit of Christ can do anything like that, but what my crime is I shall confess free and openly. Jesus Christ the King of Kings and Lord of Lords wants us to do what we are doing, namely, that the sinner shall repent and believe on the Lord Jesus and let himself be baptized in water upon confession of faith, and shall then try to obey everything that He, Jesus, commanded and has left behind openly in His Testament. If we now transgress in this against the revealed Word of Holy Scripture, be it in doctrine, life or conduct, then we are gladly willing to let ourselves be corrected. Can, however, nobody prove us guilty of this on the basis of Holy Scripture, and yet persecute us, then we want to suffer and endure everything gladly, because of the teachings of Jesus Christ; thus we want to appeal alone to the supreme judge, Jesus Christ, who on the day of His manifestation will judge aright and repay everyone according to his works without showing partiality, when Jesus will say, Matthew 25, to those on the left, "Depart from me, you cursed," because they had not fed His members, and as it continues to say, yes, what will He say to those who have persecuted them without right or trial. They will have to say, "O mountains, fall on us and ye hills cover us, because we cannot stand before Him who sits upon the throne." Therefore, I submit to you, gracious lord, my humble request to prove and investigate according to the Holy Scripture everything that happens in your country since you too have an immortal soul. You will once have to stand before Jesus, the supreme Lord, by whom you have been set over your country, and give account how you have governed your country, whether it was done according to the holy will of God or not. Because the whole world belongs to the Lord Jesus, He has to command over all elements. He who attacks His members, attacks Him. Is it justifiable to hinder the members of the Lord Jesus when they desire to be baptized in water upon confession of faith and testify that Jesus is the true prophet under whose teachings they are willing to subject themselves; to reject and to abjure the devil of the world and all sins, and to live a blameless life before God and man? How can the poor baptists help it that it is such an unusual thing, and that through the injuriously introduced baptism of children, the true baptism which Jesus commanded, [that of] penitent sinners upon their faith, has become so strange and so obscure that even the chosen ones are almost offended and repelled by it. It is not unknown to the lord count that for a long time already publicly and in books there has been and still is agitation in the country from public pulpits against child baptism. Should there now be no baptism at all since child baptism is not valid? That cannot be; Jesus has seriously commanded us, Matthew 28 and Mark 16, and has said whoever believes and is baptized shall be saved. What Jesus now has commanded, that cannot willfully be changed or broken by any creature without loss of eternal salvation. Should the true baptism not be followed by a cross, but rather a good life, honor and comfort, as is the case with child baptism, it would no doubt be defended by the scholars from Holy Scripture. But since the true baptism involves all kinds of contempt and one cannot be a friend of the world, they say against their knowledge that it is an outward performance not necessary for salvation, and at the same time they permit the poor Christians to live in all kinds of hardships while they themselves follow with a good, comfortable life and with a teaching that saves them and guards them from the cross. I do not want to become annoying through more extended writing, but will close herewith and leave everything to the examination of the lord count. As far as I am concerned I do not complain that I have to leave the country, because I had planned to do that beforehand, but I request again in humility for Eva Liss, who is a poor widow, that a little more consideration be given her. Should I, however, return to this country so I ask, if it be desired, to defend my faith. Should I be proved in error in some points by the scholars, I would gladly let myself be instructed. Can that, however, not be so, I would ask again for a trial since all kinds of disorder have occurred in this country before. Meanwhile I wish the lord count blessings and grace and heavenly light from God for his government so that he too may attain a good standing in the kingdom of Christ, which I heartily wish, and remain his humble

Alexander Mack, a member of Jesus Christ

Written on the 5th autumn month 1711

## LETTER FROM ONE FRIEND TO ANOTHER ON THE QUESTION: WHAT IS PIETISM?

The following is a translation of *La Lettre d'un Ami a' L'autre Sur La Questione Quesque La Pietisme?* The translation of this pamphlet, which was published in French in Cologne, Germany, in 1702, is the work of Professor William Willoughby, a grandson of the eminent Brethren historian, George N. Falkenstein. It is presented as the best definition and discussion of Pietism to which the present writer can point. There is no reason to doubt that the device of a letter to a friend was a mere literary device similar to the dialog between father and son, which was used by Alexander Mack.

As it is common to see that those living in a strange country are not always informed of the customs, manners, government, religion, or politics of their fellow citizens, I am indeed not astonished that you, who have traveled to Berlin, to Leipzig, through all of Saxony, and elsewhere, where there are several thousand Pietists, where their manner of life and their doctrines are known, where they are the subject of conversations in polite society, where everyone is talking about them in public places, in the towns, and in the country—I am not astonished, I say, that you asked me in your last letter what Pietism is and what kind of people are they that are called Pietists.

I shall satisfy, then, your curiosity, and since I have examined with care their doctrines, in part by their writings, in part by conversations that I have had with some of them, you can have confidence in the story I shall elaborate for you concerning them.

Although I have undertaken this, I warn you of two things: (1) That I interject none of my own ideas in the story I am going to tell, and in doing this I am purely a historian, not pretending to say anything for or against these people, leaving to you the liberty to make such judgments as shall please you. (2) I warn you that when you shall find these terms, "corrupt and imperfect Reformation," "Reformers," "Reforms," or "corrupt Protestants," the Pietists do not mean to condemn all the Reformed or Lutheran Christians, knowing indeed that in all the denominations, in all the professions and societies, there are still some good people who know God, who love Him, and who are known and loved by Him.

With these warnings I am ready to begin, and to keep some order in the story you want, I shall tell you: (I) of their name of Pietist, (II) of their doctrines, (III) of their manner of life, (IV) and finally, of their persecutions, which they have actually suffered in Saxony, Westphalia, Hesse, Wedcravie, and especially in the Comte de Hanau, Switzerland and elsewhere.

I. As for the name of Pietist, it is necessary that you understand that they have never appropriated it by assuming it themselves, for it was really their enemies who gave it to them, in mockery and opprobrium; although the Pietists mean something different even from a man who attaches himself to the Pietistic movement in order to study it. I believe, if I am not mistaken, that it was at Leipzig that they first began to call themselves by this name, and especially when Dr. Spener came into Saxony, where he endeavored to kindle in the hearts of men the beautiful fire of piety, which had seemed nearly extinguished, showing them through his good life and his shining virtues the way to true happiness. But the Pietists are not insulted by this designation, for they know that in times past others have imposed beautiful names on good people who desired to oppose vice and impure thoughts, thus mocking them, ridiculing them, and making them obnoxious, as at one time in derision they called *Euchettes* those who begged without ceasing, and *Ascetes* those who worked perpetually at their necessary tasks in clinging to stable and genuine holiness. These groups were, however, put in the catalogue of heretics, as well as the *Vaudois* who, in past centuries, were called by the Roman Catholics *Gnostiques,* that is to say, distinguished, Apostolic, "good" men, etc.

II. The above is a glance at the name of Pietist; let us pass on to consider their doctrines, which we can classify under four heads, for they concern either: (1) the Reformation in past centuries, (2) or the corruption in the morals of the Protestant Church today, (3) or the corruption in certain doctrines of the same Church, which they say is like yeast making sour the entire mass of our religion, and (4) finally, the future reform of so much of the Reformed and Lutheran Protestant Churches, as indeed of all Christianity, and all other religions in whatever part of the world they might be. This is what they call the Glorious Reign of Jesus Christ.

1. As for the Reformation—it commenced at the time of Zwingli, Luther, Calvin, Melancthon, Bezet, and others, including several princes, who separated from Rome. The Pietists say that this Reform has not been completed, nor perfected, and that it is properly regarded as the rejection of certain gross errors and outward idolatry, without touching morals and life, which ought to be reformed after the example of Jesus Christ, and the rule of His word. In brief, they say that the Reformation was a body without spirit, resembling those bones of the vision of Ezekiel 37: 2-8, which joined themselves together, being covered with skin and nerves, but lacking in spirit. In effect (one of these Pietists once said to me), if the first Reformers had wished to make a sacred and truly Christian Reform, they ought to have before everything else rooted out pride and avarice (those two sins which strengthen Babel) in the hearts of men, so that they could learn true spiritual service which is the practice of Christian virtues, the renunciation of self, and the imitation of Jesus Christ. That having been accomplished, they would have expected the Reformation to come of itself, without so much blood having been spilled in getting rid of the outward ceremonies and idolatries which to the present mark the religion of the Roman Catholics. It is thus, in their opinion, that they would have commenced the Reformation. For according to them a Christian, or a true Reformer (at least to a degree), is a man who is born of God, renewed in understanding, who after having stripped off the old Adam, walks in the light and has communion only with God. They claim that a Reformer is a temple and a vessel of the Holy Spirit, having the Word and the

Spirit of God living in his inward parts, and who acts only on the impulses and the inspirations of God himself. A Reformer, in the thought of the Pietists, is a Christian who has renounced the world, and the covetousness of the flesh, who hates himself and his own life, and, not wishing to please himself, follows the example of Jesus (Romans 15: 3), who loves his enemies and prays for them. He is a Christian humble of heart who does not seek for the honors of the world, nor for his own glory, but only for that of his God. He is a Christian who through his trust in God is conqueror of the world, not conforming to the world and not known of the world, is hated and persecuted by it (John 15: 1-8). A Reformer, according to the Pietists, is a Christian who has crucified his flesh, his passions, his self-love, his hatred, his ambition, his envying, his pride, his vengeance, and his vanity, who does not search for the riches of the world, and who considers himself more happy when he gives than when he receives. He is a Christian who carries with joy the yoke of his Savior, who bears the marks of Jesus Christ, who is neither argumentative, nor quarreling, who endures patiently his injuries, who corrects with gentleness those who err, and who bears charitably with their weaknesses. . . . according to the Pietists, a Reformed Christian is a man who is instructed of God, who speaks only of God, before God, and with God (2 Corinthians 2: 17).

It is no wonder the Pietists demand, if the Reformation or the first Reformers of the past century have had primarily in mind the production of such men as they have represented as real Reformers according to them, or whether they have worked only at separating a part of Christendom from the communion of the Church of Rome, dividing it in two, and in order to do this attacking in the beginning such errors in the doctrines as for example the traffic of indulgences, papal primacy, the cult of images, the celebration of the sacrifice of the Mass for the living and for the dead, forbidding the people from reading the Scriptures, the celibacy of the priests, the superiority of the ecclesiastics above the magistrates, and the retention of the cup from the people. In doing this the Reformers inculcated in the minds of their hearers the doctrines opposite to the ones which have just been specified, and thereby accomplishing the reforms in doctrines. But they were nearly equally deficient in morals as a Turk, a Jew, or a Roman Catholic, not to say the worst, and that is because the Spirit and the imitation of Jesus Christ were lacking. For what difference is there between the Turks and the Jews, and the Protestant Christians for the most part, if the only difference is in regard to their doctrines.

When one asks of the Pietists the cause of the evil success of the Reformation, they answer:

1. That it happened through the particular providence of God, who wished to let them form a body of bones of dry ashes of the Roman Church, although without spirit and without spiritual warmth.

2. They also attribute it to the disagreements which reigned among the ecclesiastic Reformers, who did not agree together in doctrine, were full of envy, hated one another, defended themselves from injury, and persecuted one another shamefully while they themselves were pursued with sword and fire.

3. Because the political Reformers were often very ill reformed themselves, as history makes plain, they advanced and protected the Reformation, which they called the cause of Jesus Christ, with the sword, having more in sight the seizing for themselves of revenues and ecclesiastic powers than the reforming of the Church or themselves.

4. Another reason was that many favoring the ecclesiastic and political Reformation desired to reform the Church of Jesus Christ only within certain limits, such as setting up confessions of faith touching doctrine, and in taking away from the flocks particularly the right to choose pastors. In appropriating that right to themselves they frequently provided the churches with false pastors and ravenous wolves, in which one cannot find the least sparkle of the Spirit of God. With their followers, who are convinced of their doctrines, which are for the most part hypocritical and wicked, they have fashioned a peculiar Church which they call the true Church of God.

5. Furthermore, they received into their communions quite willingly any persons who had renounced the errors of Rome, without examining whether they had also renounced the world. All of which is a different procedure from the primitive Church, for which see Spanheimius, *Orat. de Degenere Christi Ecclesia,* page twenty-four.[1] In effect, say these Pietists, most of the new proselytes left Rome for a very wicked reason, not because the authority of the Roman Church was in their sight unjust or contrary to the gospel, but rather that the yoke was too difficult to carry. One was a priest or a monk who wanted to marry, having been released from his vows, and the other was a libertine who did not wish to confess his filth to a confessor of conscience.

In a word, these new converts and pretended reformers indeed denounced the celibate, but they were not more chaste; they made fun

---

[1] Nemo non exploratus, quam exactissima, ratione admittebatur, non modo ad Mysteria, sed ne ad limen quidem, nomen Christianum. Praviae salutaribus quis lustrationi animorum, anni sae pe dati, qui ante vel cauponariae, veltheatralibus ludis, cytharae, cursui, palaestrae, venationibus, pictorumque aut gladiatorum arti dediti, vel qua cae teroquin luxum, pompam, & vanissimarum rerum sapientiam redolerant, ejurandum pruis illud vitae genus aeternum fuit.

of fasts, of prayers, and of other ceremonies of the Church which they had just left, but they were not more sober nor more pious themselves. They regarded as unholy the doctrine of the merit of works, and so the practice of them they neglected, although the gospel expressly commands it. They regarded the monks and the solitaries as fools, and yet they traveled with the world, thinking not at all of leaving it to live in solitude and to walk with God.

Finally the Pietists demonstrate with Luther's own words that most of the Protestants have been more wicked since their departure from that which they call Babylon than before, because of the preaching of grace and liberty which tends to spoil hearts and denies the principal qualities making a good Christian, which are the renunciation of self, the hatred of the world, and the love of Jesus Christ. Such things took place at the beginning of the Reformation; so it is not necessary to be astonished that the communion of Protestants is corrupted in morals and in life. Today this same church resembles the ancient Jewish Church, which the prophets called Sodom and Gomorrah, although it professed doctrines of which God was the author (Isaiah 1: 10-19, Ezra 16: 49), since it makes a show of its morals, yet walks on its traces.

For these Pietists say it is not the good doctrines which make the Church and the disciples of Jesus Christ, but the new creature, for if a person is not born again, he is not able to see the Kingdom of God. In order to be a Christian, they say, it is necessary to be reborn, to be a new man, or a new creature, to have a live faith working in love (Galatians 5: 6 and 6: 15), to do the commandments of Jesus Christ and to walk in the way as the Son of God (1 John 2: 3, 6).

They add that a good doctrine without the good life makes men more guilty before God than those who sin in error, as from wicked doctrines one is able only to bring out an impure morality; equally, good doctrines are not able for a long time to exist in impure hearts without being corrupted. On the contrary, when a Christian obeys God, when he conforms to His life and to the will of God, submitting to the order of His providence, to His grace, and to His mercy, it is impossible, according to them, that in such a man there is any damning doctrine, and what is more, God is awake to him, and makes known to him his mysteries, as David was assured. "If anyone," says our Lord, "wishes to do the will of God, he shall know, if it is of God, or if I speak by myself. Who has my commandments and keeps them is the one who loves me, and who loves me shall be loved by my Father, and shall declare him mine."

Now the Pietists, in order to demonstrate how corrupt is our own communion, say in general that all the Protestants of today endeavor to defend blindness in and through all the first Reformers as if they were infallible and had no error, adoring them to their deathbed. To wish to change something in the catechism or in the *Confession* of Melancthon or of Bezet, or in the *Rimes* of Marot is to be bold and heretical, going so far as to blame the Roman Catholics for starting the Reformation. Further, they say, the most common occupation of Protestant doctors is to write and to preach against Rome and its ritual, or against Wittenberg, or Geneva, etc., and to foment and maintain hatred among the sects. They claim that for every doctor who writes some treatise on morals or piety, there are a hundred who put people to sleep with their preaching and their writing of controversial books, of which there are so many that they are able to turn against us. For example, the Pietists believe that we dispute uselessly against the practices of the Church of Rome, who of their bishops make princes, and of their princes make bishops and heads of the Church who for the most part are quite ignorant of the mysteries of religion and piety.

In addition, they say that religion, or the Christianity of the Protestants, Reformed and Lutheran, in at least the greater part consists: (1) only in coming into a church in order to say public prayers, and hear some sermons, and in order to sing some psalms, giving lip service, while the heart is estranged from God, from neighbors, from saintly friends, and from the poor (Matthew 15: 8-9); (2) only in superficial and general confession of sins; (3) only in the outward usage of baptism, and of the bread and the sacred cup; (4) and in the usage of domestic prayers, either reading them or reciting them after having learned them by heart as a young child. For that they distinguish themselves from the Jews, from pagans, and from the Roman Church!

That is, sir, what the Pietists teach in general of the corruption of our communion, that is what they say in general, but this is what they say in particular: they say then without ceremony that these three orders, the political, the ecclesiastic, and the social are almost entirely spoiled and estranged from the Spirit of Jesus Christ. For this see the most outstanding and excellent book of a Reformed theologian, entitled *Sources of the Corruption of Our Church,* and *The Author of Sincere Letters,* etc. As to the political order, they claim that it is corrupted to a great degree, plunged in all the delights of the world, and particularly in these three things that Saint John comments on: the lust of the flesh, the lust of the eye, and the pride of life. And what is more deplorable is that they are entrenched in this way of life through the laxity of the pastors who, instead of imitating John the Baptist in their speaking, saying, "It is not permitted you!" in doing such and such a thing, the least guilty keep silence, being like dumb dogs and sleeping sentinels, where indeed they connive to their confusion; and others publicly teach that it is permitted to nobles to have gambling places with magnificent equipment, to go richly attired, to maintain great and numerous courts with splendid tables and delicate dress, where one eats the flesh of the poor peasants and where one drinks their blood, that they might not get ambitious; as if the law of the gospel, which commands humility, the renunciation of the world, sobriety, chastity, temperance, modesty, love of enemies, is given only for the weak and not for the mighty! But, sir, do not believe that the Pietists include in this state of corruption all the great of the world; they except some, as I warned you in the beginning of this letter—those that God knows and excepts Himself.

As for the ecclesiastic order, the Pietists instruct that this was never more corrupt, and that it is completely fallen from its high beginning, and from its pristine purity, that its hypocrisy is apparent in all the members of the Protestant Church, that one is able to say that this order which God said through the mouth of His prophet is come to pass: "Behold I will feed them with wormwood, and make them drink the water of gall; for from the prophets of Jerusalem is ungodliness gone forth into all the land" (Jeremiah 23: 15), without forgetting Isaiah 29: 21. They say that one does not notice in the great majority of our pastors any degree of those beautiful qualities which we have specified above in making the picture of the true Reformer, that is to say the purity of the doctrine. On the contrary, they say the great majority are worldly men, vain, carnal, friends of the world, for since they are not different from it, they are friends of it, and they gladly receive its praises. Indeed, far from being hated by it, and being persecuted as that would come upon them most certainly if they would work with zeal and sincerity for the advancement of the Kingdom of Christ, also their worldly spirit appears in their company, steps, words, and habits. If they are in worldly company they discuss only the news of the day or other trifles! Not to mention that they often hold discourses full of impurity which excites the laughter of profanity, and shames honest people, so far from reprimanding or correcting the vicious, still less their forbidding the usage of the holy words.

They are, the Pietists add, for the most part greedy or lusting for money, not recognizing the interests of others, enlivening their pastimes, their pleasure, and their high life with drunkenness, until they come to the point, to the shame of Christianity, that they reveal the flesh full of wine (Leviticus 10: 9, 10). They rush from church to church because of better benefices, using simony with intrigue and the pull of riches and of worldly men in order to enter into the sheepfold of the Savior, without thinking that Jesus Christ is the door and the Holy Spirit the doorkeeper of the sheepfold, and those who enter elsewhere are thieves and robbers (John 10: 1-5). Seeking the honors of the world and the first seats in the assemblies—so far from hating the flesh, in their sermons they preach against their colleagues and against their sheep, and against their enemies, seeking the favor of the great and the rich, and neglecting the poor, making their furniture luxurious, also their habits, and those of their wives and children. Without gentleness or charity among them, having other sentiments than these on certain matters, sometimes pure speculation, they have still less regard for those who, discovering their faults, repent of them, inspiring rage in their hearers against them whom they call Heterodoxes, although better Christians that they—the greatest Epicureans of the world, finding delights through the flesh by means of their affected and sinful manners, looking for that which tickles the ear rather than for that which touches the heart, appearing wise in theology, philosophy, history, and in the knowledge of strange languages. Preaching, in a word, an entire half century without saving a soul from the bonds of the world, and from vanity, or from the claws of an infernal lion, but, on the contrary, every day making their flocks more wicked. Finally, for this, look at the doctors and professors of theology, the Pietists say frankly, who for the most part surpass in pride, vanity, and hypocrisy all the other ecclesiastics, and which, according to Mr. Spanheimius, *Orat Cit.,*

faciendorum immemores consenescant in indagatione veri, de amore, de conscientia, de mutuis in rem Christianam officiis, non omnino aut oscitanter, de scientiae vero & inanium profectuum laude etc. unice soliciti.

That is, sir, what the Pietists say of the corruption in the political and ecclesiastical order. Listen to what they have to say about the corruptions in the economic and popular order. They teach that this order follows the outlines of pagan society, and that the Protestants are for the most part impious against God, unjust to their neighbors, and cruel to themselves.

*Irreverent to God*—In effect, say the Pietists, what greater sin can one see than that of mocking (as the children of Bethel) of good people and those who fear God, whoever they might be. Though they call themselves Reformed and Evangelical Christians, if there is anyone who grows old distinguishing himself for his virtue, for his piety, and for his tenderness of conscience, who grows old without getting drunk, or gambling, or committing other such crimes, he is a "fool," an "idealist," a "Quaker," a "hypocrite," a "puritan" or a monk, in brief, a heretic, as very agreeably says the pious Gerardus:

> Qui studium hoc ave pietatis gnaviter urget,
> Et Sophies partem tractat utram Sacra;
> Hic Stultus, Monachus, Baptista, Quakerus, habetur
> Et nota turpis ei scribitur hareseos.

It is indeed true that if there is any pastor among them who enters too much into the details of their vices, they laugh at him and pass him off as an ignorant stoic, who knows nothing but censure, at least that is what several evil souls said of *New Essays on Morality,* by Mr. La Placette, which they claim is a moral outrage. With advantage the Pietists demonstrate that our people have their hearts filled for the most part only with useless ideas and thoughts such as love of the world, and of ordinary love, loving God less, and conformity of their will to the things of this world instead of to Him. Their religion, or service of God, is but empty show, and only for on Sundays and holy days, for indeed, true religion, following the sentiment of Jesus Christ and of His apostles, consists in renouncing self, and in coming after Jesus Christ, and in visiting and loving the poor and those who are in tribulation, and in keeping oneself detached from the world.

But this is not all, the Pietists further remark that the Protestants attend their assemblies simply through custom, and often with a shameful ostentation of dress in order to be seen by all those whose faith regards the appearance of persons, which is common since the rich have the first seats and prerogatives while the poor are in the most remote place in the sanctuary. And finally, most of them commune, using the symbols of the body and blood of Christ in the manner of idols, as if the sacraments saved mechanically and by themselves, without repentance and a change of life. As a result, they do not profit much with all their meeting together; on the contrary they become worse day by day as we have already noticed for after having heard a great number of sermons, they are as ignorant in what makes the essentials of religion as a Chinese or an Ethiopian, holding fast to simple theory and speculation without passing to the practical or to the imitation of Jesus Christ. All that they do learn is to dispute against a Roman Catholic or a Calvinist, or a Lutheran, or some other heterodoxy. Never do they learn to dispute against the passions or against the anti-Christ within one.

After irreverence to God, the Pietists show our *injustice to our neighbor* by saying that each one seeks his own profit without thinking of his neighbor—lying, stealing, committing injustice without regard to the welfare of others, slandering, despising his brother, covering him

Appendix 311

with maledictions, envying him, insulting him in his misery, making
fun of him, and of all such good people whom they do not know
except by hearsay. Such are the commonest vices and works of the flesh
which are manifested (Galatians 5: 19-21). The Pietists add to that that
we never have pity and compassion for the needy, that we are insensitive
and rejoice overtly over misfortune and damage to our enemies, that
our Reformed and Evangelical Protestants, who ought to edify the
others by their discourses of common sense and by their humble and
modest bearing, scandalize even the Jews and the Papists with their
wicked and impure words, with their laughter, their eyes, their debauchery (which the devil recommends as an antidote against melan-
choly), their luxury, their evil deeds, and their lewd glances; and all
that against the exhortation of St. Paul, who does not want any corrupt
speech coming out of the mouth of the faithful—nor things villainous,
nor wicked words, nor pleasantries, which are all unbecoming (Ephesians 4: 29 and 5: 4). Equally, our meals, which ought to be love feasts,
or meals of charity for those not able to provide their share (Luke 14: 12),
are, to the contrary, only feasts of a disorderly appetite (Colossians 3),
luxury and pride appearing in all their brilliance where Jesus Christ
is forgotten and there they converse only of vain and worldly things
(John 3: 31), giving for excuse "that it is necessary to be in joy with
those who are joyful," as if St. Paul was contrary to the Holy Spirit, who
declared elsewhere that the heart of the wise man is in the house of
mourning and that of the fool in the house of mirth (Ecclesiastes 2: 2
and 7: 4).

Finally, the Pietists say, if the Protestants are for the most part
irreverent to God, and unjust to their neighbors, they are also *cruel
against themselves,* for they prefer the world and its pleasure to the
delights of heaven and the salvation of their immortal souls. For how
many are there among us who search first for the Kingdom of God and
believe in His justice that all other things might be added (Matthew
6: 33)? Who of us strive to enter through the narrow door (Luke 13:
24), using violence to take the Kingdom of Heaven (Matthew 11: 12)?
How many, who prepare to come to Jesus, are not made heavy with
greediness and the sorrows of this life? All this, sir, the Pietists use to
persuade us that we are touching the thirty days which St. Paul pre-
dicted, which he calls grievous times wherein men shall be lovers of
themselves (2 Timothy 3: 1-5).

Having heard the Pietists complain of our corruption in morals,
listen to what they say about our corruption in doctrines. However,
having passed further on, remember, sir, what I have told you concerning their teaching that a doctrine pure and wholesome is not able for a

long time to dwell in the heart of a corrupt and worldly man. On the contrary, it is spoiled, it is corrupted, it is ruined little by little by deceit of heart, illusions of the flesh, and self-love which suggest such modifications, such limitations, such interpretations as those which make this pure doctrine corrupt, as can be noticed among the Pharisees with regard to the people of Israel, and of Jesus Christ; and the Roman Catholics with regard to the Church and the anti-Christ, etc., from which the Pietists conclude that since the largest and wisest part of our Protestantism is defective and so corrupt in morals, there is no need to be astonished that the most part of them, even the wisest, understand nothing of the things which are most effective in salvation.

They do not learn it in the school nor in books, as 1 Corinthians 9, Ephesians 3, 4, 6 and other similar scriptures, which are either unknown for the most part among the common people or appear obscure and suspicious to the wisest doctors. Now if we are blind in things so essential for salvation, is it necessary to be astonished, they say, that this blindness and this corruption are produced by doctrines which have contaminated the whole body of religion? Here are some of our doctrines which they see established and confirmed in practice, and which do not please our Pietists:

1. That the Reformation is perfect—although the principal thing is lacking, as we have heard above.

2. That the Roman anti-Christ is the only anti-Christ thus properly called—contrary to the sentiment of Saint John (1 John 2: 18) and of Jesus Christ Himself (Matthew 2: 30). There are then, they say, several anti-Christs among us, for pride, tyranny of conscience, confidence in ceremonial works, and persecution, which have always been the seeds of the anti-Christ, are not far from us.

3. The Pietists also consider it an error then that we say that Rome alone, situated on the seven mountains, is the Babylon, and that we are the true Zion. Indeed, that is Babylon where is produced the works of Babel. For it is not doctrine which makes the Church of God, or the true Zion, or Babylon (that is to say, the multitude confused and assembled through violence and fear and opposed to the holy Jerusalem) but *works*. As then, Zion signifies in the Scripture the universal Church of the children of God, even so Babylon signifies the universal Church of the wicked, as St. Paul specified them (2 Timothy 3: 1-6), Canaanites, Israelites, Edomites, Amalekites, etc., in which place they might be. Although Rome is evidently the capital of Edom, and the ocean of all corruption.

4. That outward idolatry and filth is more abominable and

despicable than the inner sins such as greed, confidence in virtues, in works, in churches, in outward liturgy, in the sacraments, and in men (Jeremiah 17:5). For they say the Lutheran and Reformed detest and hate more a Papist than a miser of their own.

5. That the true marks of the Church of Jesus Christ are the pure preaching of the Word and the legitimate administration of the sacraments, although the Scripture teaches nothing about that, but on the contrary it gives another set of marks, as we have seen above. The Pietists are of the opinion that such marks had for their source the love of the sect, and that consequently all denominations and churches which hold to these marks are subject to being called sectarian, since by these they are separated from all other members of the universal Church.

6. That a pastor or a doctor loving the world and his self-interests, that is to say a mercenary or a wolf, is capable of having and hearing the Word of God, and therefore to lead a flock to graze, the sheep being obliged to hear without leaving—against the opinion of Jesus Christ, who said that a blind man is not able to lead another blind man, else they will both fall into the ditch (Matthew 15:14), and a stranger will they not follow, but will flee from him (John 10:5).

7. That faith is consenting to the Word of God and an entire confidence in the merit of Jesus Christ—although faith goes much farther, for it depends not only on the grace of God and the merit of Jesus Christ, but also on His will, His power, His providence, and other virtues of God, for this is the faith of the ancients, which is strongly praised in the eleventh chapter of Hebrews, for which the walls of Jericho fell and which closed the mouths of lions. Such faith is not nullified according to the definition which we give to it. The Pietists, thinking of this faith, say that as the bride trusts absolutely in the love, the will, the power, the prudence of her husband after having renounced both her own power and her own will, so even the faithful after having renounced his own will, virtue, and other loves, recovers and trusts absolutely on the complete power, the providence, the grace, and the will of his God, and this faith goes so far that it is capable of making miracles as Jesus Christ promised to all His disciples. "If ye have faith as a grain of mustard seed, ye shall say unto this mountain, Remove hence to yonder place; and it shall remove; and nothing shall be impossible unto you" (Matthew 17:20, Mark 16:17).

8. That it is impossible to discover and distinguish the hypocrites from the faithful—as if the hypocrite is not a bad and putrid tree that one is able to discover from its lack of good fruit (Matthew 7:15-21), and as if the good man does not gather good treasure from his heart of good things, and the wicked man does not gather evil treasure from his

heart of wicked things, and as if finally they gather figs from thorns (Luke 6: 43-45).

9. That riches give the means to advance in the understanding of God and in the cultivation of holiness. The Pietists say that this doctrine is manifestly contrary to the testimony of Scripture, which teaches that it is impossible for a rich man to enter the Kingdom of Heaven, that God has chosen the poor, that the gospel is announced to the poor, that it is not necessary to amass treasures, since where they are our hearts and our faith are also, and we are not able to serve two masters—both God and mammon.

10. That we are able to defend or search for our prestige against the sentiment of Jesus Christ and His apostles.

11. That the great and the rich are able in virtue of their grandeur and their riches to go magnificently dressed and to maintain abundant and delicate tables—against the witness of Scripture (Amos 6: 36, Luke 16: 19, 1 Timothy 2: 9, 1 Peter 3: 3).

12. That a Christian is able to enter the Kingdom of Heaven without the cross of Jesus Christ; that is to say, without hating the world, without affliction, without tribulation, and without persecution—against the testimony of Scripture (Acts 14: 22, 2 Timothy 3: 12, Hebrews 12: 2-6, John 15: 19-20).

13. That true theology is able to be learned only through the knowledge of languages or through the frequenting of schools and universities; although this understanding comes from above from the Father of light; and God sometimes gives more knowledge to his little children than to the great doctors, wise and understanding of the world. One finds evidence for this . . . in these remarkable words of Jesus Christ: "O Father, Lord of Heaven and earth, I thank thee that thou didst hide these things from the wise and understanding, and didst reveal them unto babes" (Matthew 11: 25, 1 Corinthians 1: 20, 21).

14. Finally, that in our days the Holy Spirit does not communicate directly to persons as in the time when Christianity was new—as if God would have said in this matter that His promises would have relevance only with regard to the first Christians, and not in regard to all those who are far away, and whom the Savior our God shall call His own (Acts 2: 39). Also Jesus Christ has promised that His Father shall give the Holy Spirit to those who ask Him for it (Luke 11: 13, John 14: 16, 17; 16: 7).

After having heard the complaints of the Pietists on the above-mentioned doctrines, let us see, sir, what they think concerning this new and general reform of the Church which they proclaim, and which they call the glorious reign of Jesus Christ.

They say, then, that the reign of Jesus Christ is today confined within three narrow limits—that scarcely does the Son of God reign over the thousandth part of men, since Jesus Christ is said to reign over men when they have renounced the world and their flesh, and are led by the Spirit of God, searching only for those things which are from above, and esteeming as filth the world and its glory. But the contrary is seen today, for if the devil seizes nearly all the hearts of men, is one not justified in saying that it is the reign of the dragon, which has permeated the world, including all kinds of sects, religions, and denominations (Revelation 3:3, 4, 7 and 12:9)?

Furthermore, they add that the world and Satan reign, and that Jesus Christ and His members do not reign, but are as subjects; never conquerors, but the conquered; never judges, but the judged; from the smallest to the greatest one is able to see very clearly that it is not Jesus Christ who reigns. To say it clearly as St. Paul says, speaking of Jesus and His reign—"But now we see not yet all things subjected to him [Hebrews 2:8 and 10:12-13] for he sat down on the right hand of God, henceforth expecting till his enemies be made the footstool of his feet." And finally, the rest of the afflictions which Jesus permitted to happen to His mystical body, which is the Church, which He foretold, and which He sanctified by His example, will be accomplished during the period of the interregnum (Colossians 1:24, 1 Peter 2:21), from which one is able to conclude that these afflictions of Jesus Christ are necessary during this interregnum in order to test the faith, to destroy the old Adam, to restrain the passion until that tranquil and glorious future shall arrive (Acts 14:22, and 1 Peter 17:11).

In addition to that they remember that such a glorious reign on the earth has been promised to Jesus Christ and to His Church and they prove it by the following passages and others: Daniel 7:18, 22, 27; Psalm 72:8-11; Romans 2:25, 26; Revelation 11:15. I am not going to quote the passages for you. Find them yourself, sir, if you please, for I must conclude my story.

Now as to the nature and essence of this glorious reign. Nearly all the Pietists teach (with the exception of some, who exaggerate a little too much the material), that it must be spiritual, that is to say, that it must consist in an abundant effusion of the Holy Spirit, which shall be scattered on all flesh, as a flood, which shall inundate the entire church (Joel 2:28, and following). It shall be as a fire for purification, after Satan has been bound, following the promises made by the Spirit of God (Revelation 20:23), and to that will finally succeed an outward peace, over all the world where no one will be wronged, nor anybody hurt, "for the earth shall be, etc." (Isaiah 11:6-16 and 65:16 to the end of the chapter). Many who do not believe in this glorious reign challenge the cleverest doctors in theology to show them how many and to which years the several promises and prophecies in Scripture have had their fulfillment, or when they will have it.

Now as to the duration of this reign. It is to be one thousand years. (1) Because as God worked six days and rested the seventh, so even the faithful, or the Church, after having worked through battle and through affliction the period of six thousand years, after the example of her Creator and Savior, she shall rest on the seventh day, that is to say, the seventh millenium. "For a day is with God as a thousand years, and a thousand years as a day" (2 Peter 3: 8). (2) Because the Spirit of God has promised this in His revelations to St. John, [verses] 1-6 of the twentieth chapter. In regard to this passage, our theologians try to explain it away in saying that Satan has already been bound since the coming of Jesus Christ. It is certain that this prophecy has never been fulfilled, neither figuratively nor literally, but, on the contrary, the devil has never made so much havoc as since the coming of our Savior to the present, for without mentioning the absolute control which he has had on the pagans since his coming and which he still exercises in several quarters; what damage has he not done and still does to Christians, since, except for a small number of the elect which God has known, and who have never bowed the knee to the idol of this world, all the rest of the multitude of Christians, Papal, Reformed, Lutheran, and other denominations, have taken the mark of the beast on their forehead, in their habits, in their conversation, in their business, and in nearly all their actions, having been drunk with the wine of lewdness, being either crude and flagrant, or subtle and secretive.

In conclusion the Pietists say that this glorious reign of Jesus Christ is at hand:

1. Because the six thousand years are almost past.

2. Because in nearly all the Christian States there have arisen some pious men who proclaim with vigorous voice and through their writings that this reign is approaching, for the punishment of those who love the world, but for the peace of those who love God.

3. Because it seems that the fourth monarchy draws to an end.

4. Because ungodliness reigns today in all its force, and it seems to be trying to burst its bounds in order to hasten the judgments of God on the wicked.

5. Because it is noticeable today in several parts of the world that piety, faith, and love are trying to raise their heads, since there are several good men who are trying to rekindle this first zeal and this first virtue of newborn Christianity, and who wish, at the peril of their lives

and their peace to establish with exhortation and through writing this spiritual and true faith of which Jesus Christ spoke to the Samaritan woman (John 4: 23, 24).

6. And because it seems that the archangel Michael and his angels are beginning the combat against the dragon and his angels (Romans 4: 23, 24).

7. And because one sees today revolutions more surprising and more extraordinary than anybody has even seen in past centuries.

8. Finally, because they remark that it seems that people of good-will separate themselves from the ungodly and from the worldly, making provisions of oil and lighting their lamps in order to prepare for the coming of the bridegroom while the others, insensitive, sleep amidst the delights and the honors of the world, without the oil of the Holy Spirit, satisfied with feasting on a dream, and with but the empty shell of a religion which shall fail them at the coming of Jesus Christ, who shall say to them when they think to enter, "I never knew you."

III. But enough of that in regard to the doctrine of the Pietists. I shall pass now to their morals and their manners of living. It is here, sir, that I am able to draw sincerely a picture without flattery, for I have examined these people at firsthand, and have often carried on conversations with them, and it is true that I have found among them some hypocrites and that the devil in some places has created several monstrosities and extravagances, principally among the women, as at the time of the Reformation and of primitive Christianity, but I am also able to assure you that I have seen and known several of those Pietists who seem to have reached this perfection which one notices among the primitive Christians—childlike simplicity, content with whatever might happen, fearing nothing, without anger, and without the surge of passions which disturb other men, with the charity toward God and their neighbors quite extraordinary. Nevertheless holding fast to their homes where they pass the greater part of their time in prayer with God and invoking Him, fleeing with concern the honors and the riches of the world. In a word, these persons in business and in actions breathe only an extraordinary and very solid piety. For those who have not attained the degree of perfection of the best, they remark, however, that they flee with assiduity all sorts of worldly attractions; they are modest in their habits, in their house furnishings, and they have a real frugality in respect to their tables; they are found only very rarely in polite society for fear of committing such sins as speaking evil or not reprimanding scandal or a libertine, from fear of letting their conscience become corrupt and filthy, for it would be necessary then to wash in a great abundance of tears. They are chaste in their conversations as in their actions, and say firmly that a filthy and too free word is the mark of a profane and impure heart. Finally, they leave all gambling to the people of the world, holding nothing for indifference, but saying that all words, thoughts, and actions of the Christian ought to glorify God, ought to edify His name, and to advance His sanctification, and all that does not tend to that must be avoided as useless and dangerous to eternal salvation. To say it in a word—the love of God and of one's neighbor composes all their study, the rest of Protestantism being instructed in those things which concern salvation and the mysteries of religion, until I have seen their children of ten and twelve years running in confusion from doctors with gray beards. Believe me, sir, these are not fictions nor tales of imagination. If you do not wish to believe me, examine them yourself. You will find what I have told you. It is true that their enemies publish that they serve in this beautiful outdoors of piety in order to spread the poison which they hold hidden under such a beautiful appearance, but it is hard enough, not to say a test of divinity, to judge inwardly on this matter, to know without the witness of the works of the flesh. More that I can tell you is that a great part of the Pietists never frequent our churches, nor participate with us in the sacrament of the sacred heart, and others do it but rarely. They give for reason of their seeming conduct:

1. That almost all the preachers are not instructed of God, who in place of speaking of Christ with sincerity as for God and before God, on the contrary, falsify by their comments and their distinctions the same word, and in place of preaching Christ, preach themselves (2 Corinthians 2: 17, Galatians 1: 10). Or because they are worldly with pride and greed or with debauchery, the consciences of the Pietists do not permit them to assist in the sermons of such persons whom they regard as enemies of Jesus Christ, as blind and as strangers from which one must flee (John 10), and that, moreover, they are not able to abstain from witnessing publicly their indignation against such persons.

2. Because they are scandalized with the little respect with which people come into church, where they say God is present through His Holy Spirit. They are shocked to see vanity raise its head, to see them sleeping, laughing, talking as if one were at the market place. It is for these reasons that they are not able to assist with our assemblies. For the sacrament of the Lord's Supper they say they are not able to participate in good conscience with us:

(1) Because of the above-mentioned faults.

(2) Because they do not make any separation between the ungodly and the good people at the table of our Savior, where one can see scandalous sinners of flagrant notoriety as the greedy, the argumentative,

the lecherous, the proud, etc. mingle with the true Christians without having been first censored, even once, let alone several times. They are, however, acceptable to everyone and are permitted to come in this condition to profane the table of our Lord Jesus Christ against the express commandment of our Savior, who desires that the Church hold as pagans and tax-gatherers those who are not willing to obey the Church (Matthew 18: 17). After this they say that, in good conscience, how can we commune with such people whom we recognize to be scandalous sinners, and who are recognized to be such by the pastor and by part of the assembly? And especially since St. Paul expressly commands us never to mix with such people and not even to eat with them (1 Corinthians 5: 11). "That ye withdraw yourselves from every brother that walketh disorderly" (2 Thessalonians 3: 6). Notice that the Great Apostle prohibits us business with such people in the most common actions of life. How can we without sinning mingle with them at the table of our Savior, where Jesus Christ calls only His faithful and sinners truly converted, and not false Christians and sinners by profession? Finally, they add, that if they separate (on those occasions especially) the ungodly, the worldly, the greedy, the proud, etc. that one is able according to the apostle to recognize and to distinguish them easily (1 Corinthians 5: 11) from the faithful. One could thus cover with confusion the former, and who knows if this would not be the true means of leading them to an amendment of life.

IV. I am just about at the end of my story. There remains only to tell you of the persecutions which the Pietists suffer. I believe you know something of them; therefore, I shall not prolong this very much. I shall tell you only that many of them have been sent to prison for their belief, many have been exiled and deprived of their business and condemned by their friends, not for having committed punishable crimes, by the severity of the laws, nor for having incited seditions against the magistrate, but for having found occasion to speak to our clergy and trying to oppose ungodliness, which reigns in all the orders of society, and for having (according to the dictates of their conscience) deserted our temples, or rather the false pastors or the false prophets, and for having obeyed the commandments of God. I know some even who say that they never doubt that they will die for this belief, and who are preparing every day for it with an admirable fortitude. You should know, also, in order to make them odious, there is not one crime of which they are accused that the pagans did not say of the Reformers and the Waldenses, and which they do not say today of the Pietists. They are denounced as magicians, sectarians, disturbers of the peace, enemies of the magistrate, innovators of sacrilege, and infamous heresies, etc., and as they said of the first Christians that "(in these nightly assemblies after having extinguished the candles) they mix sensually one with another, and that they mock holy objects. With such crimes as these are they accused!" See Minut Felix. That is what they say also of the Pietists today.

But, sir, I assure you that the Pietists are honorable in all their nighttime relations as well as in persecutions which they endure, and in the torture of tyranny, which is turned against them, against all human and divine rights in the countries mentioned, confirming all those who recognize the genius of the Christian religion in this truth that the Reformed and Protestant Church has degenerated and has denounced entirely the spirit of Jesus Christ and His apostles since it imitates Rome and the Babylon anti-Christ, and doing this it has condemned others for the same reason. However, it is necessary only to observe exactly what God commanded through the prophet Jeremiah: "Flee out of the midst of Babylon, and deliver every man his soul: be not cut off in her iniquity; for this is the time of the Lord's vengeance; he will render unto her a recompense." And one reads: "And I heard another voice from heaven, saying, Come out of her, my people, that ye be not partakers of her sins, and that ye receive not her plagues. For her sins have reached unto heaven and God hath remembered her iniquities. Reward her even as she rewarded you, and double unto her double according to her works: in the cup which she hath filled. Fill her to double" (Revelation 18: 4-6).

And that is, sir, what I had promised you on the subject of Pietism. I shall repeat what I said in the beginning of this letter, that I give here nothing of my own, and that I have spoken only as a historian who makes profession of sincerity. I shall make one last comment, having come to the end, and which I am not able to omit, which is that most men are living asleep and buried in a deplorable certainty, without repentance or fear of heaven.

God has made these people to see the astonishing changes in the Church and in the State. He has created them to cry with full voice that all flesh is corrupted, that there is no man who is indeed safe, that all the States, classes, and professions must be converted, that the Savior is at the door, that His day is at hand, but all this lands on deaf ears, and the song of Catullus is the song of our Christians:

> Vivamus mea Lesbia, atque amemus,
> Rumores senum severiorum,
> Omnes unius aestimemus assis:
> Soles accidere & redite possunt,

Nobis cum semel occidit brevis lux,
Nox ist perpetua una dormienda!

It is with that, sir, that I end my little story, and some other time if you
desire it we shall particularize for you a little more about the affairs
and the doctrines of these people. I am

Sir,

Your very humble and very
obscure servant,

N. N.

## Passengers on the Allen

(List 10 A) A List of Passengers Imported in the Ship Allen from
Rotterdam, James Craiges, Master, Septemr. 11th, 1729.

Alixander Mack
Johannes Mack
Felte Mack
Alixander Mack, Junr.
John Hendrick Kalklieser
Jacob Kalklieser
Emanuell Kalklieser
Andrus Ponne
William Knipper
Hisbert Benter
Peter Lisley
Hance Contee
Jacob Possart
Jacob Wise
Christian Snyder
Jacob Snyder
Johannes Flickinger
Felte Beecher
Jacob Lisley
Christopher Matten
Paul Lipekipp
Christopher Kalklieser
Christian Cropp
Andries Cropp
Jacob Cropp, sick

Christian Cropp, Junr.
Hance Slaughter
Feltin Rafer
John Jacob Knight
Henderick Peter Middledorf
Mathew Bradford )
Nicholas Bayly ) English
Johannis Pettickhover
Johannis Kipping
Hance Erick Cogh
John Michael Amwigh
Hance Urick Kissle
John Jacob Kissle, sick
Ulderick Eley
Rinehart Hammer
Samuell Galler
Conrat Iller
Hance Gasper Kulp
John Martin Crist
John Jacob Hopback
Johannes Mcinterfeer
Christian Kitsintander
Linhart Amwigh
Mathias Snyder
Joseph Prunder

Johannes Prunder, sick
Mathias Ulland
Jorick Hoffart
Johannes Perger
Johannes Weightman
Phillip Michael Fiersler
Valentine Perhart Hisle

Hance Jorick Klauser
Hendrick Holstein, Germt.
Jorick Fetter
Alixander Till
David Lisley
Jacob Possart
Daniell Cropp, sick


## THESE FOLLOWING ARE UNDER THE AGE OF FIFTEEN

Johannes Possart
Christopher Gotlip Matter
John Henderick Prundar

Johannes Ulland
Christian Hoffart


## THE FOLLOWING ARE FEMALE PASSENGERS

Christina Margaret Kessell
Anna Barbara Kessell
Eve Tabaek Elee
Susan Hammer
Dorothia Galler
Margaret Iller
Elizabeth Iller
Maria Iller
Anna Phillis Kulp
Anna Catrina Crist
Magdelina Hopback
Phronick Mickinturfer
Anna Barbara Kitsintander
Magdelina Amwigh
Magdelin Snyder
Caterina Lisbet Prunder
Anna Maria Latrine
Catrina Ulland
Anna Margaret Hoffart
Anna Margaret Hoffart, Junr.
Anna Ursella Perger
Maria Phillis Whitman
Maria Catrina Fiersler
Susannah Catrina Hissle
Anna Maria Klauser

Maria Magdelina Campbin
Anna Maria Barbara Rafer
Agnis Kalklieser
Joanna Margaret Ponne
Ferina Knipper
Anna Margaret Mack
Caterina Benter
Anna Caterina Lisley
Marylis Lisley
Susanah Possart
Marilis Possart
Susanah Snyder
Stinkee Becker
Elizabeth Lisley
Maria Agnis Matten
Christina Lipkipp
Maria Kalklieser
Anna Margt. Mackin
Phillipina Mackin
Rosina Cropp
Caterina Slaughter
Anna Lisbet Pettickhofer
Maeta Lina [Pettickhofer]
Ketruid [Pettickhofer]
Anna Kipping

Sivilla Kipping

Anna Catrina Cogh

Anna Maria Ackhorden

Christina Lisley

Eve Possart

Johanna Kipping

Caterina Iller

James Craigie [Captain]

In Council, 15th Septemr. 1729.

The Govr. present wt. Messrs. Laurence & Asheton, James Craigs made Oath to the above List.

Robt. Charles.

James Craigie

N.B. the Ship cleared from Cows in the Isle of Wight.

"At the Courthouse of Philadelphia, September 15th, 1729, . . . A List was presented of the names of Fifty-nine Palatines, who with their Families, making in all about One hundred & twenty six Persons, were imported in the Ship Allen, James Craigie, Master, from Rotterdam, but last from Cows, as by Clearance thence dated 7th of July last." —From the Minutes of the Provincial Council, printed in *Colonial Records,* Volume III, page 368.

## Items Concerning Christopher Sauer, Sr.

The following material, translated from the original German, is of interest and is included here because of our interest in Christopher Sauer. This is Sauer, Sr., referred to. It should be remarked that the Pennsylvania Hospital is the first institution of its kind to be built in America.

Note that Sauer is thought of as a representative of the *German* community of Pennsylvania.

The author is indebted to E. M. Studebaker and O. B. Maphis for this material. In some researches they made they uncovered this information in 1946:

There are four items:

1. Extract from the *Pennsylvanische Berichte,* August 16, 1751, in which Christopher Sauer encouraged young Germans to give to said hospital.

2. A letter from Matthew Koplin, a German, to Christopher Sauer. Note that he made Christopher Saur the intermediary for a gift of land to the Pennsylvania Hospital.

3. A letter of acknowledgement from J. Crosby, president of the hospital, to Matthew Koplin. Observe that the given name of Koplin is translated Matthew in his own letter to Saur, while he is called Mathias when addressed by J. Crosby.

4. The fourth translation, which is taken from the *Pennsylvanische Berichte,* is an advertisement which we find in a number of the papers published by Sauer, which indicates some things which Sauer was selling. As we know, he made some study of medicine. It is really amusing to observe that he sold "fine soft bath sponges for children to clean themselves and for other uses" and mouse or rat poison to "persons known to be honest."

*Extract From the Pennsylvanische Berichte, August 16, 1751*

Germantown

The founders or contributors to the hospital in Philadelphia have made a beginning, and already accepted impoverished sick persons, and have rented a house, wherein they will be cared for until the new building is ready. The 2000 pounds from the Public Treasury has been granted for the construction and they are preoccupied if perhaps our proprietor should not wish to present them with the site near the town, from all too great economy as it is called, so might their 2000 pounds be little enough for the site and building necessary for a hospital for the whole country: So they do not have the liberty to touch the accumulated capital of 2000 pounds in Philadelphia, rather they receive 120 pounds interest from it, and as many impoverished sick persons will be housed and cared for as the 120 pounds make possible. So is the beginning made. It does not depend on one solitary Hospital Director, chosen through influence, as sometimes happens in Germany, who can decide for himself whom to accept or not and who is more concerned with making himself and his next-of-kin rich than with the care of the sick but each year 12 persons will be chosen from among those who have contributed, who must see that it is put to the best use in so far as they recognize it.

It is well known that the Germans have to provide for a hospital every year, as they have to help so many of their known and unknown friends, who come from the ships, when the merchants must put the impoverished in prison, there is no end to the begging, complaining, and lamentations over taxes. He who knows how wonderful good health is and how yearningly human nature longs to be helped in sickness and pain will surely help in such a praiseworthy project, for he can well imagine that a destitute person in illness and pain would not wish any the less to be cured in spite of the lack of money to pay for the services of doctors, nurses and attendants.

Therefore we take this opportunity and the liberty to beg or to remind or to ask any young Germans who have either acquired the world's goods, or who have been blessed by the Lord, if they will not contribute something. It happens sometimes that one out of 10 who have been helped returns to thank God. It is not to be supposed however that only the good, or living brothers of the spiritual body of Jesus will be accepted, but also the wicked and ungrateful, for they also are human and it is said be ye merciful as your Father in Heaven also is merciful, Luke 6. He lets the sun shine upon the ungodly and the good, and the rain fall upon the just and the unjust, Matthew 5. If God were to distribute his mercies only among the pious and just, many of us would die of hunger. And because anything that anybody gives or bequeathes, will bring in more income, as long as the hospital stands and poor sick persons exist, so may many be among those to whom Christ will say Inasmuch as ye did it unto the least of these my brethren (to the sheep on his right hand) ye have done it unto me, Matthew 25. This blessed voice will be better than a 1000 pound sterling. Many on the left hand will wish he had sown in faith and love that he might hear this voice when it is too late. But he who does not gladly give or promise something will be reminded of: He who practices mercy, should do it with gladness, Romans 12: 8. God loveth a cheerful giver, 2 Corinthians 9: 7.

*Excerpts From Minutes, Board of Managers, Pennsylvania Hospital,*
*October 3, 1751*

*At a Board of Managers, met at the Widow Prat's*

. . . . .

A Letter from Matthew Koplin to Christopher Sauer was laid before the Trustees, and the Translation thereof read, which are as follows, viz.

September 2, 1751

My dear & beloved Friend,

Having seen in one of your News-Papers, that the Contributors to the Pennsylvania Hospital are earnestly concern'd about its Welfare, and have already begun to take Care of the Sick-Poor: and having also observ'd that it has not such a Foundation, nor is likely to become such a Hospital as I have seen and known in Germany, where great Sums, given as Alms, were collected, but made a bad Use of, being appropriated by the Masters of the Hospital to the enriching themselves and favouring their Friends; so that they lived in Plenty, Superfluity & Voluptiousness, insomuch that they could keep their Horses and Coaches like rich People, altho' they had Nothing before, nor any Income but out of the Funds of the Hospital; by which Means, the Poor and Needy were not taken Care of according to their Necessity, the Money being otherwise consumed. But when I consider the Noble Foundation of this our Hospital, I can't but believe it will be managed by impartial Persons; and have therefore thought fit to make a free Gift, and I do hereby accordingly give a Lot of Land for the Use thereof, situate between Germantown & Philadelphia, and have herewith sent you Deed of said Land, out of which the Managers of the Hospital may make such a Conveyance of it for the Use of the Hospital at Philadelphia, as they shall think proper, and send it to me, and I and my Wife will set our Hands & Seals thereto, before lawful Witnesses. If I should remain any longer in the Flesh, I hope they will excuse me from coming to the annual Election of the Managers, Treasurer, etc. for it may be done without me. I am the old

Matthew Koplin

P.S. Pray don't take it amiss, my mentioning the bad Use made of Alms in Germany as I have no Thoughts of any Thing of the Kind being done here.

Ordered,

That a Letter of Thanks be sent to Matthias Koplin with the Deed prepared for him to execute.

And the same being drawn and agreed to is as follows, viz.

Philad., Oct. 3, 1751

Respected Friend
Matthias Koplin,

Thy Friend Christopher Saur had communicated to the Managers of the Pennsylvania Hospital, thy Letter to him, expressing thy Intention of making a free Gift to the said Hospital of a valuable Lot of Ground situate between Germantown and Philadelphia; for which the Managers, in Behalf of the Poor, return thee sincere Thanks; and hope thy charitable and generous Donation, and those made by other well dispos'd People to this Hospital, will never be misapplied in the Manner mention'd in thy Letter as hath been usual in some Hospitals in Germany. As a Caution to future Managers against such Misapplications, they have order'd thy Letter to be copied in their Book of Minutes or Records of their Proceedings, that it may be preserved to Posterity, as a Testimony of the original Intention of the Founders of this pious Institution. The Managers salute thee respectfully, by

Thy Friend,

J. Crosby, President

To Matthias Koplin, living within        )
                                          )
     Miles of Perkiomen, near the Trapp   )

## A Sauer Advertisement for Medicines

At Christoph Sauer in Germantown the following medicinal wares are to be had: by the pound or smaller measure and weight, namely Rhubarb. Camphor. Myrrh [?]. Borax. Einhorn [Ammonia?]. Asafetida. Laurel. Jalap root. Opium. Cinnabar. Gumi hadra [?]. Gumi gutta [?]. Arcanum duplicatum. Semen stapis agria. Feihl wurtzel [?]. Oil of juniper. White petroleum. Red petroleum. Oil of turpentine. Resin. Fly poison or gnat powder. Fine soft bath sponges for children to clean themselves and for other uses. Persons known to be honest can also buy mouse powder or rat poison. Also glasergers [?].

## EXCERPTS FROM THE EPHRATA CHRONICLE CONCERNING G. A. MARTIN

The late President Winger used to assert that George Adam Martin was one of the most talented and influential men in the ministry of the early Brethren. This is certainly true. The writers of the *Ephrata Chronicle* had such an estimate of him, even though some of the Brethren may not always have appreciated him.

The following is an autobiographical sketch which is found embedded in the *Chronicle*. It is followed by some observations and additional information by the *Chronicle* writer. These excerpts are included here as being among the most informative bits of writing from the first generation of the Brotherhood. They need to be read with discrimination. Martin was sincere and of unusual depths of spiritual life, but he was also emotional and his temptations were those of a restless, brilliant man who feels himself superior to many of his associates. He never married. He belonged to European Separatist Pietism as well as to the Brethren. In these excerpts we can feel the real life of the Ephrata Community.

In the year 1733 I was strongly moved to repentance and a change of life, and all without any man's intervention, which confused me so that I did not know what to do. For my heart was troubled. Wherever I went or was my conscience was so disturbed that I avoided all company and felt grieved at any vanity I met with. I was constantly frightened and alarmed, for my conscience smote me everywhere; besides I was young, bashful and timid. I therefore went about like a lost sheep, and thought all people better than myself, which opinion indeed I still have. I never looked for much from men, and if I occasionally listened to some one preaching, I was not frightened by it, because I felt myself more damned than any preacher could damn me; nevertheless, some little hope remained, and I thought perchance I might yet be saved. Being in such a condition I was baptized on my faith in the year 1735. This I did to honor God in Christ Jesus and intended to follow him; but had no further thought about the piety of a Community, because my inner troubled state did not permit me to think about other things. All my thinking and striving were only as to how I might enter the kingdom of God.

After my baptism, when alone in the woods, I knelt down behind a tree and prayed. After I had finished, it came into my mind to open the New Testament, and whatever I found under my right thumb that should be my precept during life. Then I turned up: "Study to show thyself approved unto God, a workman that needeth not to be ashamed, rightly dividing the word of truth" (II Timothy, II, 15.) This troubled my mind excessively; sometimes I took it to be a temptation; then, again, as if I had tempted God; and again that the Spirit had mocked me. Taking all together I did not know what to make of it. To become a workman in the church of God, that I dared not harbor in my mind. Soon after I was led into such temptation for about sixteen weeks that I incessantly heard nothing but: "You are damned! You are damned!" This frightened me so that I enjoyed neither sleep, nor eating or drinking. My father asked me what was the matter with me, but I dared not tell him, for I thought that never before had a person lived on earth in such a damnable state. At last I was delivered out of this bondage, received pardon, and became a recipient of the gracious visitation of my God in Christ Jesus, and of the power of regeneration, of which before I had known nothing. Thus by grace and compassion alone I became one of the redeemed of the Lord. After this I became cheerful and joyous in my Saviour, Jesus Christ, diligently read the Bible, exercised myself in prayer, took pleasure in divine things, and meddled with nothing but what concerned my salvation; besides I held the Brethren in high esteem and had a sacred regard for everything good.

It happened in the year 1737 that my Superintendent was called upon to go to the great Swamp, in order to baptize several persons. When he announced this at the meeting and asked who was willing to go with him, I was willing to go. After our arrival, when the meeting was over, the persons to be baptized were introduced, and a passage from Luke XIV was read to them, about the building of towers and waging war, which also was customary among them even in Germany; for when I was baptized this surprised me, and I did not know what to think of it. It was done as often as persons were to be baptized; so that you did not know whether you were to build or not, to go to war or not, or whether God had 10,000 and the devil 20,000 men. As soon as you came to the water the hymn was usually sung: "Count the cost says Jesus Christ, when the foundation Thou wouldst lay," etc., which A. M. [Alexander Mack] had composed already in Germany. When these confused transactions were now also enacted here, as was customary, it suddenly seized me so that my limbs trembled, and it flashed like a flame through my whole being, and before I knew it I heard myself speaking in an overloud voice. I was frightened at myself, for I thought of nothing less than of speaking. I said that it was not the Lord Jesus' intention to bring such things before candidates for baptism, for their purpose was to enter into their covenant with God by baptism, and to build upon the rock Jesus Christ; those who wished to build a tower besides the temple of God might have such things brought before them. This speech frightened everybody, and all were silent and dumb. At last our Superintendent, M. U. [Martin Urner] of blessed memory, said, "What shall we do then, for something must be said to the people." Without taking thought I answered: "The 18th Chapter of Matthew, about exhortation and punishment, might be read;" which proposal was adopted from that hour, and is still customary with them to this day.

This was the first stumbling block I found in their doctrine. But because they adopted my suggestion throughout the whole country, and no person moved against me, but all were surprised and thought that this movement on the part of a young man which they saw and heard was the work of the Spirit of God, I greatly honored them, since they in so childlike a way gave all the honor to God. Moreover they now noticed me more, especially did my Superintendent love me until he died, and he was much grieved when he had to lose me. But I did not respect the household of the Congregation, and nothing of the kind touched me; but I was earnest in my calling to gain favor before God by my life and behavior. I took no offence at any person, nor did I seek their esteem; I only endeavored to follow the dictates of my conscience. But it happened by and by that they, contrary to my wish, chose me as their Superintendent, after I had already obediently moved across the waters of the Susquehanna. Before this occurred it happened that Count Zinzendorf and many of his Brethren came into the country and occasioned a great stir, especially by his conferences. And because all denominations were invited to them, I too was deputed by my Superintendent to attend them. When I arrived at the conference, which was held at Oley, I found there some of our Baptists, Seventh Day men, Mennonites and Separatists. The Count himself was president, and for three days I heard queer and wonderful

things there. After my return home I went to my Superintendent and said that I looked upon the Count's conference as
snares, for the purpose of bringing simple-minded and inexperienced converts back to infant baptism and church-going,
and of erecting the old Babel again. We consulted with each
other what to do and agreed to get ahead of the danger, as
some Baptists had already been smitten with this vain doctrine,
and to hold a yearly conference, or as we called it, a Great
Assembly, and fixed at once the time and place. This is the
beginning and foundation of the Great Assemblies of the
Baptists.

After this general meeting had been established, the opportunity was offered to speak of various matters whenever we met,
and since most of the Baptists who had laid the foundation of
their Congregation in Schwarzenau, were uneducated arch-
idiots and ignoramuses, their followers, of course, brought
their absurd notions also to this meeting, always appealing to
their predecessors, saying the old Brethren in Germany did so,
and we must not depart from their ways.

When I heard this I contradicted them, which occasion-
ally gave rise to disputes, in which I always had P. B. [Peter
Becker] and M. U. and most of the common people on my side.
But among other things something once occurred which
appeared to me to be heretical, for when A. D. [Abraham Diboy
(Dubois?)] who still was one of the first, once said that our old
Brother A. M. had believed the same, I was at once aflame and
boldly contradicted it. But another Brother, M. F. [Michael
Frantz] took the affair out of my hands and said: "If it had
not been for this I should not have joined the Brethren." To
this I answered: "Then you have a poor reason for your change
of religion." Meanwhile ears were pricked up and the matter
was talked about, and I said I did not know how Christ Jesus
could call himself a son of man if he had not taken upon
himself something from the Virgin consecrated for this purpose, for it was evident that she never had known a man.
Then M. F. answered that he had not received more from the
Virgin than a wanderer who passes through a town received
from the town; or than a ball which passes through a gun, or
the water which runs through a pipe. I was frightened at such
an expression. M. U. sat alongside of me and said: "May God
protect us against this!" But he whispered into my ear: "Speak
out against this, it is heretical; do not spare it." I then said
that if it were as they said it would have been all the same
whether the Virgin was holy or not; a wanton might then as
well have given birth to him since he received nothing from

her, which is blasphemous to think and far more to say. This frightened them so that they left off defending this thing; the dispute, nevertheless, lasted two days before this Mohammedan Goliath was slain. It may be thought that I have deviated too far from my reasons why I left the Baptists; but no, these are the very reasons, for I took offence at the foundation and origin, because the originators deviated from their aim and basis, which in my opinion is the love of God towards all men, and formed a sect, like the Inspired, out of the great awakening which had taken hold of them in Germany, and aroused strife and hatred by their disputes. This George Graben told them to their faces, and especially to A. M., at a public meeting in Holland, being inspired to it, saying: "You and all of you are dead, and have died to the life of God;" all which was listened to by W. K. [William Kebinger], who had just been liberated out of the prison in Gulch, where he had been incarcerated for the sake of the truth; he told me all this. At the very commencement they adopted needless restrictions, in that they did not allow anyone who was not baptized to partake with them of the Holy Sacrament. Had they not been so sectarian in this matter, and been more given to impartial love, they would have found entrance to more souls in their great awakening and largely promoted the glory of God. But, instead, sectarianism, quarrelsomeness and discord spread through their whole awakening in Germany as far as to Switzerland. Therefore, also, the incomparable teacher, J. N. [John Nass], separated from them, and stood alone, until he went to America and arrived in Philadelphia, to which place A. M. went to meet him, and entreated him for God's sake to forget and forgive what had happened in Europe; to which the same agreed. A. M. by his diligence also prevented the above mentioned J. N. from coming to Ephrata at the time of the awakening, otherwise he would have been a victim of it too, for his testimony concerning the renunciation of the world was as similar to the testimony in Ephrata as one drop of water is to another. He afterwards moved to Amwell, in New Jersey, and superintended the Community there. I visited him there several times, and was much edified by his conversation, and pleased and surprised at his great and sound mind and the gifts which God had bestowed on him. I might here mention many things which he made known to me. He told me that A. M. had been an honest and faithful man, but that he lacked enlightenment. Perhaps this was because they had fallen out with each other about the incarnation of Jesus Christ. He said to my face, "You will not agree with these people," meaning the Baptists; "either they will reject you, or you them, for a truly converted man cannot live with them; and I," he added, "should I live another year, shall again withdraw from them." But he died within that very year, and is buried in Amwell, among twenty children, all of whom lie buried around him.

With Christian Libe, who also was a preacher among them, strange things likewise happened. He was taken prisoner in Basle, where he was engaged in divine affairs, and was sold into the galleys, but ransomed after two years. At last he settled in Creyfeld, where he and the above-mentioned J. N. superintended the Community, until they at last had a fall-out, because J. N. called him a pill-monger publicly before the whole Congregation, and then left. But Christian Libe tried to continue the Congregation, although everything wasted under their hands; the Brethren who had been prisoners withdrew, the whole congregation was given up, and everything went to ruin. He himself became a merchant, and even at last a wine merchant, and married out of the Congregation, against their own rules, and not a branch is left of their Baptist business in all Europe. Such matters, and many others not mentioned, prove to me that their fundamental principles cannot endure before God and the world; for they neither know, nor are they able to conduct the office of the new covenant, because they had no true knowledge of salvation, nor of the righteousness which avails before God, and is reckoned to us as faith; but they want to force and perfect everything through righteousness, by punishing, condemning and avoiding, which is not according to the new covenant, but the letter of the law, consisting of commandments and laws.

If God had not spared a branch of the root of Hochmann from Hochenau, the whole brood would have died at birth, like the Baptists of Munster. This innocent branch was P. B., who was a spiritual son of Hochmann, but was baptized, and came to live at Creyfeld, where he energetically exercised the gifts he had received from God, in singing and fervent praying, to the benefit of the Congregation; although he was otherwise no orator, but led a quiet life. Soon after he had to experience what he had not expected, for his spiritual Father had taught him peace and love; but here he heard much quarreling and strife, which soon deeply grieved him. It happened that a young Brother, Hacker by name, who had studied, and who was full of love and an intimate friend of the said P. B., wanted to marry the daughter of a merchant, who also had been baptized into the Congregation, but still served the Mennonites as preacher, because they did not wish to lose him, and gave him a yearly salary of 800 Gulden. This man was glad for such a son-in-law, and married them with great pleasure, not thinking that it would produce such a great excitement in the Congregation. But when the affair became known the tumult in the Congregation became so great that Christian Libe, the second teacher, and with him four single Brethren rose up against it and excommunicated said Hacker, though J. N. and the Congregation wished only to suspend him from breadbreaking. This godless excommunication ruined the whole Congregation in the town of Creyfeld. I heard the blessed teacher, J. N. say that more than 100 persons in Creyfeld had been convinced in favor of the new baptism, but on account of this ban everything was ruined and killed. And since no Moses was there, who might have sent Aaron with the censer, the fire of the ban burned on and consumed the whole Congregation, which still pains my heart whenever I think of it. But it touched poor Hacker most, who took all the blame on himself. The spirits took possession of him so that he fell sick and died of consumption; as they were converted people they were able to accomplish something. His good friend P. B., however, was with him in his utmost need, up to his death.

After this P. B. concluded to move to Pennsylvania, and when this became known several others moved with him; but the spirit of discord and ban also moved with them, and so wounded and corrupted them on the other side of the ocean, that they could hardly be cured in America. But God, nevertheless, took care of this branch, that it should bear fruit from the root, and brought it about that the German ban-branches were broken off, in order that this branch might have room to grow, and at last it blossomed and bore fruit in America, as in a garden of God. But the dear soul, P. B., could not attain his object, for the wild Baptist ban-branches always tried to paint a European shadow before his eyes; so that he died having fellowship with hardly anyone, for none of them understood his nature. Now I return to our yearly meeting, at which the European ban-branch continually became a topic of conversation, so that you always had to contend with these quarrels, until A. D. and M. F. at last died. Then other and thinner branches came forth, with which it was still more difficult to deal, until at last they put me out. Then I thought the affair would end, but it only commenced in earnest; for as quiet as ever I kept they let me have no peace. I was heartily tired of their affairs. Some, however, still adhered to me and could not leave me. They also were suspected and were avoided . . ., for whoever would not ban me himself had to be banned.

Now I became puzzled, for the wild European ban-branches threw such a shade, mist, darkness and gloom over the eyes of my mind that I could not see the light of the sun in the Gospel. I still lay buried under the hellish ban-doctrine, and my conflict was very great, for I was even afraid to doubt the ban-doctrine. In Germany I should willingly have entered the highest classes of the high school, but here I had to attend high school against my will, had to learn the language of Canaan, and to begin with A. This, indeed, appeared very strange to me, because nearly everybody who knew me considered me a great doctor of Holy Writ. There I lay under a heavy rod, severely beaten both by God and men, for the treacherous dealt treacherously with me and I was so lean. (Isaiah XXIV, 16). For the justice of God pursued me and all the good in me was turned into evil, because I had taken it as my own. Here my earnestness was turned into hypocrisy, my singing and praying into boastfulness, my preaching into vanity, my journeying and visiting into an outrunning of God before He had sent me. My friendliness was dissimulation, my weeping and my tears a sectarian longing, my conversation with men on religious subjects a fraud, my piety a mere show, my reading and my studies a prying art, my desire to convert men a rebellion against God. For the cursers cursed me (namely, the old Baptist), and those who are ready to awaken the Leviathan (Job III, 8); for whoso banneth he curseth. Here I had to learn the language of Canaan, willing or not willing, like Balaam, who, whether he wished or not, was compelled to bless and could not help it, however much he wished to curse. (Num. XXIII, 20.) Here, then, God severed all fellowship of my conscience with the European ban-teachers and showed me how their foundation was laid in cursing and blessing. For, if a person does not wish to be blessed by them, they curse him like those who curse and who awaken the Leviathan, and they rejoice in the ruin of such people and say that that is the judgment of God (see A. M.'s little book, pages 107, 108, 109; also the answer to Gruber's twenty-second question), at which talk any one instructed by God should verily grieve in his heart. May God preserve mine and everybody's heart from such a doctrine, because it is so far removed from the doctrine of Christ, which teaches: "Love your enemies; bless them that curse you!" May God, the Almighty, have mercy.

Therefore I believe that the European Baptists have no business in America, but that they escaped hither as fugitives from the Spirit of God, which would not allow them to build their nest in Germany, because they were corrupt in their principles; for without knowing it they had been cheated by the spirit of Balaam, who rode and struck the she-ass before he was sent. (Num. XXII.) I further believe that it would have been better for the American awakenings if they had never come to America; but flight is permitted in the Old and New Testaments. However, had they fought out their fight in Europe, since they were there awakened, it would have been more to their honor. For although I disagree with their fundamental principles in time and eternity (except baptism, the Lord's supper and the rite of feet-washing), I nevertheless respect them before God, but especially A. M., a man who suffered much for God, in spite of the great and grave errors which he had, like many of the saints; for a man who with his congregation leaves his inherited religion, leaves Babel and Egypt, experiences what one who is no leader cannot experience, as did Moses, John Huss, Martin Luther, Ulric Zwingli, Menno Simons, Count Zinzendorf, Conrad Beissel, etc.

There never was a false prophet, who had not also some truth.

There never was a godless person, who had not before been converted.

There never has been an accuser of his brother, or a despiser of his mother's son, who has not had the covenant of God on his lips and proclaimed the laws of God.

There never was a calumniator, who had not before known the truth.

There never was one who cursed, who had not before known how to bless.

There never went a person astray, who had not before been on the right way.

There never was a liar, who did not before fall from the truth.

There never was a bitter envier, who was not before in the bonds of love.

There never was an enemy, who was not a friend before.

There never was one who recognized the truth, before he recognized the lies in himself.

Now I will briefly answer a second question: How and why I might have joined the Seventh Day Baptists? Although you might as well have asked: How and why I might have joined the children of God? For my Congregation is the largest of all, since I am at one with all who belong to the kingdom of God. (Matth. XII, 50.) But I must begin my narrative at the beginning. On my account nearly sixty souls were banished (a likeness to John IX, 22), because they would not believe in lies, nor follow the envy of their preachers; therefore, we formed a Congregation. However I continued to preach as before, and there was great commotion throughout almost the whole land, so that I was in demand at Conestoga, Philadelphia, Germantown, Conewago, Monocacy, as far as Virginia. And although I kept up fellowship with all un-sectarian souls, I, nevertheless, was not intimate with my own trusty Brethren and Sisters. About this time Brother Frederick Fuhrman held a love-feast, to which all this little flock gathered and some were baptized; this was the first love-feast. But the Congregation increased in membership by baptism, so that during a journey of four weeks twenty-six were bap-tized and twelve love-feasts held. But as the affair progressed it happened that I was expected at Conestoga. I, therefore, got ready, and three Brethren with me. I long before had intended to see the Brethren at Ephrata. When we arrived at Lititz I sent two of my Brethren by another way to those who expected me, to announce to them that I was there, and if they wished to have a meeting held the said Brethren should come to Ephrata before the meeting and notify us. I and my Brother, John Horn, however, with staff in hand, went direct towards Ephrata. Following the road we first arrived at the Sisters' household, though we did not know who lived there. We went to a worthy matron and asked where Friedsam lived. She showed us the way. We went straight to it and knocked, when old Nagele came out and asked where these men came from. I answered that we came from far, for I did not wish them at once to know who we were, for they knew my name but not my person. Then he said: "Come in then," and opened the door. The old Father reverently rose and received us with a kiss, and the others did the same, for he had visitors at the time. Then he made us sit behind the table, he sitting before it, and said: "Where do these dear men come from?" I answered: "We come from far" (for I restrained myself). He asked "But from where?" I said: "From Canecotschicken [Conococheague?]. He said: "Then you know George Adam?" I answered: "Yes, we know him well." He spoke: "Ah, how is he?" I said: "As you see," for I could no longer hold back. "Ah," he said to this, "are you George Adam? Here lies the letter which you wrote; we were just speaking about you when you knocked." We continued the conversation, and nothing was said on either side to which we both did not agree.

While conversing thus animatedly, a Sister entered, brought a tub of water and an apron, put them down, and silently left; who she was, and who had ordered her to do so,

I do not know even to this very hour. The old Father rose and said "Come Brethren, sit down here, I will wash your feet." So he washed our feet, and Brother Nagele dried them for us. Then I said: "You have washed our feet, now let us also wash yours," to which they consented; so I washed their feet, and Brother Horn dried them. When this was done, he said, "Let us go into the Sisters' house." I said I should like also to visit my old pastor M. and Brother Obed. He said that could also be done, but desired that we first should go to the Sisters' house. We went there, and they prepared a splendid meal for us, during which we all the time continued our conversation; but nothing was said on which we did not agree. After this we ascended the hill where Brother Obed lived. On the way up he said to me, "God has done this, that you had to come to us, for with us everything lies prostrate, and we have for years been unable to hold any meetings; I hope you have come to raise up again the fallen down hut." I was surprised at this candor, and thought perhaps there was some trick behind it. But I afterwards learned that it was sincerity, and through all my life until his death, I never heard of unfaithfulness in him.

When we arrived there, and had welcomed each other, he said, "How do you do, Brother Obed? How about heaven?" Such speech continued and all was harmony, which pleased my Brother Horn so much that he afterwards remarked: "You will not bring me away from these people again, do what you please;" which I heard with pleasure. At the close of the visit the old Father asked whether we would not like to visit the Sisters? I said we had no time now, we expected two other Brethren who had left us at Lititz, who were to inform us where and when the meeting was to be held. "Why, do you know what," he said, "I will make them assemble in their prayer-hall, so that you can see them all; it is also desired that you should make an address to them;" and this it was resolved to do. After this we visited our old pastor Miller, who reverently received us, and met us with all the modesty becoming an honorable man. In the course of conversation I asked him whether he did not still owe something to the R. [Reformed]. He said, "I no longer have a drop of blood in me that is R——d." I said, "That is not what I ask." "Oh!" he said, "I understand, not only to the R——d but to all men, whatever I have and can;" which pleased me.

Meanwhile it was some time before our two Brethren arrived, and reported how it was to be. At the same time news arrived that the old Father and the Sisters had assembled in their prayer-hall, and were waiting for us. Since our number of visitors was now again complete, we were all conducted thither by the old Brother Eleazar, and were shown to our seats. An inward emotion here seized me; my spirit felt the presence of a divine majesty; the veil was removed, in which all the nations are enveloped. I saw the pathway of the saints into the holy of holies; the spirits kissed each other in stillness, and a divine, holy, mutual, and profound unity was entered into without a word, voice, utterance, or speech, for there reigned silence for a long time as if no person were there. Smell, taste, feeling, even seeing and hearing, all were one, just as I have seen two small flocks of sheep unite in which there were no rams.

At last my spirit was called back again. My eyes were full of tears when the Sisters began to sing a hymn, as well as I remember: "The streets of Zion are desolate;" which brought tears to many eyes. After this was finished, I spoke: "You sang a hymn for us, let us now also sing one for you." Then we sang the "Song of the Lilies," but as it had escaped my memory, I asked Brother Horn for the words, and he told them to me; then we sang it to the end, which simplicity astonished the Sisters. After quiet was restored, I made a short address, although I felt no particular inclination to speak. I had various impressions from the spirit of prophecy, but since our time was limited we had to accommodate ourselves to it. Thus everything passed most pleasantly. A fellowship was formed, and the unity of spirits concluded without a word, without conditions, without questioning as to how or when, without care, without labor, without fear, without distrust, without consideration; in love, with love, through love, out of love, and for eternal love; and neither world nor time, neither flesh nor blood, neither friend nor foe, neither the present nor the future, neither fear nor death, neither devil nor hell can break it, for Two became One, and were One before they knew it. And thus it is with all who are truly born again; for they are children, sons and daughters of God Almighty. So far the record.

Such are the particulars of this important union, related by the Brother himself. It must be known, however, that in spite of his banishment he still had a strong following among the Baptists, who were honest people, and began to think that he had been unjustly treated; and who, therefore, were disposed to stake their lives on his innocence. The most prominent of these were John Steiner, John Horn, Peter and Abraham Knipper, Frederick Fuhrman, George Scheitler, Peter Zug, Finck, etc. But the reception of these two Brethren brought about great changes; for, in the first place, these two visiting Brethren were seized with holy wonder when they saw that the union was made in the spirit without any words, as they had thought that articles of agreement would be laid before them. Afterwards the old hatred between the two Communities was again revived on this account, for the reception of Brother G. A., nullified the ban which the former Brethren had laid on him; all of which happened in the prayer-hall of the Sisters, as above mentioned; for there the holy Mother came down from above with the oil of anointing, and healed his wounds; wherefore he was often heard to say: "Rejoice with me, for I have found the peace which I had lost." It appears that the Superintendent had received, as a trust from God, a blessing for the B——— Community, of which they would have become partakers had they humbled themselves; for he was the greatest stumbling-stone which their Community ever encountered. But because they failed to endure the test, the choice fell upon another. For we must concede to this Brother the honor that he was the first among them, who arrived at a holy harmony and yet remained a Baptist. For all of this people who had joined the Community before him, sent their letters of withdrawal to their people, but Brother G. A., above spoken of, was faithful to their statutes, and neither a second baptism, nor the Sabbath, nor any of the various other ordinances of the Community, were urged upon him. Therefore it was ordained by God that Brother G. A. was to earn the blessing, which their whole Community might have had; and the Superintendent once addressed the following impressive words to him: "You shall be blessed, and also remain blessed." When, shortly before his death, he once more visited the Superintendent, the latter said to him: "My salvation rests in your hands." All this created an extraordinary esteem for the Superintendent in this good Brother, and all the letters he wrote to him were full of special expressions of love, while the superscription sometimes contained the title: Pontifex Maximus.

Some of the Baptists who saw a little further, expected that the Superintendent's bearing towards this man would subdue him sooner than all their bans; but in the Community in and around Ephrata he occasioned great excitement, especially in the households. For up to this time the priestly office had been in the hands of one of the Solitary, but now the domestic household also wished to have part in it, which brought with it such temptations, that one house-father, J. S. [John Senseman], declared on his death-bed that this Brother would be the cause of the Community's destruction. But because the Superintendent was the first to condescend to him, there was no help, everybody had to follow suit; and if any one had not done so, judgment would have come upon him, so that he would not have dared to lift up his hands towards God. All this was not unknown to the said Brother, therefore he once declared that all the good in Ephrata rested in his hands. After the visit was now concluded with blessing, the Superintendent dismissed them with letters of recommendation to the Brethren at the Bermudian. Soon after, moreover, he sent two of the oldest Brethren, Jehoiada and Lamech, to the Brethren at the Bermudian, and expressed himself in the following manner, namely, that they should receive Brother G. A. as if it were himself. This was saying as much as that they should take him as their priest, which greatly troubled them, so that they protested that their priests lived at Ephrata. A venerable house-sister was even seized with a fatal sickness on that account, of which she died; it happened to her like to the wife of a son of the priest Eli, who, when in labor, was more concerned for the glory of God, than for her own child, and said: "The glory of Israel is taken captive" (I Sam. IV, 19). But after they had learned to submit to God's wonderful guidance they became one Community, for before this they lay under suspicion, because most of those who had moved away from the Community at Ephrata had done so for improper reasons. If you wish to build churches you must lay the foundation on the lowliness of Christ, else you build in the air.

## ANNUAL MEETING ADVICES

There were no authorized Annual Meeting minutes until 1832. There were "advices" which were passed to the members of the Brethren churches by word of mouth from those present at the meetings, especially the elders. These advices were signed by some of the leading elders. They bear resemblances to stenographic memos rather than to formal decisions of a legislative body. This accounts for the form of some of the earlier minutes.

The photostat on the opposite page shows the final page of the advices of the Annual Meeting of 1799. It is of interest particularly for the names of the elders which are affixed to it. The original manuscript of these advices was made available through the courtesy of Harry Garber of Ohio.

## EXCERPTS DEPICTING BRETHREN LIFE IN THE MID-NINETEENTH CENTURY

### A.   Travel to and From Conference

The first mention of railway travel in the columns of the *Gospel Visitor* occurs on page 82 of the issue of September 1852, in early anticipation of Yearly Meeting of 1853.

fein wixten und bewilligung fort sehen, tritt aber der bruder
gleichen Langenacker sich das dienens oder das ehrliche gemein amts
gegen die lösen des aposteln daer sagt hat gemein am amt so wurdet
er ins amt, und nennt der bruder Langenacker sich selbst, tritt
der gemeinde also dass er sich zu dienen, so da ne die versamlung
nicht beysicht, so bestimmt er sich selbst dieselbe, so das der bruder
zu gemein Raths nicht pflegen kan (wer Langenacker) die
versamlungen nicht beysicht, und demselben nachher am ehrliche
bey wohnt, so ist unser einstellige sinn das die entwägen der bruder
zug nicht solda gebunden nach gesinnet zu ihm zu seinem amt fart
zu sehen und ende auch zu richten und dem seinen eine getreue
arbeiter zu ne geben, ist aber der bruder Langenacker wesentlich
wie in einem ehrliche gemeldet, und sucht ihm amt getreulich auch
zu richten so wünschen wir so dan wir ein mögliche wochen sich gegen
ein sagen und sein dennen nicht der sündere ihm, wie meinen wägen
dann wie in die ganzen zeit geschehen ist, diese einige
dienst unserm lieben bruder zu nach sicht das zu dem unter
zeichneten bestchreib ihnen für die sach wägen sehen

Jacob Lauux
Martin Daby
Heinrich Lauux
Johannes Benib
Filip Engler
Martin Gasber
Michael Haut
Martin Barbrosi
Daniel Ult
Philip Ludwig
Valentin Heyßel

## RAILROAD—TRAVELING

We are apprized by a worthy brother and correspondent in Maryland, that a considerable advantage may be obtained in this mode of traveling, if the number of 25 persons apply for round trip-tickets. Brethren intending to travel from the West to the East next spring, we would inform, that the Pennsylvania and Ohio-Railroad passeth right through our church district, (the station is at Columbiana) that from here either the Baltimore and O. or Penn. and O. R. R. are or will be available by next spring, and that we should be very happy, if all our Western brethren would make our church a stopping and gathering-point on their way East. When the time comes near, we expect further information from our Maryland correspondent, and also from our Western brethren, who intend to come our way. For a reason obvious to the writer we did not deem it proper now, to publish his whole letter on the subject.

On page 242 of the April 1853 issue we find the promise of further information fulfilled.


## INTERESTING

To those contemplating to attend our Yearly-Meeting this spring.

When we were on the point of going to press with this form, we received a letter, from which we make the following extracts, to the exclusion of other matter set up already.

Monrovia, Md. 3d month 9, 1853.

. . . The train of cars from Wheeling to Baltimore leave the former place at 7 A. M. and arrive here between one and two A. M. next morning. Passengers may however stop in Cumberland over night, and leave there at 11 A. M. next day, and arrive here at 4½ P. M. Persons therefore leaving Wheeling on Wednesday the 11th May or next day—would be in time to be taken over to Beaverdam before the commencement of the meeting.

The fare from Wheeling to this place is $8.50, and of course the round trip-ticket will take them back without any additional pay, provided they return within the time for which the tickets are good, say 10 days, and if I can possibly do so, I will have them to extend the time to 12 days. The carriage from here to Beaverdam, for which coaches, omnibusses and other spring-wagons with good covers will be provided from Frederick, will cost one dollar, and the same to return from Beaverdam to this place. . . . "Come over into Macedonia, and help us!"

Jacob Cronise.

It is also desired by this dear brother, to urge it upon the brethren, to ascertain as near as they can the number that intend coming from their respective congregations &c. &c. and communicate the same to him during the month of April, to enable him to say to the company, what number of tickets to prepare.

We will add, that we look for further information, and will try to issue our next (May) No. as early in April as we can, to communicate it in time. Brethren from Southern Ohio &c. will probably avail themselves of the nearest route to Wheeling;—but those from Northern Ohio, Indiana and Illinois &c. will find the Northern Indiana and Southern Michigan R. R. to Toledo, thence either to Cleveland or, if the O. and Pa. R. R. should be finished in time to Crestline, aim direct for Shelby, and thence by Mansfield, Wooster, Canton, to Alliance, whence the nearest route to Wheeling will turn south to Wellsville. Those brethren, who felt disposed to stop with us on Sunday before Y. M. will have to go on from Alliance east as far as Franklin-square, near which our br. Hoke & other members live, where all will be truly welcome. In all cases, especially the last we should like to hear from our western br. soon. It is also requested by brethren in Somerset co., Pa., that some elders should pay them a visit. They will probably tell us next time more about it.

The May issue, page 266, gives the concluding information of this novel way of traveling to Yearly Meeting. It would now seem to be an unusual way to run a railroad.

Another Letter from Monrovia, Md., dated March 17, 1853.

Esteemed brother,

Since I wrote thee last I had an interview with the General-Superintendent of the Baltimore and Ohio Railroad company, who said there would be no round Trip-tickets issued, but all persons, who come to this place to attend the annual meeting, will pay the usual fare of $8.50 from Wheeling &c. &c. and upon their getting a certificate from the clerk of the meeting or any person authorized by the Society, that they had attended the annual meeting will be taken back to the place from whence they started at any time within three days after the meeting adjourns,—no matter how long the meeting may last—free of charge.

Those passengers who do not wish to travel at night, may leave Wheeling on Wednesday at 7. o'clock A. M. on the eleventh day of May, and stay over night in Cumberland, leave there next day at 11 A. M., and arrive here at 4 and a half P. M. and next morning proceed on to Beaverdam.

Say to brother Hoke and other aged brethren and sisters, that if they come here on Thursday the 12th P. M. we expect to be able to afford them comfortable lodgings to rest their wearied limbs, and next morning comfortable conveyances to take them to Beaverdam to the place of meeting.

I. C.

### B.   Appointments for Visiting Brethren

In connection with the last-quoted bit of travel news is a paragraph from page 266 of the May issue, which gives a glimpse of the intimate fraternal-family character of Church life of the days of our grandfathers.

## APPOINTMENT

To those of our beloved brethren, who will come from the West, and are inclined to favor our little church with a visit, we would say, that a meeting has been appointed at our dear brother's HENRY HOKE on Sunday before Whitsuntide, and that his carriage will be at the Depot of FRANKLIN-SQUARE, on Saturday afternoon, to take the brethren to his house. Should there be many brethren, and some of them prefer to come to our humble home, and neighboring brethren some 12 miles distant from br. H. H. they will please to notify us, and proceed on the Railroad as far as COLUMBIANA, whence our brethren will try to have them conveyed on the same day to our house, and have also a meeting appointed at our Meetinghouse, and on Monday or Tuesday all may meet again on their way to WHEELING. Please to drop a line, brethren, informing us of your intentions.

Two other such appointment notices are selected at random from the columns of the *Visitor,* the first from page 58 of the August 1853 issue and the second from page 95 of the September 1853 issue.

## APPOINTMENT

We would repeat, what we have stated already in the June number, that there will be a lovefeast held God willing in the CLARION church at br. WILLIAM MEHL's in VENANGO co. Pa. on the 11th of September next, and that members and especially ministering brethren are cordially invited to attend. Brethren from Ohio, going there, would be requested, to give us a day on their way home, say the 14th of September, at our Meeting-house, and we are further requested to say that there will be another communion meeting on the 16th of September at the house of DANIEL MOUNTZ in SANDY church, COLUMBIANA co. O. and a like invitation is extended to members and brethren, speakers in particular, in Pennsylvania, Ohio, or elsewhere.

## APPOINTMENTS

The brethren in Maryland and adjoining parts of Pennsylvania have made the following arrangements for communion-meetings this fall.

Beginning at PLEASANTHILL, (Monrovia) Md., Thursday Septbr. 29, thence at MARSHCREEK, Pa. on Saturday Oct. 1, thence to ANTEIDUM; WELTYS; BEAVER-CREEK; EMMERTS; MIDDLETOWN-VALLEY;—and on Thursday the 13th of Octbr. at BEAVERDAM, and on Sunday the 16th of Oct. at MEADOW-BRANCH.

There will be intermediate appointments; it is expected there will be a communion-meeting at each of the above-named places.

(We could heartily wish, that we in our North-East part of Ohio, could have a similar arrangement. There is now in a few days a lovefeast in Ashland co. and in a couple of weeks another in Stark co. to both of which we were invited, and would willingly attend, but our time is so much occupied. If we had lovefeasts in rotation as above, known a reasonable time before, we could perhaps prepare ourselves, so as to attend them all. For this purpose permit us to propose a plan, by which every church may secure the services of most of the laboring brethren not only in our own section of country, but even from other parts, and by which the laborers will be enabled to attend with the least loss of time. Let every church in the spring of the year express in a letter to our most aged elder her wish to have a love-feast appointed in the fall; and when this brother has received those letters, let him make the appointments at least two months before the first lovefeast is to take place, and have it published in the Visitor as the above, which would save the aged brother from a great deal of writing to and fro, and likewise save the churches from sending out a number of invitations.)

### C. Annual Conferences

Yearly Meeting is of perennial interest and its influence upon the fraternity can hardly be exaggerated. We undertake in the following from the columns of the *Gospel Visitor* to give an intimate picture of the Yearly Meeting. The first excerpt is from page 127 of the May 1856 issue.

## CORRESPONDENCE
## OUR YEARLY MEETING

Is now near at hand, and many of our beloved brethren will prepare for their journey thither before this comes to hand. Let us only not forget the true preparation, which the apostle Paul describes

(Ephes. 6: 10-18). We are all weak in ourselves, but IN THE LORD we may become strong, provided the power of his might (his word) accompanies us. Let us then put on the whole armor of God, that we may be able to stand against the wiles of the devil.

We will not be without temptation. While we will rejoice at the re-union with many, that will meet us there, we shall miss some, who will not be there;—and there will probably occur some things there, which are *not* lovely, *not* of good report, no virtue, nor any praise. Oh that every member would pray earnestly and daily: "Lead us not into temptation!"

The impending yearly meeting seems to become one of *peculiar interest* and *importance* before many others. It is to take place several hundred miles farther West than ever. This of itself is an evidence of the progress of the work of the Lord, which should rouse our hearts and souls to praise the Lord, and to pray fervently to make his servants equal to the work.

The question, Whether and in what manner our Western brethren, who were once with us, but these many years have stood alone, and during that period have become somewhat estranged in doctrine and practice, could be re-united with the great body of our brotherhood?— which will be provisionally investigated by a committee of 11 of our brethren among and with those Western brethren themselves,—this question will probably form one chief point before the yearly meeting, to which—wisdom from on high, the true anointing, and humility united with fortitude will be highly necessary.

The question, What is our duty to be done with regard to that little flock of brethren in Germany: Whether we are to consider them as brethren in the Lord? Or whether it is necessary first to make a farther investigation into their origin, condition and constitution—these are all questions of great significance, which will probably occur.

On pages 185-187 of the July 1856 issue following we find Henry Kurtz's travel sketch of the Meeting under the title

## OUR LAST YEARLY MEETING
## IN ILLINOIS

In Illinois?—Who would have thought 20 or 10 years ago, that such a meeting of our brethren would take place so far in the West?— "This is the Lord's doing; it is marvelous in our eyes." He has planted churches, where then had been none; He has blessed them from heaven above and from the earth beneath, and has made them willing, to receive in their midst the great congregation from the far East and

South, from the still farther West, and from the North, and to provide for it in the kindest and most plentiful manner. The Lord bless them for their love, and unto Him be thanks and glory for all things.

It was indeed no small sacrifice, which our loving members in Stephenson co. rendered to brotherly love by taking up the annual meeting this year. The long, cold winter and the late spring as well as the early occurrence of the feast of Pentecost has caused vegetation in that northerly region to be yet far backward. Fruit-trees and the forest stood yet bare and leafless; but little pasture for creatures had made its appearance at the time. By the preparations for the meeting the brethren there had been prevented to do their work in field and garden. Yet with joy and gladness they denied themselves, and their own interest, and welcomed their brethren from far and near with true hospitality.

This was not all. The members, who out of love gave up their home for the time being to the church, and under whose roof the yearly meeting was held, were themselves rather afflicted. The dear sister was in delicate health, and at first scarcely able to be up and about, and finally had to retire into her bedroom, and was most of the time compelled to keep her bed. What she must have felt and suffered by the unavoidable noise of a crowd of people being around and above her day and night, we leave to the imagination of those who have been ill. The loving brother too, though in good health otherwise, had met with an accident while preparing for this meeting, shortly before it took place, and had broken his arm. Yet with his arm in the sling, he never wearied to attend, where-ever his presence was needed, and forgetting self he tried constantly to make others comfortable. In these kind endeavors other brethren and sisters assisted, and nothing was wanting but favorable weather to make this first yearly meeting in what was once called the Far West as pleasant as any we have attended.

But the weather proved to be another trial of the faith, the love and patience of our dear members. Never before, at least within our recollection, and we have attended more than twenty-five of such meetings, was the weather so unpropitious and inclement, as during the time of our council-meeting this year. It was a great mercy that for the few days before the meeting commenced, the weather was pleasant, while so many were on their way to the meeting. It was a greater mercy still, that on Lord's day, while thousands were gathered to hear the Gospel preached in its original simplicity in the barn, the tent and the open air, we were blessed with a clear sky, as well as with spiritual blessings in heavenly places in Christ Jesus, and that the multitude from the surrounding country could return home before the weather changed.

For towards Lord's day evening the heavens lowered, and soon after night a thunderstorm arose with heavy rain, and from that night on till Wednesday morning or nearly noon scarcely the sun was seen, and more or less rain almost incessantly poured down. Besides the air became so damp and chilly, that those who had no overcoats suffered from cold. On Tuesday morning I had headache and felt so bad, that I thought I should have the ague, or, what is called in the west, "the chills." Our revered and beloved senior brother *George Hoke* was unwell too, and, though it was the first day of council meeting, (Monday having been consumed with the preliminary business,) for the first time in many years, neither of us could attend that day.

This was indeed a gloomy and dreadful time for such a meeting. The rich, black soil by constant rain was so softened, and by moving to and fro of so many people so much tramped and loosened, that every vestige of grass disappeared, and one step from the door a person would sink in the mud ankle deep, while the rain continued to pour down. It was impossible for people coming in the house, to clean their shoes sufficiently, and so the mud was carried into the house, up stairs, and everywhere in such quantities, that it became difficult to walk up and down stairs without slipping. I never saw a house in such a condition before. That all who attended the meeting suffered more or less during this time, was a matter of course, and in consequence many left on Tuesday.

Here I cannot withhold a suggestion, which I would present to the consideration of our brethren. Pentecost, the usual time for our yearly meeting from time immemorial, is what is called a movable feast like Easter. It will fall sometimes as early as the tenth of May, and sometimes as late as the thirteenth of June. Hence it appears that there is more than one month difference in the time our yearly meetings have been held hitherto. Its early occurrence this year was evidently the cause of much inconvenience, discomfort, suffering and loss to our beloved members, and therefore we propose the following query for the consideration of all.

"Would it not be best, instead of having a movable feast for the time of our yearly meeting, to appoint either the last Lord's day in May, or the first Lord's day in June for said meeting?"

We do not propose this question because we are fond of change, nor because we have a selfish motive. We have nothing in our eye but what might be best for all. But enough of this.

Of the transactions of the last yearly meeting the Minutes will speak for themselves. We have before observed that on account of illness we with others could not attend the first day. The first fifteen articles were transacted that day, of which we have only the papers, but did not hear the discussion. The last day we attended. Upon the whole, there was a spirit of love and harmony prevailing, and we hope and trust and pray, that all that was done will be so ruled and overruled by the glorious head of the church, as to promote the building up of the church, the salvation of sinners and the everlasting glory of our God and Redeemer.

We have said above so much about gloomy time of our meeting, that we must also say, that towards noon on Wednesday heaven began to smile again upon our meeting, things had a more cheerful aspect, and while on Tuesday and Wednesday forenoon candles had to be used in meeting all the time, by the glorious light of heaven the meeting could be finally closed. And should it be that our experience at this meeting were a token of a coming storm, or gloomy dark times, of times of affliction and temptation, (and methinks we can see and hear signs of it in the present aspect of things in the East and in the West, in the church and in the world,) may we, each and all, only endeavor to be faithful, to watch and pray, and do and suffer as the Lord sees fit to lay upon us, and we may rest assured of a happy end of all our trials; and if the Lord should frown for a while upon his people because of their sins and shortcomings, He will also smile again upon them, when they return penitent, and will be with them always even unto the end of the world.

H. K.

Lest this account give an exaggerated idea of some aspects of Yearly Meeting we follow with the report, from the same pen, of the Annual Meeting of 1857, as printed on pages 217-219 of the July 1857 *Gospel Visitor*.

## OUR ANNUAL MEETING OF 1857

Our meeting was held at the house of br. DANIEL WOLF in Washington Co. Maryland. The location was a very favorable one. The surrounding country is fertile, and well improved. A number of the brethren living near the place of meeting, accommodations for a large number of persons were offered. A more convenient house for holding such a meeting, than that of br. Wolf's does not often offer. It was commodious and convenient. The place afforded an abundant supply of excellent water. The willingness that brother & sister Wolf showed to make their guests as comfortable as possible, indicated a consciousness on their part that the service they rendered, was an offering to the Lord and his cause. The brethren and sisters who assisted on the occasion, seemed not to be ignorant of the apostolic saying, "God loveth a cheerful giver."

The church in which the meeting was held, defrayed the whole of the expense. And to meet this, between eight and nine hundred dollars were subscribed.

A large tent ninety feet long, and twenty eight feet wide was prepared for the occasion, and within this were tables and seats to accommodate three hundred persons at one time. In this tent the refreshment provided for the occasion was partaken of. On Sunday it was made one of the preaching places.

The concourse of people present on the ground was very large, especially on Sunday and Monday. The three places appointed for preaching were crowded, and a disposition was manifested on the part of a great many to hear the word of life. The service on Sunday continued from 9 o'clock A. M., till 1 o'clock P. M., and a considerable degree of interest was kept up during the whole time. We feel that some change might be made in our Lord's day service at our annual meetings, making it more useful and interesting. We therefore shall offer a few suggestions to our beloved brethren upon the subject. The time of service is too long. If our service in the morning would commence about 9 or 10 o'clock, and continue till 11 or 12, and then conclude, and we should then have an afternoon service, say from 1 o'clock till 3, we think there might in this, or in some such arrangement, be more interest given to the service. We have sometimes felt, when there have been no exercises during the afternoon, after the first service was concluded, that the time was not improved as well as it might have been. We merely throw out these hints to lead the brethren to reflect upon the subject.

During the continuance of the meeting, there was preaching in several of the adjacent places in the neighborhood by the brethren, and it is to be hoped it was not all in vain.

. . . . .

It was apparent, that there was a general disposition to close the meeting on Wednesday evening. And, consequently, business was pushed forward. We thought that a little more time might have been profitably spent upon some subjects, could we have taken it. We felt as if some subjects had, perhaps, been passed over in most too much of a hurry. We design to call the attention of the brethren hereafter, to the limited time we allow ourselves to do our business.

The time for the parting having arrived, it was evident that many felt the solemnity of the occasion. We had enjoyed a very pleasant meeting together. We had felt in some degree the presence of the Head of the church, and likewise the presence of the Holy Spirit, the delightful and welcome guest of the church. We could not resist the impression, that that meeting would be the last of the kind, that some present would enjoy. This impression drew our hearts nearer together. It awakened stronger affections towards one another. No doubt, for every censorious thought indulged in, and for every unkind word spoken, there was sorrow felt.

We had been in some degree separated from the world for a few days, and thrown among that society whose prevailing element, at least in profession, was Christian. We had felt considerable inward peace and comfort. But we were about separating from each other to meet the duties and trials of life.—A recollection of heaven's blessings to us in the past and a sense of our dependence upon the same source for future supplies, called us to a throne of grace. We united in prayer, and parted with pleasant reminiscences of our meeting which had just been brought to a close, and with joyful anticipations of meeting in heaven, to separate no more for ever.

The Yearly Meeting probably never met in more dramatic circumstances than when it convened in the Beaver Creek meetinghouse in 1861. There had been some debate about the wisdom of holding the meeting. But we let Daniel Miller tell the story as he told it in the July 1861 *Gospel Visitor*, pages 210 and 211.

## THE ANNUAL MEETING

Having been to the Annual Meeting and having returned from the same, and being requested by some of the brethren while there, to write a piece for the Visitor; I will for their satisfaction, as well as for others who were not there; and as it is not certain whether the proceedings of the meeting can be sent through soon in consequence of a rumor that the mail south is stopped, I will be a little more particular than I should otherwise be. On Monday the 29th of April myself and wife and brother Jacob Early and wife, started for Rockingham county, Virginia, the place the Annual Meeting was to be. In consequence of missing several connections, we were a good while on the road. We arrived at brother S. Ziglers near Spartapolis Thursday noon, May 2nd., where we commenced visiting our old friends and relatives, through Rockingham and Augusta counties. We found the friends generally well with one or two exceptions. We spent the time very agreeably among our friends until the 19th inst., when we went to the Beaver

Creek Meetinghouse, the time and place appointed for the commencement of the Annual Meeting, where we met with a very large concourse of people. There was public preaching on Sunday and Monday till noon, after which time the meeting proceeded to discuss the queries brought before the meeting, which required till Wednesday about 11 o'clock, when the meeting broke up and we started for home. We got to Harpers Ferry next day before 11 o'clock, and had to wait till after 7 in the evening before a train came. There we were all day among ten thousand soldiers. We talked with a good many of them, and they talked clever, and did not seem in the least to manifest any desire to molest us. We started from there that evening, and on Friday night at 12 o'clock we were at home. Now as respects the meeting more particularly, there was very good order during the meeting. Union and love was manifested, and I believe that surely the Lord was there. But the churches were poorly represented. There were a good many churches represented by letter, but personally there were only three or four churches represented out side of the state of Va.; namely, this one, and South English church, Iowa, and one in Kansas, and perhaps one in Indiana. I suppose the brethren generally were afraid to go in consequence of the excited state of the country, but they should not have been so easily scared; for there was no danger, or at least we saw none. Some of the soldiers at Harpers Ferry said that they looked with eager eyes, to see the brethren go through. They said they should not be molested. I talked with a captain while there, he said that such people as we could travel in the South where we please. The brother from Kansas, namely, brother Eichenbury said that he was nearly a day in Washington, and no one molested him. So that upon the whole, I believe that if the brethren generally had turned out that it would have had a very good effect. The proceedings of the meeting had all to be transcribed, and consequently were not ready to send when we left, or they would have been sent. The arrangement is such, that in case the mail is stopped, they are to be brought to some brother near the line, and he take them across to some brother in Pa. near the line, where they can be mailed and sent to the Editors of the Gospel Visitor. I just mention this because it has been reported in some papers quite recently, that the mail south is stopped. According to request, the brethren in Ehrback's district, Montgomery county, Ohio, have the grant for the Annual Meeting on Pentecost 1862. Please give this a place in the Visitor . . ., and oblige yours in the bonds of love.

                                        DANIEL MILLER.

Lima, Ohio. May 28, 1861.

## BEGINNINGS OF CITY MISSION WORK

Wilbur B. Stover, Germantown, 1892-93—what a strange conjunction of personality, place, and time. Verily history is a unity, but of what a complex pattern!

The name of Wilbur B. Stover stands today for foreign missions. It was he who opened the India mission in 1894, launching the Church of the Brethren on missions to the non-Christian world. But the conjunction of W. B. Stover and Germantown brings together this young missionary and the city mission movement.

It is impossible for the present generation of the Church of the Brethren to recapture the strange starry-eyed admiration and veneration of a generation ago for the "big cities." The cities were a wonderful land to be taken for Christ. Of the goal and of the ability of the dreamers to achieve it, there was no doubt.

The "city mission" era dawned in the 1880's and—well, it seems to have merged with the landscape. Closely connected with the advent of city missions were the beginnings of the professional pastorate. *Professional* was (and in some places may still be) an evil—or at least a doubtful—and offensive word. The very term *pastor* was under suspicion in some parts of the Brotherhood. The term *missionary* came to be a hallowed designation. Christian service or full-time Christian service became the ideal—but, no, never professional service. It was in Philadelphia that there can be located the beginning of the paid ministry. It is claimed (with no definite documentation) that as early as 1861 occasional payments as help or assistance to the minister had been paid. At any rate, it is clear from a letter of Roland Howe, dated March 5, 1938, and printed *in extenso* in a Bethany Seminary thesis by F. C. Hollingshead, that "Tobias Timothy Myers was the first pastor of the church at the new site just then completed at Carlisle and Dauphin Streets, and became our first regularly full-time salaried pastor, beginning April 26, 1891 at sixty dollars a month." This is the year before the coming of W. B. Stover to Germantown.

Wilbur Stover had been living in DuPage County, Illinois, when J. G. Royer discovered him and enlisted him to attend Mt. Morris College. Wilbur entered college in 1884, completing the commercial course in 1885, and then the academic classical course with the class of 1889, and then the seminary course in 1891. In March 1891 he was elected to the ministry by the Mt. Morris congregation.

He had confessed Christ during a series of meetings in the college chapel and had been baptized by D. E. Price on March 8, 1885. From the day of his baptism he had been an active, growing, vibrant Christian and long before his election to the ministry was an advocate of foreign missions. He went east to study at Temple College (since 1907 known as Temple University), which had been established for those who were compelled to work and study.

The documents which follow largely unfold their own story. As a prelude we quote from O. C. Slifer's story of his travels from his home in Bird City, Kansas, to Annual Meeting at Hagerstown, Maryland, and then of visiting various places, as it was printed in the *Gospel Messenger* for July 21, 1891.

From Washington I started for Baltimore, Md., where I arrived June 25.

Here is where Brother J. T. Quinlan has been laboring so earnestly for the poor boys and girls of the city. Brother Quinlan welcomed me very kindly, and on the evening of the 25th I had the pleasure of being present at the "Young Folks Prayer meeting" which was conducted in an interesting manner. I also met our zealous missionary,—sister Eliza J. McGaughey,—who is doing a good work by distributing tracts, not only in Baltimore but elsewhere.

From Baltimore I took the steamer "Elizabeth" for Philadelphia, to visit my old friend and playmate,—Bro. T. T. Myers,—who has charge of the Brethren churches in Philadelphia, on Dauphin Street. I certainly had a very enjoyable time among the brethren and sisters of this place. They are very energetic workers and deserve much credit, for they certainly work under great disadvantages in this large city. They have finished a new stone church and have very encouraging prospects. Four were baptized June 28—one brother and three sisters, all young. May the Lord keep them safe from the snares of the evil one until the end, is our prayer.

I did not get to visit Brother Reiner's congregation [the extinct congregation of Dover Street or North Philadelphia] very much, but those I did meet, including Brother Reiner and family, were wide-awake Christians. I also visited our old stone church,—"the church primeval"—at Germantown, adjoining Philadelphia. I found the ancient edifice still in a good state of preservation. The church stands back from the street, making room for a beautiful lawn, which is kept in good condition by Brother Bigger and wife, who kindly showed me through the building and graveyard. The grave of that venerable "soldier of Christ"—Alexander Mack—may be seen in the adjoining graveyard. As I gazed upon the old stone church, the birthplace of the Brethren's church in America [it will be perceived the good brother took his history rather uncritically!], I wondered if posterity will not revere the dear old spot even more, a hundred years hence than we do now. I have had a pleasant time in Philadelphia and am reluctant at leaving, but tomorrow, July 1, I start for New York City and, after visiting Saratoga and Niagara, I expect to return home via Northern Illinois and Central Iowa to Bird City, Kansas.

O. C. Slifer

From the pen of W. B. Stover the following appeared in the *Gospel Messenger* of December 22, 1891, under the title "From Edgemont, Md."

Several weeks ago I went to Philadelphia to be with the Brethren there during their lovefeast and the series of meetings to follow. The feast was a very pleasant one. During the meetings, continuing for three weeks, brethren J. T. and T. T. Myers did the preaching, with an immediate result of seven applicants for baptism.

I am again impressed with the fact that city mission work and country mission work are two things, and the ways and means for the one, may not suit the other; neither do the men successful in the one, always promise success in the other. The work in Philadelphia is encouraging. Brother Myers says he has never preached straighter doctrine, and yet the congregations are growing steadily. The church is growing in sympathy with the General Brotherhood, and, I understand, has expressed a desire to be regularly represented in the deliberations of that hereafter. The spirituality and sociability of the Philadelphia members are commendable.

I also had the pleasure of visiting the church in Germantown,—the mother church,—built in 1770 or before. In the well-kept little cemetery there, lie the remains of many of our forefathers. It is a sad thought, indeed, to see that first church in its stand-still condition. Take the cemetery away and there is not much left! Yet if there is any place that ought not to be forgotten when we pray, it is those first churches. With it all, I believe the place could be built up again, but somebody must go there to *stay* [italics in the original], and then exercise untiring effort and patience. While the tide goes westward, God bless our eastern churches.

W. B. Stover

The realism of this article is quite in contrast with that of the former visitor quoted. We wish we might fill in certain data that seemingly is forever lost; however, the relevant part of the story survives, dated April 19, 1892, but published in the *Gospel Messenger* of May 3, 1892.

## From Germantown, Pa.

I am glad to say our work here in the city, is progressing encouragingly. Four weeks ago closed a short series of meetings in the Philadelphia Church. From then until the present time, ten have been added by baptism, and will be soon. During the same time two have been added by letter. The church has decided to be represented at both District and Annual Conference, and has chosen Bro. T. T. Myers as delegate. Plans are submitted for an addition to the present house of worship, and it is expected that the structure will be completed during the summer. The progress and prospect of the work makes it very encouraging for anyone in anyway connected therewith.

Following the above mentioned revival we also had a short series of meetings in the Germantown church, Brother Myers returning the favor for assistance given him. Three were baptized and others are manifestly near. The attendance and interest in the work are increasing gradually. Two weeks ago we began prayer meeting. With earnest and careful work we have bright hopes for the future. Brother Landon

West hits the mark in his notes on city work. A little actual practice is sufficient to upset a good deal of theory.

Wilbur B. Stover

In the issue of July 12, 1892, the first page tells of the travels of the editor, H. B. Brumbaugh, who proceeded from his home and office at Huntingdon, Pennsylvania, to a special meeting at Philadelphia. We quote only that part relevant to our theme.

Last week we had a very pleasant visit to the "City of Brotherly Love." Though exceedingly warm, we had a pleasant stopping place in the house of sister L. Krupps, familiarly known there as the Brethren's "Headquarters" as quite a number make this place their home. Here it is that our two ministers, T. T. Myers, of the city church, and Brother Wilbur Stover, of the Germantown church, stay, with quite a number of members who have employment in the city. . . .

On Sunday morning we attended their church services and had a good audience, though somewhat smaller than usual, on account of the very warm weather. This congregation has been growing very encouragingly under the ministry of Bro. Myers, and their Sunday School has so enlarged that they were necessitated to make more room, which they are now doing by building an addition to the main building, 36 x 84. The foundation is already done and the work is being pushed rapidly forward, so that, in a short time they will have ample room for their large and growing school. . . .

Brother Stover is laboring faithfully to build up the Germantown church, but he has many difficulties to contend with and needs all the encouragement that can be given him. He is hopeful, and if he receives the necessary help and sympathy, we believe that even that which has been dead may be made alive again.

When we think of those whose bodies are sleeping within speaking distance of the old stone church, made sacred as the place where once was voiced the Gospel by such godly men as the Macks, Keyser, Fox, and others a prayer arises in our soul; "O Lord, wilt thou not restore thy work at this place?" Let us all pray that the Gospel Sun, that once shone so brightly at this place, may again rise with healing in his wings and that a soul saving prosperity may fall upon the old Germantown church.

In the *Gospel Messenger* of October 4, 1892, is a travel sketch by Daniel Vaniman, chairman of the Mission Board. It is so packed with information and we feel throws such light on the city mission atmosphere of the times that we quote from it.

## CHIPS FROM THE WORK-HOUSE

A visit to Philadelphia, North Philadelphia, Germantown, Norristown, and the three New Jersey churches has furnished timber for many Chips. The nice point is to make such Chips out of it as may be of some use. If this cannot be done, it were better left alone.

That all the above churches need help and encouragement is freely admitted by all with whom the writer had opportunity to converse about the situation. In New Jersey we held two preaching services with each one of the three churches, the members being as kind and hospitable as members can be. The old brethren who, years ago frequently visited these Far Eastern churches, have died off or gone westward with the march of empire, as have also some of their own number, until they feel somewhat forsaken by the large Brotherhood in the West. This causes some of them to feel rather neglected. . . .

A visit to the Germantown church and graveyards was of much interest. Here stands the first Brethren church ever built upon American soil. It was built one hundred and twenty-two years ago. Adjoining it is the neat and well-kept graveyard, and also a parsonage belonging to the church. In the cemetery lie buried a number of our pioneer brethren and sisters, including Alexander Mack, Jr. who died in 1803. We also visited the old graveyard where is the grave of Alexander Mack, Sr., marked with a very common stone, 18 inches high and 13 inches wide. Five have been baptized into this church since Bro. Stover came here as minister last January. The little band now numbers twenty-five. Twenty-eight have been baptized into the first Philadelphia church since Brother T. T. Myers went there as minister last May one year ago. They now have a membership of about one hundred members, a large, substantially-built house, with large addition now nearly completed, preaching services and a live Sunday-school each Lord's Day, and a weekly prayer-meeting.

In the *Gospel Messenger* of January 10, 1893, occurs the following item:

Brother W. B. Stover, 2029 N. 13 St., Philadelphia, Pa., whose desires are, in the near future, to be engaged in active mission work in India, would like to correspond with those whose secret desires are for the same work.

In the *Gospel Messenger* of June 6, 1893 (although the item is dated May 16), is the following brief item. The heading is simply "Germantown, Pa.," and the signature is "W. B. Stover."

We held our love-feast last Thursday evening. Forty-one communed. We had a full house and an impressive meeting. Brother T. T. Myers officiated. One more baptized recently.

We know that on June 29, 1893, at Mt. Carroll, Illinois, W. B. Stover married Mary Emmert. Sometime between May 16 and June 29 the heroic and radiantly dreaming young pastor closed his work with Germantown and did not return after his marriage.

Missionary work and professional pastoral service are here found to be branches from a single root—the root of professional religious work. Professionalism in general is the necessary and inevitable corollate organization of society, resultant of our capitalist industrial social order. This order began with the commercial revolution and after growing slowly for five hundred years has grown rapidly the past two and a half centuries, especially during the past century of increasing tempo of industrialism.

## Congregations and Membership in Recent Years, According to the Yearbook

| | Congregations | Membership in U.S. and Canada | Membership on Mission Fields | Total |
|---|---|---|---|---|
| 1939 | 1,024 | 169,571 | | |
| 1940 | 1,021 | 173,783 | | |
| 1941 | 1,017 | 176,908 | | |
| 1942 | 1,019 | 178,271 | | |
| 1943 | 1,019 | 179,843 | | |
| 1944 | 1,020 | 180,033 | | |
| 1945 | 1,019 | 180,287 | 10,472 | 191,759 |
| 1946 | 1,021 | 181,087 | 10,595 | 192,682 |
| 1947 | 1,018 | 182,497 | 11,822 | 194,319 |
| 1948 | 1,021 | 184,584 | 11,821 | 196,405 |
| 1949 | 1,023 | 185,799 | 12,503 | 198,202 |
| 1950 | 1,025 | 185,088 | 10,595 | 196,683 |

## STATISTICS OF BRANCHES OF THE CHURCH

| Name | 1890 | 1906 | 1916 | 1926 | 1936 | 1946 |
|---|---|---|---|---|---|---|
| Church of the Brethren (Conservatives) | | | | | | |
| Membership | 61,101 | 76,547 | 105,102 | 128,392 | 153,516 | 182,497 |
| Congregations | 720 | 815 | 997 | 1,030 | 1,031 | 1,018 |
| Brethren Church (Progressives) | | | | | | |
| Membership | 8,089 | 17,042 | 24,060 | 26,026 | 30,636 | 17,687 (y) (z) |
| Congregations | 128 | 202 | 201 | 174 | 163 | 109 |
| Old Order German Baptist Brethren | | | | | | |
| Membership | 4,411 | 3,388 | 3,399 | 3,036 | 3,589 | not |
| Congregations | 135 | 68 | 67 | 62 | 67 | available |
| German Seventh-Day (Beisselianer) Baptists | | | | | | |
| Membership | 194 | 167 | 136 | 144 | 137 (x) | 125 (b) |
| Congregations | 6 | 5 | 5 | 4 | 3 | 2 |
| Dunker Brethren (v) | | | | | | not available |

Church of God (New Dunkers)

| | | | | |
|---|---|---|---|---|
| Membership .............. Existent but the census | 929 | 650 | 549 | 526 (a) |
| Congregations .............. has no trace of them. | 13 | 9 | 8 | 8 |

(v) This group came into existence in 1926.

(x) By their request in 1936 they were involved in Baptist returns.

(y) Report of National Statistician, *Brethren Evangelist*, November 29, 1947.

(z) The Brethren Church split in 1939, and for the church year 1946 the "Grace" division reported 16,077 in the U. S. in 101 churches; in Africa, 7,098; and in Argentina 360—a world total of 23,535.—*The Brethren Missionary Herald*, November 1, 1947.

(a) 1944 statistics, *Yearbook of American Churches—1949.*
(b) 1942 statistics, *Yearbook of American Churches—1949.*

Population Growth in the United States, Urban and Rural, 1790-1947

| Year | Total | Urban* | | Rural* | | Rural-Nonfarm | | Rural-Farm | |
|---|---|---|---|---|---|---|---|---|---|
| | | Number | Per Cent | Number | Per Cent | Number | Per Cent | Number | Per Cent |
| 1790 | 3,929,214 | 201,655 | 5.1 | 3,727,599 | 94.9 | | | | |
| 1800 | 5,308,483 | 322,371 | 6.1 | 4,986,112 | 93.9 | | | | |
| 1810 | 7,239,881 | 525,459 | 7.3 | 6,714,422 | 92.7 | | | | |
| 1820 | 9,638,453 | 693,255 | 7.2 | 8,945,198 | 92.8 | | | | |
| 1830 | 12,866,020 | 1,127,247 | 8.8 | 11,738,773 | 91.2 | | | | |
| 1840 | 17,069,453 | 1,845,055 | 10.8 | 15,224,398 | 89.2 | | | | |
| 1850 | 23,191,876 | 3,543,716 | 15.3 | 19,648,160 | 84.7 | | | | |
| 1860 | 31,443,321 | 6,216,518 | 19.8 | 25,226,803 | 80.2 | | | | |
| 1870 | 38,558,371 | 9,902,361 | 25.7 | 28,656,010 | 74.3 | | | | |
| 1880 | 50,155,783 | 14,129,735 | 28.2 | 36,026,048 | 71.8 | | | | |
| 1890 | 62,947,714 | 22,106,265 | 35.1 | 40,841,449 | 64.9 | | | | |
| 1900 | 75,994,575 | 30,159,921 | 39.7 | 45,834,654 | 60.3 | | | | |
| 1910 | 91,972,266 | 41,998,932 | 45.7 | 49,973,334 | 54.3 | 18,118,341 | 19.7 | 31,854,993 | 34.6 |
| 1920 | 105,710,620 | 54,157,973 | 51.2 | 51,552,647 | 48.8 | 20,159,385 | 19.1 | 31,393,262 | 29.7 |
| 1930 | 122,775,046 | 68,954,823 | 56.2 | 53,820,223 | 43.8 | 23,662,710 | 19.3 | 30,157,513 | 24.5 |
| 1940 | 131,669,275 | 74,423,702 | 56.5 | 57,245,573 | 43.5 | 27,029,385 | 20.5 | 30,216,188 | 23.0 |
| 1947† | 143,400,000 | 84,800,000 | 59.1 | 58,600,000 | 40.9 | 31,200,000 | 21.8 | 27,400,000 | 19.1 |

* Adjusted to 1940 census classification of urban and rural.

† Based on published estimates of the Bureau of the Census, with persons in the armed forces allotted to the residence groups in the same proportions as veterans of World War II were distributed in April 1947. Used by permission of the Bureau of the Census.

## Brethren Schools Which Have Operated

*Opened Closed*

| | | | |
|---|---|---|---|
| Kishacoquillas Seminary, Mifflin County, Pa. | 1861 | 1866 | Sold |
| New Vienna Academy, New Vienna, Ohio | 1861 | 1864 | Suspended |
| Salem College, Bourbon, Ind. | 1870 | 1873 | Suspended |
| Berlin College, Berlin, Pa. | 1872 | | Never opened |
| Plum Creek Normal School, Elderton, Pa. | 1874 | 1878 | Suspended |
| Brethren's Normal College (first name, Huntingdon Normal School) Huntingdon, Pa. | 1876 | 1894 | Rechartered as Juniata College |
| Juniata College, Huntingdon, Pa. | 1894 | | |
| Ashland College, Ashland, Ohio | 1879 | | Taken over by "Progressives," still operating |
| Mt. Morris College, Mt. Morris, Ill. | 1879 | 1932 | Merged with Manchester College |
| Spring Creek Normal School, Spring Creek, Va. | 1880 | 1889 | Rechartered as Bridgewater College |
| Bridgewater College, Bridgewater, Va. | 1889 | | |
| Mountain Normal School, Patrick County, Va. | 1882 | | Sold; continued by others |
| McPherson College, McPherson, Kan. | 1887 | | |
| Daleville College, Daleville, Va. | 1890 | 1937 | Merged auxiliary of Bridgewater, 1925 |
| La Verne College (first name, Lordsburg), La Verne, Cal. | 1891 | | |
| Manchester College (first name, North Manchester College), North Manchester, Ind. | 1895 | | |

| | | | |
|---|---|---|---|
| Hebron Seminary (Prince William Normal School — 1897-1905 — revived), Nokesville, Va. ......... | 1908 | 1924 | Suspended |
| Fruitdale Seminary, Fruitdale, Ala. | 1896 | 1901 [02] | Suspended |
| Citronelle College, Citronelle, Ala. .. | 1896 | 1901 [02] | Only built building |
| Plattsburg College, Plattsburg, Mo. | 1897 | 1899 | Suspended |
| Smithville Collegiate Institute, Smithville, Ohio ......................... | 1897 | 1900 | Suspended |
| Maryland Collegiate Institute, Union Bridge, Md. ..................... | 1899 | 1910 | Moved to New Windsor and re-named Blue Ridge College |
| Blue Ridge College, New Windsor, Md. ..................... | 1910 | 1937 | Sold to non-Brethren; prop-erty bought in 1945 by Breth-ren Service Committee |
| Canton College and Bible Institute, Canton, Ohio ............................... | 1904 | 1907 | Suspended |
| Elizabethtown College, Elizabethtown, Pa. ..................... | 1900 | | |
| Bethany Biblical Seminary (first name, Bethany Bible School), Chicago, Ill. ................................. | 1905 | | |

## CHRISTIAN HIGHER EDUCATION
## COMMITTEE ON HIGHER EDUCATION

In the formation of the General Brotherhood Board with the different commissions the interest of the church's program of higher education was assigned to the Christian Education Commission. To care for this assignment the commission has recognized the presidents of the six colleges and the seminary as the Committee on Higher Education. The Committee brings an annual written report to the Christian Education Commission.

## EDUCATIONAL INSTITUTIONS, AS OF 1950

Bridgewater College, Warren D. Bowman, Bridgewater, Virginia
Elizabethtown College, A. C. Baugher, Elizabethtown, Pennsylvania
Juniata College, Calvert N. Ellis, Huntingdon, Pennsylvania
La Verne College, Harold D. Fasnacht, La Verne, California
Manchester College, V. F. Schwalm, North Manchester, Indiana
McPherson College, Desmond W. Bittinger, McPherson, Kansas
Bethany Biblical Seminary, Rufus D. Bowman, 3435 Van Buren St., Chicago 24, Illinois

## FINANCIAL STATISTICS
### *Balance Sheet Totals*

Assets and Liabilities

| *Name of Institution* | *Endowment Funds* | *Plant & Equipment Funds* | *Total Assets* |
|---|---|---|---|
| Bridgewater | $ 421,922.69 | $ 789,718.05 | $1,372,456.57 |
| Elizabethtown | 212,695.34 | 357,639.34 | 686,245.89 |
| Juniata | 837,902.71 | 1,331,125.75 | 2,359,172.83 |
| La Verne | 57,317.31 | 793,169.04 | 886,640.43 |
| Manchester | 621,323.49 | 1,324,730.85 | 2,302,067.22 |
| McPherson | 445,154.00 | 760,132.00 | 1,496,889.00 |
| Total | 2,596,315.54 | 5,356,515.03 | 9,103,471.94 |
| Bethany Biblical Seminary | 69,689.59 | 413,705.73 | 729,371.58 |
| Grand Total | $2,666,005.13 | $5,770,220.76 | $9,832,843.52 |

ENROLLMENT STATISTICS, 1948-1949

| Name of Institution | Regular Session | Extension and Special | Summer Session | Members of the Church of the Brethren | Members of Other Denominations | Not Affiliated With Any Church | Ministers (Brethren) or Preparing for the Ministry | Ministers (Other Denominations) or Preparing for the Ministry | Total Number of Students Exclusive of Duplicates | Faculty Members—Church of the Brethren | Faculty Members—Other Denominations | Total Faculty |
|---|---|---|---|---|---|---|---|---|---|---|---|---|
| Bridgewater | 526 | 18 | 105 | 264 | 228 | 34 | 21 | 20 | 570 | 20 | 17 | 37 |
| Elizabethtown | 377 | 39 | 400 | 113 | 256 | 8 | 22 | 21 | 494 | 19 | 13 | 32 |
| Juniata | 709 | 12 | 305 | 190 | 531 | 6 | 10 | 24 | 788 | 18 | 32 | 50 |
| La Verne | 240 | 51 | 0 | 142 | 136 | 13 | 13 | 4 | 291 | 24 | 13 | 37 |
| Manchester | 872 | 13 | 333 | 446 | 360 | 66 | 55 | 10 | 1,049 | 31 | 21 | 52 |
| McPherson | 376 | 39 | 162 | 206 | 138 | 32 | 41 | 2 | 554 | 21 | 12 | 33 |
| Total | 3,100 | 172 | 1,305 | 1,361 | 1,649 | 159 | 162 | 81 | 3,746 | 133 | 108 | 241 |
| Bethany Biblical Seminary | 239 | 20 | 0 | 195 | 44 | 0 | 97 | 23 | 259 | 11 | 1 | 12 |
| Totals | 3,339 | 192 | 1,305 | 1,556 | 1,693 | 159 | 259 | 104 | 4,005 | 144 | 109 | 253 |

# INDEX

## A

Abelard, 18
Adams County, Ill., 122
Adams County, Iowa, 130
Adams County, Ohio, 119
Adams County, Pa., 113, 114
Adventist chiliasm, 23
Africa, 217
*Agriculture in Modern Life,* 152
Allegheny College, 214
*Allen,* passengers on, 321
*Allen,* The, 40
American Friends Service Committee, 228
American Revolution, *see* Revolutionary War
American Sunday School Union, 221
Amick, Joseph, 195
Amish Mennonites, 137
Amwell, 75, 76, 79, 88, 331, 332
Anabaptists, 15, 22, 26, 27, 38, 39, 42, 164, 276
Anglo-Catholicism, 23
Annual Conference, *see* Annual Meeting
Annual Meeting (general), 68, 69, 157, 160, 162, 165, 166, 167, 168, 169, 170, 171, 172, 173, 174, 175, 176, 177, 178, 179, 181, 183, 184, 187, 188, 191, 241, 250, 256, 257, 258, 271, 273, 277, 279, 283, 330, 340, 345
Annual Meeting (specific years)
1763—77
1783—161
1785—96
1789—221
1791—68, 69, 252
1794—115
1797—115
1799—78, 340
1803—78

1804—78, 252
1810—91
1813—68
1817—254
1822—161
1827—155
1829—91
1834—254
1837—161, 172, 254
1838—221
1840—254
1845—161, 254
1846—72, 155, 169, 171
1847—91, 161, 162, 170, 254
1848—162, 254
1849—102, 114, 159, 254, 256
1850—188
1851—158, 281
1852—203, 231, 281
1853—155, 203, 257, 280, 281, 340, 342
1854—257, 281
1855—282
1856—127, 158, 161, 162, 194, 280, 346
1857—160, 203, 221, 257, 349
1858—103, 160, 210, 257, 280, 281, 282
1859—281, 283
1860—116, 281
1861—277, 351
1862—161, 222, 280
1863—161, 194, 257
1864—121, 158, 270, 281
1865—158, 162, 237, 280, 281, 282
1866—91, 158, 173, 238, 278, 280
1867—160, 282
1868—280
1869—103, 160, 280
1870—103, 130, 162
1871—162, 280, 281

## B